D1403264

NEWS
OF
MY DEATH

NEWS
OF
MY DEATH
. . . Was Greatly Exaggerated!

HOW I SURVIVED THE TEXAS DEPRESSION

MY FINANCIAL STRATEGIES FOR THE '90S

CRAIG HALL

ST. MARTIN'S PRESS
N E W Y O R K

Design by Bob Bull

Jacket photo by Dan Sellers

Library of Congress Cataloging-in-Publication Data

Hall, Craig.
    The art of survival : staying alive during the Texas depression of the 1980's / Craig Hall.
      p.   cm.
   ISBN 0-312-04440-2
    1. Hall, Craig. 2. Businessmen—United States—
Biography. 3. Real estate investment—Texas—History—20th century. I. Title.
HC102.H33A3   1990
333.33'092—dc20
  [B]   89-77897
                                         CIP

First Edition

10 9 8 7 6 5 4 3 2 1

CONTENTS

THE HARD ROAD

To live for tomorrow, existing today,
To be bound by superficial righteousness,
To invest in guilt,
To be less than you can,
To have the unusual, make it common, let it die.
To waste in dreams of what could have been,
To fear truth, deny love,
To feel and hide, all of this is
To exist and die. But
To seek truth,
To dare and
To follow,
To challenge,
To love and not lie,
To meet the lows yet see the highest highs.

—Craig Hall, January 1976

PREFACE

1985 WAS A VERY GOOD YEAR. In fact, the Hall Financial Group had a record year, exceeding even our most optimistic forecasts. We were the largest private-placement real estate sponsor in the United States. My personal non–real estate investments were also doing great, and my most recent audited net worth was more than $200 million including a substantial amount of money in cash. Having become very active in the Dallas community, I was even a part owner of the Dallas Cowboys. In 1986 almost overnight the price of oil declined from twenty dollars a barrel to nine dollars a barrel. The tax law was changed retroactively. By mid-1986, what in 1985 would have seemed impossible was happening. My financial holdings were teetering on bankruptcy, and I was rapidly heading toward being flat broke. The *Wall Street Journal*, front page, April 25, 1986, read:

PROPERTY DAMAGE
SYNDICATOR CRAIG HALL STRUGGLES
TO SHORE UP REAL ESTATE EMPIRE

. . . His $3 billion financial empire, which includes two savings and loan associations, a controlling interest in an oil company, 10 percent of the Dallas Cowboys and extensive real estate holdings is crumbling.

The news of my financial death was on the tips of many tongues at cocktail parties and in financial circles alike throughout 1986. Yet even though I never filed personal or corporate bankruptcy, our restructuring effort was larger than the Chrysler government bail-out.

The *Journal* story, like many others that would follow, predicted the corporate and financial demise of the Hall organization and Craig Hall. Although I was quoted as saying in regard to my effort, "His objective, he says, is to solve problems and work in the best interests of all parties: 'I don't want to run away from problems. I'm concerned about the lenders as well,' " the next paragraph reported the industry's attitude and quoted a securities analyst. "But many real estate and financial experts see little hope for successful bailout. 'Craig Hall is only trying to rearrange the deck chairs on the *Titanic*.' " That colorful statement, comparing my business to the *Titanic*, was picked up by other national publications immediately.

This is the Hall Financial Group story and my personal story, one of a boom and a near bust and then a comeback. In a broader sense, this is the story of the Texas depression, when in the latter part of the 1980s the oil, banking, savings and loan, and real estate industries crashed simultaneously. Between 1985 and 1990, the pillars of society in Texas were shaken to the crumbling point. Corporate executives and small business owners to multimillionaires or even billionaires—including Clint Murchison, Dr. Denton Cooley, Herbert and Bunker Hunt, and the former Texas governors John Connally and Preston Smith—fell to bankruptcy.

The depression didn't just crush individuals, but in an unprecedented manner it also toppled virtually the entire Texas financial system. Its fierce devastation, which was limited to the geographic region of Texas and a few surrounding states, was in some ways worse than even the 1930s. In the early 1980s, the regional banks in Texas were considered the strongest in the country; by the mid-1980s, they too were broke. The almighty RepublicBank first merged with its archrival InterFirst, became insolvent, was bailed out by the FDIC, and then eventually sold to North Carolina National Bank. It was the largest bank failure in history, surpassing Continental Illinois. Other large Texas banks, including MBank, Texas American Bancshares, and BancTEXAS, all suffered similar fates. For the savings and loans, the situation was even worse. Virtually all of the larger savings and loan institutions and most of the smaller ones went through some form of insolvency. Only a very small handful will survive without a government bail-out.

My company's, as well as my personal, multibillion-dollar holdings in real estate, oil and gas, venture capital, and savings and loans, which I had worked very hard to build, turned out in the mid-1980s to be diversification of the wrong kind in the wrong place at the wrong time. A Texan by choice, I moved to Dallas in 1981 at the height of the boom, when the "freeze a Yankee" mentality and Texas inflationary spiral were creating an image of endless prosperity. Texans are different. Texans have a unique "can do" spirit, a confidence that seems unsinkable. I liked that enough to make Texas my home and I'm glad I made that decision.

Then a funny thing happened on the way to endless prosperity. In December 1985, we started to see the economics of our company's 60,000 apartments starting to crumble, so we decided to re-examine our financial future. We realized in January 1986 that there was a localized real estate depression on the horizon. Yet even then we had no idea how severe the depression would turn out to be. We immediately contacted our largest lenders, while still current on all loans, to describe our concerns. What we found out was that most of our lenders were quietly under one form or another of government supervision and fast on their way to financial institution bankruptcy.

Being a sponsor of more than 250 real estate limited partnerships, we felt that it was our duty to contact our investors. As soon as our financial review was complete in mid-January 1986, we issued a letter to 10,000 investors describing our serious concerns for the future. It was then that I decided to bite the bullet and announce the problems which we foresaw in an interview with a local newspaper. I still believe it is better to face problems head on and communicate with the media rather than to have rumors begin and then have the media search for quick answers on short deadlines. We didn't have any idea how much attention this announcement would draw. The letter and our announcement, together with the very public profile the Hall Financial Group had attracted for many years, led to numerous front-page stories in the Dallas area papers, the *Wall Street Journal*, and many other publications throughout the United States. Many initial stories speculated about the potential failure of our company, but they were, in the big picture, addressing the fact that Texas was well on its way to a deep depression. I initially called it the "Depression of the Rich," but as time went on, the savings and loan and banking collapse affected virtually the entire country and people on all socioeconomic levels, making it front-page news on a daily basis. Though my announcement of debt restructurings was viewed as highly unusual and even somewhat shocking at the time, such announcements eventually became commonplace in the Southwest's crash of the eighties.

As the inflationary burst of the 1970s gave way in the mid-1980s to a deflationary correction, those in oil and gas, real estate, and banking, particularly in the Southwest, felt the pain of the economic depression.

The reaction of the government in our case, and in the cases of others who were early to fall, was to try to place the blame rather than face the realities of the market. This led to intense involvement of the Federal Home Loan Bank Board. It is my opinion that the chairman at the time mishandled the savings and loan industry's problems. Hall Financial Group's story is one that shows how some of the savings and loan problems occurred and, more important, how they were compounded and worsened by mismanagement.

Finally, with the help of Congress (including senators and congressmen, Republicans and Democrats, and a cast of lawyers) we were able to re-establish communication and work out problems with our lenders.

Our story doesn't end with the trials and tribulations of dealing with a government agency; that was just a part of our surviving the depression. The grinding pressures of a depression in real estate and the savings and loan industry have affected the entire economic and social structure of Texas. Washington's early reaction to the crisis was mostly that of pointing fingers at Texans for fraud and mismanagement rather than dealing with the depression of real estate values. No doubt there were individuals who had committed fraud and other serious offenses which contributed to the crisis. They should be punished. But the economic depression was the major cause of the savings and loan crisis, and it brought with it changes in business ethics and morality as Texans dealt with a bust of Texas-sized proportions.

This story is also a personal one of how an entrepreneur can triumph over adversities. From the lessons I learned, I hope readers can gain insight to their own economic challenges. The story combines another chapter in the giant saga of Texas, the real estate depression, and how Hall Financial, as a large real estate company, and I, as one entrepreneur, dealt with specific business pressures and eventually won.

Most of all, this story exemplifies the fact that even in the worst of situations, with honest, hard work there is always hope. We all can turn around the worst of problems if we persevere and refuse to let those problems overcome us.

PART ONE

AN
ENTREPRENEUR
COMES
OF
AGE

CHAPTER 1
WHAT A DIFFERENCE
A YEAR MAKES

IT WAS A SMOOTH FLIGHT. Cruising along at 35,000 feet on a perfect sunny day with almost no wind, my wife MaryAnna and I were relaxed and happy, sitting in comfortable seats on the chartered commercial jet. Across the aisle from us, in the other front row of first class, were Tex and Marti Schramm. Tex was fiddling with the antenna on the battery-operated television that he had brought along. The picture cleared just in time for us to see Michigan score a touchdown against Notre Dame.

Tex watched analytically, but MaryAnna and I cheered loudly. We both had gone to the University of Michigan and, although we attended different campuses at different times and didn't meet until years later, we liked to think of the university as part of our romantic past.

During the flight the four of us and others in the Dallas Cowboy entourage talked football business and just plain had a good time. Behind us were Tom and Alicia Landry and, as usual, Coach Landry was quiet and self-contained, always thinking. It was Saturday and we were flying from Dallas to Detroit, where our Cowboys would play the Lions on Sunday. The plane was an American Airlines charter devoted solely to transporting the Cowboys' organization. And with this in mind, there was a very specific protocol in seating: Tex Schramm, president and general manager, and his wife sat in the front row of first class on the port side. Owners who wanted to see an away game sat in the other front row seats, followed by the head coach and other coaches, and the players and team personnel sat in the regular seats.

I suppose for most on the plane, this was just another game, but in many ways, I felt this was a special flight taking me home as victor. My company, Hall Financial Group, had opened an office in Dallas in 1981 and, since that time, I had been splitting my time between Detroit and Dallas. The Detroit area had remained my business headquarters until the fall of 1983, when almost one hundred key people with Hall Financial moved to Dallas. Since the move, the real estate syndication business had grown and prospered beyond all expectations. I was feeling great about life. As a relatively new Texan, I couldn't help but feel proud making this trip, knowing that the next day my wife and I would be sitting in the visiting owners' box, hopefully watching our Cowboys beat the Lions.

About a year earlier, I had first talked to the Cowboys' long-time owner, Clint Murchison, about buying the entire team. I backed away when I found out I would have to hold at least 51 percent ownership in my own name, and frankly, I just wasn't that much of a football fan. But I was reasonably sure the team would be sold in the near future. I wanted to make sure the Cowboys would stay in Dallas and in the hands of a quiet, concerned ownership that would carry on the proud tradition that Clint, Tex, and Tom had fostered together for more than twenty-five years.

I remained interested in the Dallas Cowboys for a number of reasons. First, MaryAnna loved football and the Cowboys in particular. Second, I had a great deal of enthusiasm for Dallas as my chosen home—a city dedicated to success. Since the Cowboys were truly a Dallas institution, I felt that becoming involved with them showed my appreciation for Dallas and would be a good indication of my Texas loyalties.

But there was another reason. The Cowboys were a well-oiled, excellently-managed machine. The Cowboys' management had always done a great job of putting together a clean-cut, dedicated group and over the years they had earned far more than their share of victories, championships, and glory. I admire that kind of effort in a business. I couldn't help wanting to become a part of it—even in a passive role.

In 1985, Bum Bright, a highly regarded Dallas businessman whose fortune began in oil and real estate, organized a group to purchase the Cowboys. I was one of those fortunate enough to be invited to participate. I purchased 10 percent of the team, borrowing all of the money required —as did others in the group—from RepublicBank in Dallas. It was a personal, unsecured loan for $6 million with favorable terms. At the time, that was quite an easy loan for me to get. I had earned excellent credit and was already a good-sized customer of Republic's.

I had reached the point where my family could enjoy some of the perks of success. I had come a long way since 1968 when, as a teenager, I started my real estate business with $4,000 in savings. Now, in 1985, my company owned 60,000 apartments, 3.5 million square feet of office space, and controlled $3 billion in total assets. Owning part of the Cowboys was a relatively small business venture, but it had special meaning to me as a tribute to MaryAnna.

The Cowboys' owners took only a passive interest in the team, so it was never difficult to arrange to attend an away game as an owner representative. Most of the owners had too many regular business commitments to travel to games frequently, but when we did, the flights were always great fun. From the time we arrived at the airport until we got back to Dallas, every arrangement and detail was handled perfectly. At our seats were goody bags full of candy bars, fruit, pretzels, and much more. The meals were often lobster and steak, two to three times normal size. While the players could eat it all, we were stuffed after the first course. American Airlines used the same senior crew for each trip, so we soon got to know one another. At take-off and landing, I was occasionally invited to sit in the jump seat of the cockpit.

As the plane landed in Detroit that day, I was looking forward to the quiet evening we had planned with two of our closest and dearest friends in their new home in a fashionable suburb of Detroit. The next day I planned to host a business brunch and then, of course, go to the game. I had given most of my extra seats in the visiting owners' box to friends, but I had a couple of tickets left and figured I could find takers at the brunch. Our Detroit office manager for Hall Financial Group had bought more than 150 tickets for securities salesmen and investors to go to the game. After the brunch and my scheduled "State of the Economy" speech, we would take off for the stadium. It was going to be a great weekend.

Two buses awaited the players and coaches as we got off the plane, and a long, black limousine was waiting for MaryAnna and me. I would rather have ridden on the bus and made a mental note to let the person who arranged these things know that in the future we would rather not be singled out. The limousine drove us from Metro Airport to downtown Detroit. The buses followed. As we pulled up to the new Omni Hotel, TV camera crews were waiting with lights and microphones. I guess it was common knowledge that the Cowboys were staying at this hotel, but I was amazed at the size of the crowd gathered behind the police ropes to get a glimpse of the team.

As we entered and walked through the onlookers, I couldn't help but wonder if people were thinking, "Who's that?" or maybe even, "Is he the kicker?" I was obviously too small to be anything but a kicker, or maybe a water boy. We got to the table where all of the envelopes and keys were organized for the team, and an assistant manager of the hotel very nicely asked me who I was. I guess I was still dreaming about being the kicker, because his question momentarily stumped me. I was rescued when one of the coaches volunteered, "This is Mr. Hall, one of the owners." That quickly produced the hotel manager, and in a matter of seconds we were whisked up to our luxurious suite.

We had time to relax before dinner, so I opened a copy of the *Detroit Free Press* newspaper that was in the room. The cover of the magazine section shocked me—on it was an illustration of me! I immediately turned the page and started to read. The lengthy cover story was a profile on me, a favorable one, and it was just one more thing that made the weekend special.

The press hadn't always been so kind. Some months earlier, both of the large Detroit papers ran major stories on me when the chairman of First Federal of Michigan, Jim Aliber, started litigation to try to stop what they thought was my takeover interest in their savings and loan. I was by far their largest shareholder. The litigation at that time was at a boiling point. Several Detroit and national reporters had interviewed me in Dallas during the previous several weeks. The result of one of those interviews was this favorable story. What a relief. At this point in my life I was getting far more press than was desirable, but it seemed to come with the territory in the kinds of business activities I had been pursuing lately— like the takeover of First Federal Savings and Loan Association.

The evening with friends and the brunch the next day were great. At the brunch I saw more than 250 people who had been the core of my business life in Detroit, and since our move to Dallas, I had fully realized how much these friends meant to me. I had tried to maintain the relationships. It was gratifying to have so many of them turn out that morning to hear me speak.

In my speech, I talked about the softness in the real estate markets of the Southwest. Then I compared those problems to the difficulties the Midwest had suffered only a few years earlier. I reported on how well our properties in Michigan were doing and what that meant for the large number in this group who had invested in those properties. I compared the comeback of these properties with what we were hoping to do in the Southwest, explaining that, in our view, down cycles generally presented the best opportunities. The Hall Financial Group had been buying aggressively in the Southwest. We felt we might be in for some tougher times than originally expected, but we had no idea what the future would actually bring. At that time we still thought this was just a normal, temporary down period. Cycles are the norm in real estate and in the fall of 1985 this seemed just like any other. In 1986, however, we learned it was far worse than we had believed the previous year.

After that I talked about football and made the big mistake of predicting a strong Dallas win. The Cowboys' performance wasn't particularly brilliant that day and they lost to Detroit. On the trip home everyone was silent, which was usually the case after a loss, but I was preoccupied wondering about my takeover of First Federal. Would it go through, or would I make as much as $15 million on the stock I had accumulated? As I think back, it is funny that I became so upset over what clearly—by my current perspective—was not a problem worthy of much worry and frustration. Coincidentally, weeks later, when my real estate partnerships needed more cash, I had just sold out of the First Federal investment for a $12 million profit.

Perhaps that weekend in Detroit was prophetic of things to come. It may have signaled the beginnings of a turning point that I couldn't see at the time. No one had expected Dallas to lose that game and probably no one expected the Hall Financial Group winning streak to turn stone cold. In a very short time it did.

SEPTEMBER 14, 1986: A YEAR LATER

A year later I had learned what real frustration was all about. Once again the Cowboys were in Detroit to play the Lions. But I didn't go to the game. I wasn't even an owner anymore. In April, RepublicBank came to me and essentially called my loan on the Cowboys, forcing me out. On September 14, I put in a typical sixteen- or seventeen-hour day at my office. I was halfway listening to the game on the radio at my work table and occasionally glanced at the portable TV that my secretary had brought into her area. It sounded like a good day for the Cowboys, but the game was far from what was really on my mind. On that day, things were a little bit more upbeat than they had been during the first part of 1986. My life then had been reeling past me as if I were a bystander. Yet on that day things were bleaker than I could have ever, even in my wildest nightmares, imagined a year earlier.

I was absorbed with planning various workout restructuring strategies and preparing a report to give to Federal Home Loan Bank Board (FHLBB) officials in Washington the next Wednesday. This preparation and that meeting the next week were crucial to the future of my companies—just as so many other days and weeks of meetings were that year. Still, it was clear that if on this particular Wednesday the meeting did come through, it would be the first break in the Federal Home Loan Bank Board's stonewalling. The Federal Savings and Loan Insurance Corporation (FSLIC), a subsidiary of the Federal Home Loan Bank Board, as conservator of one of our lenders, Westwood Savings and Loan, had started foreclosure and receivership actions against fifteen of our properties in mid-July.

Savings and loan associations, financial institutions separately chartered by Congress, are a specialized form of banks. Savings and loans (S&Ls) were originally established to make sure home-mortgage loan money was available, but as laws changed, they were granted more and more powers. In 1982, a new law, known as the Garn–St. Germaine Act, allowed too much freedom to the ill-equipped savings and loan managers, and this was one of the major causes of the problems that led to the savings and loan bail-out legislation in 1989.

As a result of wrongful proceedings to foreclosure on fifteen of our properties, we had been doing nothing but fighting back in courtrooms all over the country. We refused to let a few government representatives be above the law and treat our investors unfairly. Since mid-July, I had been trying to get the Federal Home Loan Bank Board's chairman, Edwin Gray, to meet with us and explain why government representatives were reneging on an agreement that had been signed by Westwood in June. We had paid $1 million at their request as a good faith consideration of the agreement at the time of the signing, and now they were reneging. We wanted to know why we were being aggressively attacked in the courts instead of being allowed to complete the agreed-upon restructure of our loans. We were prepared to do everything possible to meet our financial obligations. We just needed a little breathing space for a chance to pay back the loans. Moreover, the government, through Westwood, was causing the downfall of a restructuring plan that it had been involved in negotiating for seven months, and which was about to be completed. The restructuring plan, or "workout plan" as it is sometimes called, is simply the changing of debt terms to allow for new circumstances surrounding the loan, such as the devastated market in Texas, and to avoid a bankruptcy. Foreign debts are frequently restructured or worked out with the big U.S. banks that have made billions in loans to Mexico and others. Somehow Chairman Edwin Gray seemed to prefer to force us—along with several savings and loans—out of business altogether. It made no sense, since the government would eventually have to pick up the tab on those failed institutions. I got a strange message from seven unanswered letters and numerous unreturned phone calls to Chairman Gray.

While we were in the thick of serious financial problems, news stories with misleading headlines like "Hall Financial Group Files Bankruptcy" appeared in the papers. (One small partnership we controlled, *not* Hall Financial Group, had filed for bankruptcy and, ironically, it was our smallest affiliated property a 114-unit apartment complex in Greenville, Texas.)

This caused a dramatic loss of business for us. Those headlines threatened to become a self-fulfilling prophecy.

We first began realizing our potential problems in December of 1985, but we had no idea how serious they would become and, until the spring of 1986 when reports were beginning to show the seriousness of the decline, we still saw the problems as just ordinary business difficulties. Our fundamental business was to buy property, usually large apartment complexes, that we believed could be improved or "turned around" over time. We would increase the profitability of operations, sometimes by physical changes, sometimes management improvements, or by both. We would then sell the properties at a profit. The properties were purchased with capital provided by limited partner investors, whose investments were in great part tax benefits. We improved the properties with the investors' capital and the residents lived in better apartments at more affordable rents due to the tax incentives the investors received, which encouraged the needed capital to be invested into the properties. Hall Financial Group had raised more than $1 billion in equity and borrowed an additional $2 billion to acquire the many properties. The limited partner investors would share in the profit when each property was sold, which, over the years, proved very profitable for many of them.

Often these properties would need extra cash to carry them through difficult periods because operations would fall behind projections. Experience over two decades had shown that these short-term loans were enough to get through the temporary down periods. By late 1985, I had a substantial amount of my own money in short-term loans to partnerships to keep the properties current on their mortgages. In hindsight, 1985 had been a tougher year than we thought along the way, but we thought we had seen the bottom. I thought my loans would be more than the properties would probably need, but soon I discovered that it wasn't enough. In late December, I thought we might have to restructure some of our debt to avoid problems paying back mortgages on some properties. In 1986, we analyzed our properties and found, to our surprise, that we would be short as much as $120 million—if we paid everything according to the original mortgage requirements without a restructuring.

Restructuring is a widely accepted financial technique used when debts face temporary cash-flow problems. Payment reductions, lowering of interest rates, or delaying payments on principal become options in times of unusual economic strains for home owners and business people alike. In some economically hard-hit farm communities, farmers were forced to restructure their mortgages to survive and avoid foreclosures or, worse yet, personal bankruptcy. The restructuring process can help both the borrower and the lender get through the tough times. From a business perspective, one of the most famous large restructurings is that of Chrysler Corporation. Hall Financial Group's restructuring, as it turned out, was actually larger and more complex than Chrysler's government bail-out. A well-organized restructuring plan avoids bankruptcy for the borrower, saves lots of wasted legal accounting and other costs of a bankruptcy, and maintains more value for both the creditors and debtors.

What we at Hall Financial Group did not realize until 1986, and even beyond, was how severe our problems would become and the extent to which we, as a company, would become the focal point of broad troubles in the real estate business in general. To make matters worse, the restructurings were put in jeopardy by the FSLIC foreclosures. The lawsuit for receivers and foreclosure was the first step in taking the ownership of the properties away from our investors and us. If we had failed to convince the Federal Home Loan Bank Board to back off, huge losses would have occurred, with a terrible ripple effect throughout the economy. It was possible that I could have lost everything, but more importantly, so could many of the investors who had trusted me, and our lenders would have suffered huge unnecessary losses. Attorneys had urged me to take actions to protect myself financially, such as putting assets in trusts or moving monies offshore away from U.S. laws. With the exception of paying off my home mortgage, I ignored their advice. I didn't want the foreclosures to happen and I was determined to put all of my money and my heart and soul into protecting the investors. For me, Westwood was a symbol of a domino effect that would follow—one way or the other. Because of this, 1986 had been a miserable, frustrating year.

On September 14, 1986, I only half-heartedly listened to the Cowboy's game, probably because I was no longer part owner. And I had work to do. On that particular Sunday, like so many others in 1986, I was working in my office with a substantial number of wonderfully loyal managers and staff members. We were all determined to try everything we could think of to save our investors from loss.

It had been fun being an owner of the Cowboys and living on top of the world in 1985, but September 1986 was a time to look ahead to our upcoming meeting with the Federal Home Loan Bank Board officials. It was frustrating to work hours preparing a report for people who were stonewalling us. It was enough to make me ask myself if the end could ever justify this pain. But at those times I would think of the investors who had trusted me and I knew we would have to keep trying to make our situation work.

SEPTEMBER 13, 1987

With less than two minutes to go, the Cowboys were ahead of St. Louis 13 to 3 as I drove to Bachman Lake for my regular 3.5-mile run. This simple fact gave me enough confidence in the outcome to turn off the car radio and go jogging. Driving back refreshed, I turned on the car radio and was surprised to hear that St. Louis had managed to totally turn it around and beat the Cowboys 24 to 13. Well, that just goes to show the fine line between success and failure. It was like the city of Dallas at the time. Success in Dallas was regularly turning to defeat for a lot of people. You'd think I would have learned by then never to take anything for granted.

Although I was in my office working that particular night, I had spent most of that Sunday at home relaxing with my family. That was certainly unusual for me at any time, but it sure felt good. As the sunset faded and the lights of the city began to twinkle beyond my office window, I was preparing for several important meetings on Monday.

The first meeting was with the head regulator of the Federal Home Loan Bank of Dallas to talk about my potential interest in acquiring some of the failed savings and loans under his jurisdiction. I had put together $100 million from investors who had approached me seeking the opportunity to acquire and run failed savings and loans in Texas. The irony of the situation staggered me. In 1986, we had been fighting for our lives with the Federal Home Loan Bank Board, and then, just a year later, we were going to walk in and offer those same regulators a deal that could help get them out of hot water.

I felt, undoubtedly, that I could be of service to them. It seemed at the time that we had worked our problems out successfully, though not without some casualties and losses, and had developed a relationship of mutual respect in the process. All of our loans were current under the restructurings and we truly had saved the savings and loans and the regulators a huge sum of money by avoiding a massive bankruptcy and collapse of all of our holdings. Indeed, things worked out well for the vast majority of our investors and for the financial system behind the savings and loans—just as we had hoped. While we did not have a perfect scorecard, we did save almost all of the properties from foreclosure and loss for our investors. I was still confident that in the long run, the same positive outcome would be true for Hall Financial Group and for my personal financial situation. But that was certainly down the road.

My second meeting that Monday was on a debenture (a type of

corporate borrowing) we were trying to put together for Hall Financial Group. We had been working hard to recapitalize Hall Financial Group with $50 million in subordinated debentures. If successful, it would have greatly increased our ability to move forward in a continually difficult market. But what I couldn't have foreseen that Sunday was the stock market crash to come the following month. All of our work on the debenture was to prove for nothing. Our plan was ruined when the market tumbled dramatically in October. Another more ambitious plan of ours, a merger of the Hall corporations (then my private real estate companies) with May Petroleum (a company in which I had 54 percent ownership), would eventually take the place of the proposed debenture.

All of our problems were certainly not out of the way in September 1987. We still were involved in some restructurings (also known as loan workouts) from time to time, but we were substantially on course. We had closed most of the loans with our largest lender, Westwood Savings, but a few still lingered. We had also settled our differences with the government and with our other lenders. Now the press saw us as a sign of a market that was becoming healthier. I had received many requests to speak, to tell my story of how I made it through the last year. Tough times were still with us and many real estate investors were groping for ways to survive. In my own way, I hoped we were part of a trend toward lenders and debtors working together so that the economy didn't get any worse and spiral downward.

Despite a tight cash position and the real estate market being still worse than we projected, Hall Financial Group had begun expanding through acquisitions of other troubled real estate companies. In the six months preceding September 13, 1987, we had purchased Knoxville Associates, Combined Properties, what was left of a big financial failure called Vesteq, and others. In all, we purchased companies with a total of 17,000 apartment units. We had looked seriously at as many as thirty real estate companies, most of which were run by people who had been in the business fifteen or even twenty years and were going broke. The shakeout had driven them all out of business. It was sad to see not only the financial loss but the personal cost that the economy was inflicting on so many people in Texas. Yet, we were an example of the fact that people can survive.

In fact, by September 1987 we really had come back. I had come back personally from having very little cash to having more than $10 million in stocks, bonds, and cash. The Hall Financial Group also had available cash, May Petroleum had cash, and my two stock special funds were also liquid with more than $20 million in cash. Until September, I had been bearish on the stock market. I had most of my personal cash in a short position (this is a bet that the stock market will go down) in the Standard & Poor's futures market in an effort to take a big risk, but I hoped to make a big gain. I badly wanted to get back into the big league. However, things were going against me because the stock market had been going up. I was feeling pretty stupid because I had lost $3.5 million of my hard-earned, turnaround money. Some very aggressive stock brokers had convinced me that the Dow Jones stock average really was going to 3600. Repeatedly, they told me I should get on the bandwagon or I would lose my shirt. One of them constantly repeated, practically chanted, "The trend is your friend."

In September 1987, I was back on my way to recovery. I had a plan to merge my real estate companies into May Petroleum, which would give Hall Financial Group a substantial added liquidity and economic power. That, combined with the cash position I had already established personally through liquidating my investments, put me in a position of relatively good economic strength.

SEPTEMBER 1988

I was not listening to the Cowboys' game. A joke that was going around Dallas at the time told it all: "A voice comes over the loudspeaker at Texas Stadium and says, 'Would the lady who left her eleven children please come back to the stadium and pick them up? They are beating the Cowboys 49 to 0.' " In fact, one joke after another about the Cowboys not only depicted their worst season in years, but also, more or less, told the tale of Dallas and the general economy of the state of Texas.

The largest owner of the Cowboys in 1988 was Bum Bright. He must have wondered if the jinx that was on Clint Murchison was at work on him. Clint went broke after selling the Cowboys to the group made up of Bum, a few others, and myself just three years earlier. Now Bum Bright, who only a few years earlier was listed by *Forbes* as being worth $600 million, was trying to sell the Cowboys to gain needed personal liquidity. Bum, a very savvy investor, had bet heavily on the savings and loan and real estate business in the mid-1980s and was now seeing it crumble. His Bright Banc grew to over $5 billion in assets but was rendered insolvent and acquired in early 1989. Despite his problems, Bum survived and surely will come back strong.

Looking back from the fall of 1987 to the fall of 1988, I realized this was an unkind period of time to many individuals in Texas, as well as many institutions. First RepublicBank, in a merger put together primarily by Bum Bright, its largest shareholder, failed and was taken over by the FDIC, causing not only Bright to lose his entire stake, but all other shareholders to lose their stakes as well. Savings and loans were being taken over, merged, and liquidated like crazy. The financial system was in chaos, caused by lower real estate values and numerous bad loans. The so-called Southwest Plan became the highly public and highly controversial bailout program of FSLIC. This plan tried to help solve the S&L crisis in Texas, which has since escalated to being the most costly financial disaster in U.S. history.

Shortly after my uncertainty about being bearish on the stock market in September 1987, I allowed my personal insecurity to be overcome by the confident, strong statements of those stockbrokers who "knew what was happening." They knew for sure the market was headed to 3600. I reversed my position from being "short" in the stock market to going "long." This meant that in October 1987, I was betting in a big way that the market would go up. Just days before the crash that I had been predicting would occur, I went against my own intuition. This was certainly something I would never have done before the disastrous times of 1986. The pain of 1986 had caused me to lose a great amount of confidence.

In the stock market crash of October 1987, I lost a huge amount of money, and in a short span of two years was forced once again into such a deep hole that I thought there could be no recovery. In fact, in many ways I was economically in worse shape than at any point in 1986, but my pressures were different. The newspapers weren't running full-page stories and didn't know about my financial travails in the stock market, which made it somewhat easier for me to cope.

Throughout most of 1988 the real estate market continued its downward spiral, putting further pressure on rents and occupancies in the Southwest. New market problems started to develop in Arizona as well as the Southeast. The overall government involvement in the savings and loans and commercial banks further added to the cloud over the market, as virtually no loans were being made and a sense of economic gridlock had taken hold in the marketplace.

The difference for us in 1988 was that we were more prepared for these types of problems. For us, 1987 provided a false recovery which was further accented on the downside by virtue of our stock market losses. From a business standpoint, 1988 was a tough year but it was not nearly as difficult as 1986. The year 1988 involved more restructurings and a constant vigil over cash and cash flow.

AUTUMN 1989

Jerry Jones from Arkansas bought the Cowboys for $147 million in 1989. Boy, have things changed. Texans never thought anyone in Arkansas could have that much money.

The Cowboys have changed in many ways. At that time, Texas, in its own way, had changed. Just like the Cowboys. Tom Landry was no longer the coach; the fans had to swallow hard as they saw the legendary and only coach of the Cowboys for twenty-nine years fired by the team's new owner. Jerry Jones even managed to get into a scrape with the fans over changes he wanted to make in the uniforms and rules regarding the Cowboy cheerleaders. The venerable institution of the Cowboys was downright being shaken up by the new folks from Arkansas.

Just like Jerry Jones from Arkansas, North Carolina National Bank (NCNB), Banc One from Ohio, and numerous other outsiders from all over the world were coming into Texas with their money to buy the bargains. Texas was changing, there was just no two ways about that. While the Cowboys might never be the same, neither would the banks and the savings and loans. Nor would real estate be played with the same high-leverage, handshake relationships that once existed.

For Hall Financial Group, 1989 was a transitional period. It seemed like everything was so close yet so far away. As in the Dickens line, it was the best of times, it was the worst of times. Lawsuits and lots of legal entanglements characterize the whole depression mentality, which certainly continued throughout 1989. Further restructurings and additional economic problems in Arizona and other markets added to the "worst of times" side of the ledger.

But on the bright side, 1989 was a year of great progress in many areas. The operations of the properties improved dramatically and the trend in Texas was clearly upward. Opportunities to buy properties finally started to shake loose. With the passage of the savings and loan bail-out legislation, and the establishment of Resolution Trust Corporation, the cleanup began.

The light at the end of the tunnel was clear and it truly was sunlight, not a freight train. Although the headlines of the local papers continued to press onward with the doom and gloom of financial failures such as the financial problems of Lomas Financial, a multibillion dollar real estate and mortgage company, some good news also began to appear. Hall Financial Group was beginning to raise new capital and to buy new properties. The opportunities and the purchases were absolutely phenomenal. All in all, Hall Financial Group and its investors fared well, although we continued, like everyone in real estate, to have some losses.

On a personal note, in the autumn of 1989, I truly could look back and understand what a difference a year makes. The last few years have each seen dramatic change—the distance from the severity of '86, the temporary recovery of '87, the continuing difficulties of the market in '88, followed by a combination of continued challenges and vast improvements in '89—and this gives me a greater perspective for time and change. Perspective also allows me to reflect on the amount of dramatic ups and downs of the last few years with a sense of peacefulness and gratitude. Through the help and efforts of many, we at Hall Financial Group have not only survived, we have done so without selling out in any way. I believe that good guys do win in the long run. Sometimes the pain can be awfully strong in the short run, but hard work, integrity, and perseverance are the elements that make winners.

SPRING 1990

Texas is getting better. Hall Financial Group is buying property again, now with investment from Japanese partners, pension funds, and sophisticated individuals from all over the United States. At the same time, we, like the industry, are still working through old problems with loan defaults and needed restructurings.

The bad times aren't completely gone; in fact, real estate deflation is now spreading to other areas of the United States. The flip side of the problems is that we are now taking advantage of great opportunities caused by the problems. The 1990s will see a transition from problems to prosperity in real estate. Hall Financial Group will continue to solve old problems (fewer as time goes on), and hopefully with our new partners prosper in the future from today's opportunities.

CHAPTER 2
THE MAKING OF AN OPTIMIST

AS A KID I had never intended to become a businessman or an entrepreneur of any kind. To the contrary, I was determined from a very young age to avoid business. Though I had always had great love and respect for my father, I watched him as he climbed the corporate ladder, and despite his success, decided early on that a life like that was not for me. I wanted to be a writer and a poet.

When I was three, I was diagnosed as having a form of childhood epilepsy. Though I eventually outgrew the condition, I was treated with phenobarbital, the prescribed remedy for epilepsy in the fifties. Doctors assured my parents that the drug would produce only helpful results, but despite their assurances, this strong depressant produced many harmful side effects that dulled my childhood development physically, mentally, and emotionally. Throughout my grade-school years until I was taken off of the drug at age thirteen, I was a poor student. I had severe problems with reading because the drug, I later learned, affected my eye-brain coordination. That didn't help much with baseball either. I was often lonely and frustrated and remember many times going home to sit alone and think when the other kids were out playing.

After my brother and I were born, my mother decided to go back to college to get a degree in art education. Though she was either at work or in class when I came home from school, she channeled my energies into art projects. I spent many afternoons alone at home writing poetry or drawing when both my parents were at work and my brother was off with his friends. Eventually my frustration and sadness, caused both by the natural cruelty of other children and the depressants I was taking, gave way to an inner strength and determination born of long hours of self-reflection. I used to sit for hours planning how to overcome my difficulties and eventually I did.

In school, I was the typical class clown, always disrupting the teacher and never paying attention. When I was thirteen, one of my teachers took a special interest in me. She suspected that my clowning was a cover-up of a far more serious problem. Together with my parents, she started a full-fledged effort to get to the bottom of my reading problems. A reading expert was called in, and within a matter of minutes after her arrival, she phoned my parents to find out if I was on some sort of medication. My pediatrician had told my parents not to inform schoolteachers that I was being given phenobarbital because they might misunderstand. As a result of the prescribed drugs, I was practically illiterate.

I stopped taking phenobarbital, which new doctors found I no longer needed. That year my family moved to Chicago. I was excited to start a new school and have a fresh beginning. There I progressed rapidly both mentally and physically and, for the first time in my life, I tried out for sports. I also ran for class president and won. However, at the first football practice in seventh grade, I ran to tackle a dummy, hit too high, landed awkwardly, and broke my leg. That was the end of competitive sports for me.

When I wasn't falling on my leg tackling dummies, I was writing poetry. My family spent only two years in Chicago before moving back to Ann Arbor in 1965. Ann Arbor is a traditionally liberal college town and the war in Vietnam was beginning to tug at the national conscience. Much of the spirit of these turbulent times was felt at University High School, where I started ninth grade. University High was set up by the University of Michigan as a learning lab for teachers in advanced training. It was somewhat of an experimental environment and I took full advantage.

I'll never know how Dougie Stewart, a young teacher there, responded with such kindness to the high-strung, rude teenager that I was. She taught English, a subject I hated because of the reading. I cut her class more than most, and when I was there, I was an adversary. One day after class, Dougie asked me what I would like to study in English. I told her about my interest in writing poetry, and so after some negotiating, we agreed to a reading schedule that gave me plenty of time to write. Instead of my having to go to the class, Dougie arranged with the principal for me to spend time with her on evenings and weekends. I grew to become close friends with Dougie and her husband and was deeply influenced by her.

Between my interests in writing poetry and my liberal political views, influenced by my experiences in Ann Arbor, the last thing I ever expected to be was a businessman.

I had negative feelings about the business world—I thought you had to step on people to get ahead. Yet despite my feelings, business was something that came naturally to me. In hindsight I see business differently. "Business" as I defined it when I was young was more in the image of Beaver's dad, Ward Cleaver, on "Leave It to Beaver"—staid, corporate, conservative, and bureaucratic. Today, I think, business people in our society generally have become more entrepreneurial—risk takers who are more creative and exciting. The stakes are high and entrepreneurs can grow faster and create more jobs for society, but they can go broke a lot quicker, too. Business today is very different from my youthful view. To me it is truly more of an art form when it works and works right. Business is action.

I have always been infatuated with money, and even as a small child I held on to it fiercely instead of spending it. I remember more than once, when I was very young, looking at a menu that my father was holding and preaching to him that what he had ordered was too expensive. Naturally, my parents thought this fixation was a little strange for a small boy and quite annoying. Eventually, they sent me to a psychologist to figure out why I had this fascination. Nothing ever came of those sessions, although I sure looked at a lot of Rorschach inkblots. No one ever figured out my unusual attitude toward money. Ever since I was twelve years old, I have always had a job of some sort and I have always saved almost everything that I earned.

My first all-out business venture, when I was twelve, was a somewhat elaborate version of the proverbial lemonade stand. A local drugstore had just gone out of business, and I saw an opportunity. For fifty cents, a quarter down and a quarter to be paid later, I bought the entire inventory of Green Rivers—a soft-drink syrup from the drug store—and began selling the beverage made from the syrup around the neighborhood. My only problem was, when the syrup was gone, so was my business. Not so different, I later found out, from the oil and gas business. Soon after that, I went into business with a friend of my brother's, distributing coffee for automatic coffee makers to offices in the Ann Arbor area. I got two-thirds of the business for doing the work and he got one-third for putting up $600 in capital in order to start the business. To this day, my former partner in this coffee service is still my friend.

But the real money in those days was in lawn mowing. I started mowing neighbors' yards before I could drive and an increase in revenue depended on a larger customer base, which was beyond walking distance. I negotiated with my Dad and we came to an agreement: he supplied me with the transportation for a percentage of any earnings. This big scheme of mine also depended on a riding mower, which I had already picked out. I approached my dad for the money and learned something I then hadn't heard of but am very familiar with now: interest. He loaned me the money for the mower at 2 percent above the interest rate the bank would charge him. This, he explained to me, was because I had no established credit record.

By the time I was eighteen, I had $4,000 in savings, thanks largely to my lawn-mowing business. In 1968, I was living in Ann Arbor and there was a tremendous struggle going on between students at the university and landlords. I read newspaper stories of high rents and poor maintenance and was outraged. It seemed to me that something was drastically wrong with private enterprise taking advantage of students, so I decided to use my entire life savings to buy a rooming house. Before I graduated from high school, I had my plans set. As a first-semester freshman at Eastern Michigan University, I planned to operate a rooming house on a part-time basis and prove that business could be done in a fair and honest manner. Of course, I planned to do that, make a profit, plus hold down a full-time job. Idealistic, young, and naive, I began my journey into real estate. I looked at more than a hundred properties before I finally settled on the first one. But after the first, the rooming houses multiplied like rabbits. Within a fairly short period of time, I had acquired twenty of them and secured management contracts for several other properties. Beginning with my second building, I always had partners. I used to sell limited-partnership investment interests in the rooming houses to other students in $250-per-investment units. Throughout my three years of college I did, in fact, work a forty-hour job at a hospital, as well as rent the rooms, clean the halls, maintain the buildings, and acquire new properties.

Limited partnerships are partnerships in which the general partner does all the work and takes all the liability and risk and the limited partners invest most or all of the capital, but their risk is limited to losing their agreed-upon capital and no more. The limited partners depend on the general partner for the day-to-day decisions. In turn, the general partner usually gets some ownership (usually 25 percent after the limited partners have gotten their money back) and fees for his efforts. If the investment succeeds, the limited partners can receive outstanding returns, both in cash flow and sale proceeds. In these early partnerships, I found a few students with some extra money and a few family friends willing to bet on me and the buildings I had found to buy.

Those were difficult times to be in the apartment business. There were rent strikes, landlord-tenant relationships, consumerism, and Nixon's Wage and Price Controls, which froze rents at a very low level and almost forced us into bankruptcy. I found that while I was determined to be a "good guy" landlord and make an honest profit, the tenants union, however, wasn't playing by the same rules. I never had understood why other owners wouldn't talk to the tenants union representatives. They seemed like nice enough people to me. I had always believed that tenants' complaints have merit and they had some legitimate complaints, so I always agreed to meet with them.

The members of the tenants union had various agendas. Some of those agendas were filled with legitimate gripes like "fix my leaky pipe" or "provide better security." I thought that I could come along and provide a fixed pipe or security and everything would be wonderful. But I later found that I was missing the whole point. The brains behind the union really had no interest in fixing leaky pipes or even a fair profit and fair rents. They just wanted to tear apart the system of private ownership of housing. Their goal was to have enough rent withheld that they would, one by one, bankrupt the private owners of real estate with the theoretical result of "free housing for the people." They were, to my surprise, socialists—even though they didn't openly say so. I thought I was liberal, but I found I was anything but liberal when it came to the basis on which free enterprise is built.

The University of California at Berkeley and the University of Michigan were the two campuses that had really radical, powerful tenants unions. Their strategy was similar to that of the United Auto Workers, who concentrated their strike efforts on one auto maker at a time in order to force each into either an agreeable labor contract or bankruptcy. Similarly, the tenants union decided to go after one landlord at a time and bankrupt them. But their strategy fell short with some of the bigger landlords. They would deposit the rent money into an escrow account in Canada to try to force the landlords into collective bargaining (similar to what the United Auto Workers had done with General Motors, Ford, and Chrysler). By the time the school year would end, the unity would break down, some tenants would stop paying rent into escrow, and most would just split and go home for the summer. The effort would fall apart.

Well, there I was, this young student, nineteen years old, and I was the one who talked to the members of the Tenants Union Steering Committee. Therefore, they thought I was the weak one. I didn't know it at the time, but I was the next target. The steering committee of the tenants union went to the *Michigan Daily*, the big student newspaper, and told the paper that they needed to do a story on this Craig Hall, a rotten rat fink who had sold out to the establishment. The next thing I knew, a couple of reporters came over and I had my first exposure to the world of journalism. These reporters were really after me. They were very antagonistic and asked me to justify this or that rent increase. At one point one of them just came out and asked me how I could be such a capitalistic pig. I didn't avoid one question, and I must have done an okay job because the next day on the front page of the paper was a story about "Craig Hall, Youngest Landlord."

It was a very favorable article, and I was just naive enough to be pleased. The press has often been a double-edged sword for Craig Hall: the article made the tenants union furious. If they hadn't already decided to come after me before then, the article clinched it.

So that next fall of 1970, on any one day between twenty and thirty people were picketing my house where I lived with my first wife. The tenants union was putting leaflets full of false allegations under the doors of every building I owned or managed. The tenants responded in force by not paying rent. Even then, as a young landlord, I wasn't about to give in. I spent my evenings going around to talk to my tenants, convincing them to pay rent. I also fought back in the courts, suing those who hadn't paid. But I wasn't always successful. That year I sold my blue Corvette for a thousand dollars to make payments on the properties. It was one of the worst times of my life physically and emotionally, and I wouldn't be under that kind of intense pressure again until 1986. In retrospect, it was good, though minute, preparation.

The school year ended and I had survived, somehow, but I was still in deep financial trouble. President Nixon then passed the 1971 Wage and Price Controls Act on August 25, 1971. Under the controls, rents had to be rolled back to May 25, 1971, or be frozen on August 25, whichever was lower. The timing was really bizarre. I had a new property of 128 apartments. This property, called Eastern Highlands, was my big jump. I was finally getting away from what I called the "old haunted houses," rooming houses with high maintenance and lots of problems, and was acquiring a modern apartment complex. I created a marketing plan for the property around a Scottish theme that included a character named Scotty, named after my brother, Scott. I printed yellow bumper stickers with Scotty sayings. They were helpful in marketing the apartments.

Eastern Highlands wasn't without its problems. Nobody else wanted to buy it, which is the reason why I ended up owning it in the first place. The people who owned it previously had three mortgages, all of which were in default at the bank, and I had to take over all of the loans. It was a financial mess. I bought this property with a co-general partner, David Mackstaller, who was in his late twenties and, at the time, was my business law professor at Eastern Michigan. He was also a full-time lawyer downtown. We had become good friends after he tried to throw me out of his class. It was a class for seniors and I was a freshman but had begged to stay. Senior partners of David's law firm owned nineteen banks and a lot of real estate all over Michigan. His firm, the Parsons Group, was in a lot of financial trouble, and as the empire was about to topple, I found out that the firm owned Eastern Highlands apartment property. Of the 128 apartments, 100 were vacant! Whole halls had not been open for two years and there were cobwebs everywhere. I was undaunted though, and thought this was the greatest property. God, it even had a real parking lot, which was big stuff for me. What I didn't know was that the Parsons Group was ecstatic about getting rid of it.

I talked David into getting me an appointment with one of the partners and at a second meeting I got to talk to the executive vice president of the bank that controlled the property. I'll never forget the banker asking me how much I wanted to put down on the property. My answer was simple because I didn't have any money. He put his arm around my shoulder and said, "That's all right, if you want it this bad, you should have it." The first mortgage on the property had been in default for six or eight months, the second mortgage had been in default for a year and a half, and the third had been in default for two years. They rolled all the mortgages together and put it in my name together with the names of my friend David Mackstaller, who had quit his job at the law firm to work full time with me as an equal partner, and a third partner I brought in, Duncan Robertson.

After buying the Eastern Highland complex, I made needed improvements. We wanted to buy new furniture for the apartments, but we didn't have the money. Before the students went home for the summer that spring, I told them if they rented their apartments at the new, higher rents we had established and gave me a security deposit and first and last months' rent, then when they returned in the fall, the apartments would be fixed up and furnished with all new furniture. We even painted and furnished a model to show them what we would deliver.

Well, we did all kinds of improvements on the property that spring and summer of 1971 and then came the Wage and Price Controls. We had rented the places for $320 a month for eight months or $240 a month for twelve months. They were 1,100 square feet and had brand-new furniture. But the price controls were going to skew the rents in the building dramatically—even though all of the units were the same. Rent on some units would not change at all, since I had already improved them and rented them at the higher rates prior to May. Other apartments that I had improved since May, with the now illegally high rent money, would have to lease for $108, or some even as low as $78. There was no logic to it at all, and before I knew it, I was being sued—not only by the tenants wanting their money back, but by the United States of America. The tenants union had gone to a Senator in Michigan who had called the Justice Department and the IRS. The government's lawsuit was in the amount of $22,000 for alleged violations of the Wage and Price Controls.

It was ludicrous, but more importantly, it was an amount that could have bankrupted me then. I never could have come up with $22,000 in those days, considering I was already running behind 90 to 120 days on my bills just trying to make payroll while students refused to pay rent. I struggled and scraped my way through. Six years later, I settled the lawsuit by paying $2,000 to a charity. The whole thing seems so silly in retrospect, but it was only a taste of things to come.

Meanwhile, the bank that had financed the apartment for me was having huge problems and had been taken over by the regulators. We were in default on the loan because we were having trouble collecting rents, so the bank was suing us. Those were not all of the problems. The building started having structural problems and was falling apart in places. Then, to add insult to injury we found out we were being taxed doubly by the municipalities since the property was on a city/township border, and we were being sued for nonpayment of those taxes as well.

We did all kinds of things to make money to keep the Eastern Highlands going. We managed housing projects for HUD and even for a man who a lot of people thought was in the mob. Basically, we'd manage anything—no matter how bad the neighborhood, how horrible the property, or how tough the landlord.

Picture, if you can, a property with dark, dingy hallways, no doors on the individual apartments, graffiti everywhere, and smelly carpeting. This was one of the properties we were going to manage. The first day, I walked into the main office of the apartment complex and announced to the men sitting there that I was the new management. One guy picked me up a couple of feet off the floor and held me against the wall, and the other one took a gun out and held it to my head. Then they said, "Call Joey and see if this guy is telling the truth." These were the kind of people I was working for. I did become sort of pals with Joey, even though every month he asked me how much I was stealing from him. I told him I wasn't that crazy.

Student housing was an interesting business, to say the least. When marijuana was popular back in 1968 and 1969, it was good, believe it or not, for student housing; it mellowed people out and they didn't do a lot of damage. But when beer came back into fashion around 1971, you could judge how good the parties were from just the trash in the hallways. If there were less than fifty or sixty kicks through the drywalls, it was a slow weekend. I finally got tired of picking up beer cans on Monday mornings and fighting the tenants union, so by the end of 1971, I got out of the student-housing business and went into real estate for "real people."

In late 1971, we began to purchase non-student apartment buildings. We used the same basic formula of our doing the work and taking the risks—being the general partner. The investors put up the capital and were limited partners. We bought Van Dusen Apartments, a 72-unit property, and raised $70,000 of investor capital to capitalize it. That partnership took a long time to put together. Our investors were always kept well informed and we were making a lot of money for people, so our following grew rapidly. As the size of our investor following grew, we were ready to buy the larger properties. To really make the jump to bigger deals, we needed the help of other people in raising the investor capital.

When I was twenty-three, I was introduced to Peter Nunez and Bob Flynn, who were insurance and securities salesmen. They taught me a lot about raising money. At the end of 1973, we put together a partnership that raised $1.1 million of equity to buy Woodcrest Villa, a 458-unit apartment complex with an indoor swimming pool. I was so excited. That year we held our company Christmas party there and, except for two employees getting drunk and into a fight, it was an almost perfect night. At the time of the Christmas party we hadn't finished raising the limited-partnership capital. It was Peter and Bob's way of letting me live on the edge. They said, "Don't worry," but the money didn't come in as expected. However, on December 31 at the last possible minute, they brought in the needed investors. Peter and Bob are still with us seventeen years later, only we've raised more than a billion dollars in equity since those days and we've climbed a lot of mountains together.

In 1974, money was raised for limited partnerships right up until midnight on December 31. This meant that limited partners could claim tax deductions on the property for several months in that year based on when the partnership actually bought the property. So much of our business was done the last few days before January 1. By December 31, 1974, we had raised $2.5 million for a property called Honeytree. To me, if Eastern Highlands was heaven, Honeytree was nirvana. Like Woodcrest Villa, it had an indoor pool, but it had much more, such as three- and four-bedroom townhouses, and there were 744 units—huge! Nothing could ever be bigger than this property, I thought. So, ecstatic from raising the money for Honeytree and in a rare effort to spend vacation time with my wife, I decided to go to Jamaica. As we were driving to the airport, we passed a property called Knob On The Lake. It was beautiful and big, had a golf course, a 150-acre property on a lake, and I turned to my wife and said, "When we get back, I'm going to buy that property." True to form, when we returned, I told my top associates that we were going to buy it. This was to become Lemontree.

The property was 56 percent occupied and was owned by a seventy-nine-year-old man named Frank Volk. He had been in business as a builder since he was a teenager, and this particular property was sixty years of building experience rolled into one dream. But as we learned, he had overextended himself to build it and now he was in financial trouble. I knew he needed to sell to someone who could turn it around. I thought to myself, I'm a turnaround artist, I can do it. I immediately thought of new ways to market the buildings on the property and fill them up.

My first meeting with Frank Volk didn't go too well. He said he was interested in selling, but when I told him I didn't have any money he literally threw me out of his office. But I kept coming back. At one point, he almost sold it to someone else. However, before the deal was closed, the buyer made Frank mad when he came onto the property acting arrogant and announcing that he was the new owner. I also explained to Frank that, even though this new buyer was going to put a million dollars down, Frank would still be personally liable on a lot of debt in that deal and still would be at risk to go bankrupt. He needed a deal with someone he could trust and who was capable of turning around a complicated financial mess. Frank would still be liable on the loans even after a sale. If a buyer just milked the place—that is, took the rents and let it go downhill—Frank would be in worse shape. He needed someone with management talent, willing to work hard, and most importantly, he needed someone with the highest level of integrity. He needed a much younger version of himself. I convinced Frank that I would, first of all, pay him a million dollars over time, but most importantly, that I wouldn't cheat him. I did insist, however, that I had to have free reign to fix the problems. He agreed. I wrote a good faith note for $300,000, which we both knew I wasn't good for at the moment. There were six mortgages on the property, all in default by six months to two years. We closed our purchase on March 5, 1975. I was twenty-four years old and had just purchased a $25 million property —it felt great.

One of the problems with the property, I thought, was nepotism; two people running the place were related to Frank, a son-in-law and a grandson-in-law. I was wrong about that one. They both agreed to work for me for the ninety-day transition period. Bill Poore, the son-in-law, worked with me for nine years after that, and we're still friends. Ron Berlin, the grandson-in-law, is still with me now as President and Chief Executive Officer of the Hall Financial Group, Inc. He is also a very close partner and friend.

Still, success with Lemontree didn't come easily. At the end of 1975, we had just barely raised the $3.3 million needed to syndicate the property. In fact, I had to have a friend open the county clerk's office in Wastenaw County at almost midnight to get the correct filing time, date-stamped and registered for 1975. This property was such a long shot that I actually had told all of the investors up front that they were probably going to lose all of their money.

Ten years later, we sold Lemontree to Southmark Corporation for $42 million cash. We had made a huge profit just from tax benefits and cash flow, but having paid $25 million for the property with nothing down meant the sale, at $42 million in cash, was very profitable. One reason people put money into Lemontree was that it offered, over the life of the investment, a 4.4-to-1 tax loss; this meant that for every $10,000 invested, the investor could write off $44,000 of tax losses. This was much higher than normal and was due to the high leverage (excessive amounts of debt) and, therefore, had a very high risk to it as well. The sales pitch was more than just tax incentive—we always had that drive to turn the property around and make money. Those were great years when my experience as a nuts-and-bolts real estate entrepreneur began to really pay off. Our investors were getting great returns of between 23 and 200 or more percent on their money. The returns were a combination of cash flow from the properties, tax benefits, and profits at the time of sale.

The hard-won expertise took its toll. By the end of 1975, barely twenty-five years old, I was burned out. I retired temporarily from my company, but retained ownership. The business had also affected my personal life and, with the pressure mounting, I got a divorce. I am fortunate that my first wife has remained a very good friend, and I am very close to our daughter, who was born in 1972.

I left for Europe after the divorce for a few weeks and when I returned I had an idea for a book about my company's methods to revive financially distressed real estate. My dad helped me write *The Real Estate Turnaround* and it proved to be great therapy and fun. The book was published in 1978 and finishing it helped me begin a new chapter in my life.

After getting back from Europe, I was sitting around one day with my friend Marty Rom, talking and thinking about what I was going to do for the rest of my life. Racquetball was a national craze then and everybody was playing. We decided to go into the racquetball business, but we needed cash. Marty and I made a list of seventy-five corporations to approach with partnership propositions. The first one on the list was Time Inc. because we thought it would be great to use the name *Sports Illustrated* in the name of the clubs.

Marty is a lot more outgoing and gregarious than I am, so his contribution to the deal, for 10 percent, was to get the corporate investor. I would do all of the limited partnership work, manage the clubs, and put some money in for my percentage. Marty decided to go after Time, so he just picked up the phone and called the son of Time founder Henry Luce. He got through right away, even though he didn't know him, and just said, "Hank, Craig and I are going to be in town next week. Let's go to lunch." Unbelievably, it worked. Within ninety days, Time Inc. had given us a million dollars and a name—Sports Illustrated Court Clubs.

This fairy tale doesn't have a happy ending, though. A year and a half later, we knew the business wasn't working! We had caught the crest of the wave. While we had become the largest chain of racquetball clubs, the business was simply overbuilt and the demand in the sport itself was declining. We started liquidating. Time Inc. bought the name back and gave us some operating money so the clubs wouldn't be an embarrassment to the corporation. Our investors had poured $14 million into the clubs, and we didn't want them to lose a penny, so we hung in there and put our own money in to support the business.

In 1978 and 1979, though my advisors were telling me to file for bankruptcy on the racquetball business, my real estate business was going great guns. To protect those investors, I supported the court clubs with profits I made from the real estate business and my other investments. When we went to closings to sell the clubs, we wrote checks to get people to buy. Though it may appear to have been throwing good money after bad, it was just my philosophy at work. I felt a sense of commitment to those individual investors. They had made their investments relying heavily on me, and I knew saving them from loss was the right thing to do. Those investors may not have made money, but we did everything we could to see that they didn't lose any. Today I'm still voluntarily paying back the last of some corporate loans for the racquetball business we started in 1975.

In 1979, now married to MaryAnna and rejuvenated, I decided to return to real estate full time. In the early days of the company, then called Hall Real Estate Group, we started a ritual of having partnership meetings and keeping in close touch with our individual investors. In good times and in bad, through the ups and downs, we tried to be consistent in our dedication to the people who made our business possible. This was one important key to our growth—our ability to keep investors happy and to honor their trust in us. This consistency remained as our guidepost throughout the toughest experience of my business and personal life—the restructuring workout experience on which this book is based.

In 1981, Hall Financial Group opened a small regional office in

Dallas. It was our first attempt at an office outside of Detroit and we were having trouble breaking into the good ol' boy network in Texas. I made a calculated decision. Toward the end of 1981, I decided to buy a house in Dallas and start spending a lot of time there in order to try to make Hall Financial Group work. The longer I was in Dallas, the more I began to like it—both the people and the area. Eventually, I moved my family to Dallas.

Cracking the solidly established Texas network was not easy. There's much more to being a Dallasite than wearing boots and speaking with a Texas accent. You don't see cowboy hats and boots on the streets of downtown Dallas like you might in Houston or Fort Worth, but the importance of being a native is strongly ingrained in the business world here. I think my straightforwardness is what enabled me to be accepted. Texans appreciate honesty in a person. They respect a person who'll state his opinion loudly and clearly, without hesitation, and I've never had any trouble doing that.

Our move to Texas was timed perfectly. In 1981, after Congress passed a new tax act, the Economic Recovery Tax Act (ERTA), I wrote an article for *Barron's* that explained how the new bill would be a boon to real estate investors. What I saw was huge tax benefits from the shorter depreciation that would encourage tax-oriented investment in real estate and push prices up. Congress had decided that we needed more capital in real estate. We quickly transformed our real estate company with a history of turnaround successes into one of the largest real estate companies in the country by riding the wave that we correctly saw as resulting from the 1981 Tax Act.

Our business took off like a rocket in 1982 and 1983. We grew geometrically in employees, investors, and apartment units owned and managed. In 1982, we had 1,016 employees, 2,168 investors, and 16,043 apartment units. By 1985, we had 2,913 employees, 7,235 investors, and had amassed 60,000 apartment units and several million square feet of office space. In 1982, we raised $55.3 million in limited partnerships. By 1985, we were the largest private-placement real estate operator in the country and that year raised $320 million. Our corporate revenues, not counting rents, had skyrocketed to $72.3 million. Hall Real Estate had offices from coast to coast and in Europe. We were in San Francisco, Newport Beach, Washington D.C., Dallas, Houston, and eight other U.S. cities, as well as Amsterdam. We were growing so quickly primarily because we focused on one product—private-placement offerings of some office buildings and many apartments—and we didn't diversify. We had an extremely good team of people marketing and putting together those partnerships. Nobody in the business had better people than the Hall Financial Group.

Hall Financial Group was a young, aggressive company. We were ripe to do something in a big way. I had an optimistic personality that matched the booming Dallas optimism. Detroit, by comparison, was stuck in the Midwest blahs.

But by 1986, the Texas real estate depression was in full rage—and instead of counting our profit, we were putting all of the money we could back into the business. We had amazing momentum, like a freight train moving faster and faster but headed for the wrong place at the wrong time. Maybe I should have seen more of the signs, but it seemed like just another cycle. In 1985, when I began to pour money back into the partnerships, I thought the huge amount needed—upward of $40 million—was a function of our size and this was just another cycle. We thought 1985 was the bottom, but it turned out to be the edge of a cliff. By the spring of 1986, with our people redoing numbers again and again, always revising, adjusting downward with the plummeting economy, I came to the realization that this was not just another cycle. In hindsight, one of the reasons we suffered so in 1986 was because we chose to do only one thing at which we were very, very good. When the apartment markets turned bad, and inflation went to deflation, and the tax law changed, all within the same eighteen months, we were in deep trouble. We would have been much better off had we diversified. Luckily for the company, though, I had begun to diversify my interests personally, and the profits I reaped helped keep Hall Financial Group alive.

CHAPTER 3
THE WINNING STREAK

DURING THE 1982 TO 1985 period of major growth for our company, I began to spend more and more of my time on other business. Activities that I'm told "normal" people call "work," I call "hobbies." Luckily for my real estate business, my hobbies have sometimes been very profitable. In those days, I was working seven days a week, many hours a day, spending fifty to sixty hours a week on the real estate business and fifty to sixty hours a week on non–real estate business interests. It was all great fun and I loved what I was doing. It always confused people around me because they would find out I was doing all of these different things and wonder how I found the time, but I thrived on it. I've always had people tell me that you should stick with what you do best. Well, I think that's not necessarily true for everyone. Some people find that they can do two or three things if they try. Most of my acquaintances think I made all of my money in real estate, but that's not true.

In 1978, I was introduced to seven people and together, with a small amount of capital from me, we founded one of the earliest for-profit Health Maintenance Organizations in the country. In 1983, I helped these individuals, who did the day-to-day work, take the company public. The Independence Health Plan, as we called it, was a great success. I sold part of my shares when we went public and some more in 1984. I made more than $30 million profit on that one deal. While most people think of me as a real estate investor, I was quite fortunate in my success in non–real estate activities. Later, I was able to use the money I made from Independence Health Plan to become involved in venture-capital investment in the medical field. I was involved at one time in a company that came up with a new formula to stop wounds from bleeding. Taking the money from Independence and putting it back into medicine and other venture capital was fun and sometimes profitable. It was consistent with my philosophy that being successful in business can lead to a positive outcome, not only for the business person cashing the check.

In 1984, for approximately $20 million, separately from Hall Financial, I personally bought 4.9 percent of the stock in Southland Financial Corporation, a Dallas-based real estate development company known for its world-class mixed-use project, Las Colinas. This mammoth development was a new city with all the amenities. I bought the stock because I thought it was a well-run company and because I thought Southland's founding family, the Carpenters of Dallas, or someone else would take it private. I never planned on going over 5 percent, the point when I would have to show my hand and go public with an SEC filing form called a 13-D. The SEC rules were to keep the marketplace informed of who owned more than 5 percent of any public company. I planned to stay at 4.9 percent and make whatever profit I could. That fall, I was in France on vacation with my wife. We were to leave the next day for a cruise of the Greek Isles to celebrate her birthday. But before we made it to Greece, I got a call from my office that the Carpenters had made an offer to take Southland private. Based on their offer, I could have made an immediate $7 million profit on my stock, but I didn't like the offer. I thought the vast assets of the company, primarily raw land strategically located between the Dallas–Fort Worth International Airport and downtown Dallas (in the then-booming Dallas real estate economy), were worth much more than what the Carpenters were offering. I estimated the per-share asset value of the company to be between $80 and $100. I thought a better offer in the $40 to $50 range would come along.

Anyone else probably would have taken the $7 million, gone to Greece, and bought an extra bottle of champagne, but I got on a plane, went back to the States, and bought another 5 percent of the Southland stock. I still didn't plan to buy the company, although I also didn't rule anything out. I just wanted to get in the fray and see what might happen. I certainly didn't want to fight with the Carpenters. Ben Carpenter, the patriarch of the current generation of Carpenters in Dallas, was a dream maker who took the family ranch and turned it into one of the great real estate developments in the world. In the beginning, they called Las Colinas—which took its name from the nickname that Ben's mother, Flossie, bestowed on the ranch, *"El Ranchito de Las Colinas,"* or "Little Ranch of the Hills"—Ben's folly, but Ben's 12,000-acre little ranch soon proved the naysayers wrong. By 1985, just ten years into its development, Las Colinas was a city alive with some 45,000 inhabitants and a nighttime population of nearly 20,000. I had a lot of respect for what they had built at Las Colinas. I had worked hard to earn acceptance into the Dallas community, and I didn't want to tangle with one of Dallas's oldest and most respected families. Later I had several opportunities to join forces with people who wanted to attempt a hostile takeover of Southland, including another 9.9 percent holder, Ivan Boesky, who wasn't yet infamous. But I didn't want to see the Carpenters lose their company, so I made a gesture to try to get together with them, and we arranged a meeting in New York. Ben Carpenter, his son John, and I had never met before. Despite the circumstances, we got along very well. They bought my stock for $62 million (just a little below the stock's market high) and, with a $14.5 million profit, I more than doubled what I would have made had I sold out and gone to Greece. As a result, I threw a party for 500 in Dallas to celebrate MaryAnna's birthday and to make up for not going to Greece.

I continued in 1984 and 1985 to take a number of positions in the stock market just under the SEC 13-D filing level of 5 percent ownership in a company. At any one time, I would have between $50 million and $100 million in cash invested in companies I believed to be undervalued. I was very, very liquid in those days. When the Carpenters bought me out for $62 million, I had no debt on that stock. The funny thing is, I have never learned to spend my money on personal fun. My family never flies first class. I always wanted to buy a boat but never let myself. At one point, I had the money all ready to put into CDs to maintain a large yacht that I was going to purchase. I even had the yacht picked out. We went to London and met with the lawyer for the yacht, but before going to Spain to finalize the transaction, I chickened out. That little boy looking over his dad's shoulder and preaching about ordering something too expensive is still very much alive within me.

Cluett-Peabody is another undervalued stock I purchased. I took a 9.9 percent position in the company, made an offer to buy it, and lost. But with $5.6 million in profits, I cried all the way to the bank with the Cluett-Peabody bid. I also became better acquainted with Paul Bilzerian, whom I had met casually some months earlier. As a result of his repeated attempts to get me to join him in his bid for Cluett-Peabody, which I repeatedly declined, we became acquainted. Although he was charming and likeable in his own unique way, something about Paul had bothered me so that I was hesitant to do business with him. Then, when management of the company tried to put up unfair defenses to stop a takeover by anyone, I agreed to lend Bilzerian's group $30 million—as a debenture if his bid succeeded. This is similar to the role T. Boone Pickens played in Bilzerian's takeover of Singer Company in 1987. Ironically, later I would end up suing Bilzerian over the Singer Company deal, but that is getting ahead of my story.

I was both intrigued and obsessed during this period with stock and commodity market trading. It was fast, exciting, exhilarating. In a room next to my private office I installed all of the latest Quotron equipment (a computerlike screen that gives up-to-date information on stock and commodity trading) so that I could keep up with the market at every moment. Futures trading is the riskiest and most complicated part of the market and when it beckoned, I answered the call in a big way. While competing in futures, I would often trade silver, gold, oil, and other interests, sometimes holding as much as $100 million in futures positions at a time. My success at times was substantial, but only because of my intense interest. I remember days during those frenzied bull years when I would rush through the end of a luncheon speech, leave the podium as quickly as possible, and rush to the phone to get the latest quotes.

Part of my motivation was to diversify. I had always heard that diversification was a prudent and smart thing to do. On the one hand, it helped me because I didn't have all my money in real estate and could liquidate diversified assets when I needed the cash, but overall, my advice to most people would be not to diversify. Concentrating on what you know best is the way to succeed. Today I am spending all of my time, and all of my capital, concentrating my efforts in real estate.

Those times were by far the most fun I had ever had in business. Hall Financial Group was growing phenomenally with the changes from the 1981 tax bill that had brought billions in private capital into the market. We knew exactly what Congress wanted when it used the buzzword "capital formation" and we wanted to be the best at finding good real estate for private investors. Congress's strategy was to get the country out of a recession, and it worked. From 1981 to 1985, we raised approximately a billion dollars in equity. In 1985, we were the largest private-placement syndication company in the country. In total we raised $320 million that year.

Meanwhile Texas was booming at the time and I was caught up in the mania. Money was free and easy in the late 1970s and early 1980s. Investors were happy-go-lucky. Dallas was, for the most part, a materialistic, conspicuous-consumption haven with lots of foreign cars, including many Rolls-Royces, dashing the beautiful people to the numerous charity balls. Slightly intoxicated, happy, young multimillionaires from oil, real estate, and banking would bid greatly more than fair market value for auction items they'd never use. Western art, bronze sculptures, vacation trips, and cars all brought handsome prices. At one auction I saw a friend bid $90,000 for a $45,000 airplane glider. That was several years ago and I don't think he ever used it—it just collects storage bills and dust.

Texas was really on a winning streak. Everything seemed to be working. Whatever anyone tried, it worked. Making money was easy and it was, socially, a part of the culture. Most people mixed friendship and business, while countless deals were made over a barbecue or a small neighborly get-together. For instance, I bought into a number of different partnerships that owned control of dozens of banks. It was a fashionable and, I hoped, profitable thing to do. I owned 50 percent of the bank of Quitman, Texas, was a part owner of several New Mexico banks, a new start-up bank in downtown Dallas, and on and on. Yet, like so many friendship deals of the early 1980s, I didn't have to pay in cash; I just signed notes and 100 percent of the investment was borrowed from a bigger bank. For a long time, these deals made money for everyone—the investors and the financing bank as well. However, in the depression a few years later, those loans were one of the worst types of loans for banks, second only to oil and real estate. Many of us who had signed these notes learned what joint and several liability really meant when most of the co-borrowers went broke and the banks looked to those of us who were left. Joint and several liability means you're responsible not just for your share of a note, but you can also get stuck for your partners' liability if they don't pay.

For Texans, the winning streak of the 1970s and early 1980s seemed like it would last forever. Texans were riding high and they let the world know it. Oil was at $35 per barrel in 1980, and, according to most experts, on its way to $100 per barrel by 1990–1995. Some Texans touted "Freeze a Yankee" bumper stickers to express their attitude toward the "cold and brusque" northerners who had invaded their territory.

The Texas winning streak was a long and great ride. The 1982–1985 oil decline seemed like a rest period in the expansion, an expansion that everyone figured would cleanse the excesses and allow Texas to move on again. Surely $20 per barrel would hold as a downward low price. In retrospect, 1985 was the top of the overall Texas economy. Despite the troubles with oil and the cracks in the banking system because of oil and real estate, the overall economy of Texas was strong in 1985. While the outside appearances looked and felt good, the foundation of that economy was weakening fast. In 1985 we surely couldn't see it.

In the spring of 1985, I had quite a bit of excess cash, more than $60 million at various points. The real estate business was not very demanding of my time; seemingly, it was doing very well. I was still looking for diversification, and the oil and gas business sparked my interest. The popular view at the time, and the view I held, was that oil and gas prices, having declined from 1982 to early 1985, were now bottoming out, making this a good time to get involved in the oil and gas business. This was in keeping with the contrarian "buy when things are down" philosophy, but the problem was that the timing was off. That summer I bought a little more than 8 percent of May Petroleum and became its largest shareholder.

My stock market investments and sometimes battles were indeed preparation for my bigger battles of the next four years. In 1985, I also had taken a position in First Federal of Michigan. First Federal was a stodgy old savings and loan with a great market position but poor management. I knew the savings and loan business, and I knew the real estate business. I saw this company selling at $5 and $6 a share, and I thought that was very low. I was critical of some of the things it was doing, but overall, I thought it was a good investment. The oncoming changes in the market, I believed, would increase the company's value. I had very little interest in buying any more stock, let alone taking the company private after my purchase of a little less than 10 percent. But I bought the stock and filed the required SEC forms and said I may or may not buy more stock, or sell, or do anything at all. This was my way to give myself flexibility in the SEC 13D form, since it truly represented my view of the First Federal investment. Well, the next thing I knew, First Federal filed an inflammatory lawsuit and went straight to the press with it. They actually wrote the lawsuit more like a press release. Evidently, they thought I was a lot more interested in taking over the company than I really was. I guess they were trying to scare me away. Well, that's exactly the wrong thing to do with me, because I don't scare easily. All they did was make me mad.

Often I make notes about ideas or when I'm in a meeting. Even though I never had any serious intention of taking over First Federal, I had made plenty of notes on my dreams and wildest ideas for the company. As part of the lawsuit, First Federal subpoenaed all of those notes. Lots of times, people conveniently lose things. In my case, I always play the game straight, and I sent them hundreds of pages of documents, many of which were apparently incriminating because it appeared that I really intended to take over the company. It looked like I had spent a lot more time on this deal than I actually had in comparison to my other work, but that's just my obsessive nature. I'm sure the bulk alone of what I'd kept on the company was overwhelming. Notes of thoughts on a business situation can, in hindsight, be taken out of context and therefore be very misleading. While I believe in living my life such that the truth will always be on my side, it is complicated by smart lawyers who can twist anything in writing by taking the parts out of context of the whole story.

The First Federal fight got quite intense, but eventually we came to a settlement and I got something that all of my lawyers had said would be impossible (they had urged me not to even ask): Jim Aliber, the chairman of First Federal, wrote a public letter of apology to me, to my family, and to my associates. That was only part of the first settlement. It also included $250,000 in legal expenses and a board seat for anyone but me. I chose my father. Later the chairman, still worried about my 9.9 percent interest, sold to someone another 9.9 percent of the stock below the market value. The stock was selling for $17, and he had sold it for $14. The board was also holding meetings clandestinely to exclude my father. So I fought back with another lawsuit. I fought back in the newspaper, taking out full-page ads in the *Wall Street Journal* and the Detroit papers, and I gave the names and phone numbers of all the directors in the ad, letting everyone know what the chairman had done. Eventually, the company found a friendly buyer for my stock, and I sold out and went away. The sale came just in time, even though I hadn't planned it that way. The $12 million profit I made from First Federal would be swallowed by Hall Financial's problems in a short time. It proved to be only be a Band-Aid remedy.

In August of 1985, while the First Federal litigation was in full swing, the management of May Petroleum, Inc., approached me and said that they were going to sell May for $5.50 a share to another public oil and gas company. They said that if I wanted to buy the company and would bid $6, the board would support me. On the strong recommendation of one of my advisors, I arranged the financing to purchase the balance of the company. Unfortunately, I made some mistakes. Before I completed buying the remainder of the shares, I also agreed to invest $14.25 million in the company, which I borrowed short-term from MBank Dallas. Both MBank and First City had loans to May Petroleum and the money I put into the company went to pay down those loans. With my long-standing MBank relationship, I felt certain they would tell me of any problems they knew about with May. I didn't make any moves without consulting MBank.

My loan from MBank was to be paid back in three weeks out of other monies I had coming in from stock sales. I was given a fast sales pitch, but I was depending heavily on the honesty of the individuals and the strength of the relationships. The MBank people had known the management of May Petroleum for years; in fact, the president of May Petroleum was on the board of MBank.

The bulk of my cash infusion into May Petroleum came on September 24, 1985. Less than three weeks later, I found out that in the third quarter, which ended September 30, the company showed its largest loss in history. There were major problems with two oil wells that I believed management, with any reasonable business knowledge, should have known about and should have told me. Hindsight is always a clear way to look at anything.

They may not have known and what seems reasonable in hindsight may not have been at the time. But by November, my relationship with May management was anything but friendly. After a grueling four-day board meeting in November, I bought control of the company and paid in another $5 million that was sorely needed to solve May's growing emergency cash problems. May was in far more trouble than I or the other shareholders knew, and it was about to get much worse than I realized. Without a good choice, I jumped in with both feet (arms, legs, body, and soul).

I gave the management until January 18 to sell the company at the highest possible price. If they couldn't, I was going to exercise my legal right to take control and make big changes quickly, in order to save the company. That's what happened. On January 18—upon my return from meeting with the Home Loan Bank of San Francisco—I became chairman, president, and CEO of an oil and gas company that had big problems. More problems than even I knew.

In looking back, perhaps I was ill-advised or moved too fast in getting into May. I didn't do enough homework and perhaps I let friendship and trust come before good business judgment. The management was in a tough spot and, in retrospect, I suppose they did what they thought was right. I'll never know who knew what about the asset problems. The board members were clearly a good and honorable group. Even today, I am blessed with the guidance and friendship of the directors who are still involved with me in the now-merged May Petroleum, renamed Hall Financial Group, Inc.

When I became Chairman, President, and CEO, I immediately cut the overhead of May Petroleum in half. The overhead had been running over $14 million a year and we cut it to an annualized basis of about $7 million. It was difficult and required terminating many employees, but had we not done that and had I not put cash into the company, May Petroleum would have been in bankruptcy liquidation in a matter of months. In 1985 and 1986, the company lost over $50 million and the banks were constantly knocking at the door. Before we came along, May was a whisker away from failing.

Immediately upon my takeover, First City and MBank started squeezing me on the May loans. The May Petroleum loans stood at $82 million. After I put money into the company, cut overhead, and accelerated loan pay downs, the loans were reduced to $24 million. In addition to the debt on May Petroleum, we had some $22 million in debt on May Energy, another company in which May Petroleum was the general partner and guarantor of loans. We eventually were able to trade May Energy to a larger company and get relieved of the $22 million in debt. But with oil and gas prices falling by more than 50 percent throughout that spring down to less than $10 a barrel, we were, like most independent oil and gas companies at the time, rapidly becoming insolvent. So here I was in early 1986 trying to run a business I didn't know a lot about, and the bankers hounding me for money were from the same bank that had led me straight into this deal. The management at First City was now telling me they had been worried about the excessive overhead at May Petroleum for two or three years.

At the same time, May had a very expensive geological staff always talking about visions of sugarplums. They had drilled a series of wonderful "company saving" wells—very expensive, deep wells—and one by one they all came in dry. It became clearer and clearer to me that to save the company there were only two courses of action: one was to get bigger and at the same time keep the overhead where it was; the other was to sell the oil and gas reserves and consolidate. Consolidation became essential to survival. As with many public companies with management that doesn't own much of the stock, May's management had been running the company like it was Exxon when it was not. I changed all of that as quickly as possible. When I took over, May Petroleum had about sixty-three employees; that number was eventually reduced to eight.

While I was on a winning streak, May Petroleum was an overnight transition into a losing streak.

In just a few years, my profits from the stock market and venture capital investments had exceeded the profits from my entire real estate organization—built up over many years. Though *Forbes* magazine didn't put me in their *Forbes* 400 wealthiest individuals (a list I really didn't want to be on), the facts were that, at the time, I would have easily qualified. It was a lucky thing I had as much cash as I had because it later gave me the ability to put more than $145 million into helping my investors in real estate partnerships and $24.25 million into saving May Petroleum from liquidation.

At times, the irony of Hall Financial's situation was overwhelming. One of those was a black tie awards banquet held at the Helmsley Palace in New York on February 19, 1986. On that evening Hall Financial Group was presented the Forum Award, a prestigious sales award in the real estate industry. All of the largest real estate partnership sponsors in the country were there. The audience watched as my company was described as the largest private-placement sponsor in the country in 1985. I was too busy with problems to even attend and accept the award. In fact, by the time we received the kudos in 1986, our new problems had already been plastered across the pages of the *Wall Street Journal*. Our problems were very public and, even while applauding our efforts of the year before, everyone knew we were in deep trouble. They also knew that their own bad times were ahead.

I have always attracted media attention, whether I wanted it or not, dating back to my days as a student landlord and even further to my childhood when I was Mayor for a Day in Ann Arbor. So it was again in 1986 when the bottom fell out. Although when I began to realize the severity of the market downturn and the oncoming depression I chose voluntarily to announce to the media the problems that my company was preparing to face, I didn't realize that I would come to represent the area's economic plight in the national and local media. Nor did I realize that the worst of my fears were, in fact, understated in comparison to what would eventually occur. I wanted to announce the problems as straightforwardly as I had announced positive strides we had made over the years. That is far better than having reporters hear half-accurate rumors and try to put the pieces together at the last minute on deadline. And, of course, it was important to maintain our credibility in bad times as well as good. For the media, I was the first to admit the problem that so many people were beginning to face, and I became the biggest example of the tumbling real estate market. Even as I was willing to admit our problems publicly, I had no idea how bad they would get.

PART TWO

TEXAS STUMBLED AND I FELL

CHAPTER 4
WHEN TEXANS FALL

TEXAS WAS BOOMING in 1981 when we opened our little regional office in Dallas. We weren't the only ones who liked what we saw in Dallas. Corporations like Diamond Shamrock, The Associates Corporation of North America, Caltex, and American Airlines were all making Dallas their new home, drawn to a city with a pro-business attitude, comparatively low taxes, and an expanding economy. Although the oil business was already showing some signs of trouble, Dallas was firmly embedded in a growth pattern. High-tech companies led by giants like Texas Instruments were booming. The banking industry was fueling construction, hurrying to meet the needs of prospering businesses and a growing population. Manufacturing companies were realizing the logic of Dallas as a distribution point—central in the nation, made efficient with the resources of the Dallas–Fort Worth International Airport, at that time the fourth busiest airport in the world (now it is closer to second place).

When our company first came to Dallas, we couldn't afford to compete with all of the big guys who were aggressively buying in Texas. We didn't really do much business until the economy started to turn sour. That's the way I like to do business. I would rather move into a bad economy than a good one, the idea being to buy properties at depressed prices, improve them, and sell at a profit when the cycle turns up again.

The expanding Texas economy in the early eighties was like a rubber band being stretched—first by a natural increasing demand for real estate product and later by an artificially induced demand. Finally, the increase of product became a self-feeding frenzy, with projects being built to meet the artificial needs of a real estate–driven economy. Far from anyone's mind was the inevitable need of the true real estate user—or the lack thereof.

The passage by the U.S. Congress of the Garn–St. Germaine legislation in 1981 deregulated the liability side of the savings and loan industry. One of the problems the savings and loan industry had in the seventies was that interest rates in other financial markets were climbing steadily, but savings and loans were still limited by regulations to paying only 5.25 percent on passbook savings. Liquidity was going out of the business as savers took their money to the highest bidder. The Garn–St. Germaine legislation allowed savings and loans to pay whatever they wanted to pay for funds. Thus, Congress legislated new powers and regulations to allow the savings and loans to compete with other lending institutions. But Congress forgot to legislate new brains and expertise for the people that ran the thrift business. Congress gave new liberal powers to an under-managed, undereducated industry full of people who were used to taking money in at 5 percent, loaning it out at 7 percent, and keeping the difference—then going to their country clubs to have drinks at 3:30 in the afternoon. But just allowing savings and loans to pay higher interest rates didn't solve their problems. Now, savings and loans had the ability to get money back in the door because they could pay anything anyone else could pay. Being "smart," they paid higher and higher rates (CDs were as high as 16 to 18 percent), and racked up even larger losses because their loan portfolios were primarily single-family mortgages earning only 7 or 8 percent. There was a severe mismatch. Mortgages in some savings and loans averaged only 7 to 8 percent earnings—far less than the new deposits at 12 percent to 14 percent.

To solve that problem, the Federal Home Loan Bank Board regulators encouraged entrepreneurs to come into the industry. They changed the regulations to allow savings and loans to sell off their mortgages and convert them to cash. They created new accounting for savings and loans whereby they could write off the losses over a long period of time. The regulators were using creative accounting to put off the true problem. They were betting that by allowing savings and loans to invest their new-found cash freely, the savings and loans could make a profit and recover their losses. But this was just regulatory chewing gum to hold the industry together. Some of the entrepreneurs who discovered this newfound source of cash were good and honest in their endeavor; many of them were just real estate gunslingers betting with FSLIC's money (heads, they won—tails, the FSLIC and taxpayers lost); and worse, a few were out-and-out crooks. But any way you slice it, savings and loans were made to be attractive to entrepreneurs who could bring energy, ideas, and a little capital. I bought a savings and loan in 1983, Resource Savings, and I don't fit in those last two categories.

With the new savings and loan owners being entrepreneurs, a whole change of culture occurred in the once staid and conservative industry.

Young, fast-moving real estate entrepreneurs now had the keys to the money version of a candy store. While probably well-intended, and having been encouraged by the regulators, most of these entrepreneurs-turned-bankers had no experience in this arena. They were not the ones to solve the industry's problems. Some, like me, built their savings and loans in a reasonable and prudent manner and avoided the conflicts of interest. Others found themselves in that candy store full of delicious goodies with no one minding the cash register. In some cases, legitimate lines of right and wrong were not carefully drawn, and some alleged wrongdoing is a matter of hindsight interpretation. However, too many of them couldn't help themselves and, one way or another, fell to temptation. In fact, the temptations to take advantage of the cash availability of financial institutions caused the decay and decline of the savings and loan and banking industries in the mid-1980s in Texas.

There were good times, though. No one knew how to throw a better party than the nouveau riche savings and loan owners (after all, the S&Ls had plenty of money to spend). There were parties, parties, parties, and more parties. During the early 1980s, I was invited to several dove hunts in Mexico by savings and loans or commercial banks who were taking their best customers in their private jets to their ranches. There were always the typical large get-together parties for no reason at all and, of course, the normal holiday parties.

Christmas 1984 was typical of the times. Sunbelt Savings sent out their Babes in Toyland invitations. It was their only Christmas party that my wife and I attended, but it was a memorable event. As we pulled up to the Las Colinas motion picture studios (the largest outside of Hollywood), the place was packed. The valet took our car and we walked into what was an unbelievable mob scene. The several thousand square feet of studio space had been transformed into a Babes in Toyland odyssey. All the guests were requested to bring a toy as a present to be donated by Sunbelt to the underprivileged. The waitresses were dressed as toy soldiers—in rather skimpy outfits, I might add. Dry ice provided a smoke-like atmosphere and several bands performed on different stages. Huge stage sets had been created, with giant toys you could walk through. The whole atmosphere was a cross between Disneyworld and the Twilight Zone. Food was available at food stations throughout the thousands of square feet of space.

The evening's festivities featured nationally known stars such as Ben Vereen, The Commodores, and Sha Na Na. At this particular Christmas party, the guest list of two thousand had swelled to over five thousand attenders. The smell of prosperity was in the air. It had been a good year for all of those in the real estate and banking fields and everyone felt like letting loose and celebrating. As the times went on right up until 1986, the parties kept getting bigger and bigger. Parties costing between $500,000 and $1,000,000 were all too common. One savings and loan tried to outdo another. These parties were often attended by young Southern Methodist University graduates who had the typical real estate uniform of a Rolex, sometimes a diamond ring, and for the really successful new broker, a Rolls-Royce or at least a Mercedes. To say the least, there was a feeling by all that the good times would last forever.

The new savings and loan owners, the entrepreneurs, knew that they could never make money paying 12 and 14 percent for savings and making single-family home loans at half that rate. Still, Congress allowed them something other financial institutions could never do—to participate in the deal with the debtors, to actually own a piece of the deal. In Texas that meant commercial real estate. The reasoning was to own a part of an office building since everyone gets rich doing that; lend the developer the money at 14 percent, plus get the ownership and two to five points up front (points are fees charged on mortgages). Each point, as it's called, equals 1 percent of the total amount of the loan. The savings and loan owners got greedier and greedier, and nobody ever stopped to think, "Is there a consumer to use this building?" They just saw the fun in it. All these points! This high interest rate and half of the building to boot! The developers liked it because they could get the lenders to pay them huge development fees up front. They didn't care if the lender ended up foreclosing and thereby owning 100 percent of the building—which is what usually happened. The outcome was that the savings and loan ended up owning 100 percent of a building that produced a 2 or 3 percent return instead of owning half of a building that they thought would produce 14 percent. Worse still, most of these buildings fell in value, along with older competing properties, by 30 to 70 percent from the early eighties, when they were built, as the market depression in 1986, '87, '88, and '89 caused a complete downward re-evaluation of assets, particularly with new, empty buildings.

This newfound source of funds for developers stretched the real estate market to the snapping point. Savings and loans in Texas became major players in the real estate market overnight. This new breed of savings and loans did costly damage to the real estate market, damage that has hurt us all. And Congress, which gave savings and loans the investment power in the first place, would later be trying to clean up the mess. Since our company's problems with the government were solved, a whole new set of head regulators has been appointed, and even today they are struggling with the problems. They sure have my best wishes. It's a monumental task.

In 1987, the S&L industry reported a $7.7 billion loss nationally. Much of the loss was attributed to bad real estate loans in Texas and the Southwest. For that same period, savings and loans in Texas, Oklahoma, Louisiana, and Arkansas posted an $8.44 billion loss. The depression was truly specific to Texas. While savings and loans in thirty-six states were profitable, much of the regional loss in the Southwest was concentrated in Texas alone. And the losses got larger and larger. During all of 1986, Texas savings and loans lost $3.2 billion. In the first three quarters of 1987, Texas savings and loans lost $4.4 billion—and by year end the losses grew worse and worse.

Once I had a naive belief that market demand controlled the real estate building process, but it's money that really controls it. It took me years of being in business to realize that simple fact. You would normally think that supply and demand would have something to do with it, but supply and demand is not of the consumer—which would be logical—but of the availability of money. Why, you might ask, would lenders keep lending money when a market is obviously overbuilt and headed for problems?

My view of the Texas market in 1984 and 1985 was that it was a buying opportunity due to temporary softness in the market. Although there was no way to know it at the time, in hindsight, I was wrong. We continued to buy real estate right through that period, but the rubber band continued to be stretched. Savings and loans were growing and, at least temporarily, prospering while the market became more and more overbuilt. At the same time, Texas had very aggressive tax-exempt bond financing, much more liberal here than in other areas of the country, which flooded the market with product. Tax-exempt bond financing was a method of providing lower-cost mortgage money by having the mortgage owned by investors whom the government allowed not to pay tax on the interest earned. The theory of this government program was to encourage development of low- or moderate-income apartments, but in practice it was more of a benefit to real estate developers than renters. For several years, this type of financing accounted for more than 25 percent of multi-family housing starts and was another bountiful source of real estate development capital. Favorable tax laws for investors participating in limited partnership commercial projects also added to the inventory. The tax laws were extreme in their favorable nature and developers and syndicators pushed the laws to their limits and beyond. All of this meant that ample equity was readily available to invest in real estate with or without any economic promise from the property.

This was an era of huge growth for the limited partnership industry. It seemed that the environment was perfect for both general partners and limited partners to prosper. The partnership format has tax and other legal benefits that are better for owning real estate than a corporation. Many people think real estate syndications are a recent event, but actually they have been in practice for a very long time. The Empire State Building, for example, was owned by a limited partnership, as were many other great real estate investments. Since 1981, though, limited partnerships became far more popularized and grew at a much more explosive rate directly as a result of the first tax-law change of the Reagan Administration in 1981.

Savings and loans and partnership sponsors were more aggressive in Texas than anywhere else in the country. I think it all goes back to that can-do attitude. Texas was a growth market. It seemed to most Texans, including me, that we wouldn't have a serious downturn in real estate because of the overriding strength in the area economically. However, while supply continued to grow much faster and much more aggressively than it should have, growth and demand began to fall rapidly. The oil and gas industry was having problems in '82, '83, and '84. The year 1985 was harder, and then, when many people thought the market had bottomed out, 1986 was devastating. In less than six months, oil prices fell from about twenty dollars at the end of 1985 to ten dollars. We had already had huge decreases in employment in the oil and gas and related industries through 1985, but the continued loss of jobs in 1986 was much more severe than was ever foreseeable. A lot of that unemployment was structural and permanent; for the first time in recent Texas history, people were moving out of the state in large numbers to find jobs elsewhere.

Like everything that goes to extremes, one moment there was way too much money chasing every deal in Texas, and the next there was none. The money simply dried up and the rubber band snapped. Locally, lenders were having problems of their own, riddled with bad energy and real estate debts, and in the money centers in New York and around the world, Texas suddenly became a dirty word while properties badly in need of cash to stay alive tried to find new sources of relief. Texas's arrogance during the seventies oil-boom decade, flaunted with bumper stickers, came back at us in full force. In the last half of the 1980s came news of bankruptcies of people whom I had come to know and respect as bright individuals—

movers and shakers like the Hunt brothers and former Governor of Texas John Connally—and with scandals like the Southern Methodist University pay-for-play debacle and the uncovering of grossly negligent and, in some cases, criminal lending practices on the part of some Texas savings and loan owners, the rest of the country snickered at the once-proud Texans. The prevailing attitude in the Midwest and on the East Coast was that Texans had finally gotten their comeuppance.

Private limited-partnership sponsors were hit with a double whammy. Not only had the real estate and financial markets been devastated, but Congress once again changed the rules, and in 1986 we were hit with new tax laws. In 1985, Hall Financial Group had the dubious distinction of being the largest private-placement sponsor in the nation. We raised $320 million of equity that year, and while I'm proud of our accomplishments, they later amounted to burdens and frustrations. Almost all of that money was raised in installments payable over the next six or seven years, and all of those investors were counting on a law that existed at the time that allowed losses generated from these investments as tax deductions. "Tax reform" was going on in the House and Senate, but in the industry we had faith in the Republican Senate—that it wouldn't go the way of the House and its liberal bill that passed in late 1985. Even if a bill did pass, we all knew that it would never be retroactive (applying to partnerships already sold); we knew that wouldn't be fair. Congress had never done it that way before. We were all wrong and shouldn't have bet on this "sure thing."

Senator Robert Packwood of Oregon came to Dallas in early 1985, and Trammell Crow hosted a fund-raiser for him that raised more than $500,000. I even paid $5,000 to have dinner and cocktails with the man. The subject on everyone's lips, of course, was tax reform. The House bill could be devastating to our business, but little did we know we were chatting with the real enemy. Later, Packwood, accused of being bought off by the real estate industry's big contributions, used his position on the Senate Finance Committee to show the country that he couldn't be bought. Like a guillotine coming down upon us, the tax incentives and, more importantly, the decades-old tax structure for our business were chopped off. This wasn't just a change, it was a complete overhaul without any common sense being applied to the implications. The bill that Packwood sponsored was an overnight end to the way we did business. It was our worst nightmare. The new laws were terribly unfair to many hardworking Americans who had trusted Congress and were now betrayed. Limited partnership sponsors quickly tried to regroup and begin to sell partnerships that weren't "tax oriented," but the buyers just weren't there in the numbers needed to support the business. The business began to fall. The industry, as we all had known it, was now history and with it many thousands of people's lives were turned upside down overnight. Limited partnerships, as a form of real estate, will come back in time as a smaller industry with different players and with different goals. In the long run, this will result in higher rent levels for the consumer.

The tax law was called the Tax Reform Act of 1986. Its theoretical agenda was simplification and fairness, but the reality for many investors was exactly the opposite. Deductions for real estate were not going to be allowed to be used against regular income anymore. This meant that people who bought tax-advantaged investments with an agreement to make payments for a number of years in the future had been betrayed by Congress retroactively changing the law. The law itself was approximately 1,000 pages (of small print) and has so far required thousands of pages of regulations and explanations that are still being issued. It is anything but simple, and to many it sure wasn't fair.

The new tax law was quite a blow to spirited Texans (especially the entrepreneurial real estate types), who found themselves working to save themselves, rather than building wealth. Real estate "developers" became dinosaurs. As time went on, I wasn't the only real estate entrepreneur in the headlines. Giants like John Eulich's Vantage Companies, LTV, and the Carpenter family's huge Southland Financial Corporation were humbly making public their debt problems and, sometime later, the solutions. Where the big guys had leverage with lenders, the little guys found themselves waiting in long lines that would extend out of the courthouse and around the block to file for bankruptcy on the day before monthly foreclosures. Many watched their office buildings being auctioned on the courthouse steps. The morality of the borrower-lender relationship went out the window. Texas was operating on a crisis mentality—it was every man for himself. Lenders and borrowers alike were stabbing each other in the back, rifling through each other's pockets, and taking anything they could get away with. No one was thinking about the future, about trying to preserve some sort of business relationship; people were just trying to survive the day at hand while each day was getting worse.

Bankruptcies in Texas reached record numbers, pushed higher by speedy foreclosure laws. For example, in the Northern District, which includes the Dallas–Fort Worth area, Lubbock, Abilene, Amarillo, San Angelo, and Wichita Falls, bankruptcies in 1980 to 1982 averaged 3,078 per year; in 1986 they went to 10,415, in 1987 to 12,999, in 1988 to

14,934, and to approximately 15,000 in 1989. In Texas, it takes as little as three weeks for a lender to foreclose on a delinquent property, as opposed to months and even years in other states. Some say it is the state of the debtor. With its very lenient homestead laws, which allow individuals to keep a major nest egg to start over, Texas has always had big debtors. The homestead laws allow a bankrupt Texan to keep his or her house and a lot of personal property. Ironically, in contravention to the protective nature of the homestead laws in terms of real estate, Texas is the fastest foreclosure state in the nation.

Many Texans faced foreclosures and personal and corporate bankruptcies. The Hunt brothers lost billions of dollars and ended up in bankruptcy. Except for Hall Financial Group, virtually all of the Texas limited-partnership syndication companies ended up in bankruptcy—Sunderman, D.R. Walker, Equity Management, and Southmark, just to name a few. Some of these, such as Equity Management, were good, well-run companies overcome by events over which they had no control. The syndication industry was destroyed, and so, too, were numerous developers. John Connally, formerly Secretary of Defense, Governor of Texas, and candidate for President of the United States, owned a real estate company with Ben Barnes, the former Lieutenant Governor of Texas. They ended up with both of their companies filing for bankruptcy and they filed for personal bankruptcy as well. Former Governor Preston Smith succeeded John Connally as Governor of Texas and subsequently in bankruptcy. Then there was the famous heart surgeon Dr. Denton Cooley, who, despite a purported annual income of $36 million from surgery, was taken into bankruptcy as a result of his real estate problems.

To say it was a blow to Texas egos is an understatement. Still, an underlying optimism continued to pulse. Though never in this magnitude, the old pros had seen it before; in the mid-seventies giants like the Trammell Crow Company came dangerously close to going under. But the depression in real estate that began in Texas in 1986 was different from any before it—worse even in many ways than the Great Depression of the thirties for those in real estate, oil, or finance. And while Texans couldn't share their woes with the rest of the country, the most devastating blow was the lenders selling off prime properties in Texas to outsiders. In fact, very few Texas real estate companies would end up surviving the Texas depression.

It's never been a sin to go broke in Texas. There's always a fine line between being fabulously wealthy and flat busted. It's all a part of the wildcatter heritage and philosophy of this state: To make it big, you often must risk everything. And the tables turn oh so quickly.

I have a lot of faith in the Texas spirit and in each of the markets in Texas. They are coming back and partly because the Texas bravado lives on. With the true believers, the boom attitude doesn't die. It just rests awhile, mending after the bust, rejuvenating, watching and waiting for opportunity, finding new ways to make money, and knowing that the prosperous times are bound to return.

CHAPTER 5
WE'VE GOT A PROBLEM

ON DECEMBER 10, 1985, I walked through the hallways of the Hall
Financial Center building, just wandering around as I often did, checking
on the tempo of our team of associates. I was in an up mood for several
reasons. I had just completed the First Federal of Michigan stock transaction
and would soon be coming away with $12 million in profit, and I was
looking forward to the holidays. My wife and I had planned a family
vacation with our four daughters and all of the grandparents at our Florida
condo, and it would be nice to leave town on a positive note.

The $12 million I had just made would come in very handy. With
the real estate market depressed, I figured the $12 million would give us
plenty of liquidity to carry us through another year. This seemed like
previous temporary real estate downturns.

As I walked into the finance department of the company, I passed
Don Braun, our then assistant treasurer for Hall Financial Group, and
Cheryll O'Bryan, manager of accounts payable. They said they were just
on their way to see me. The tone of Don's voice indicated it was something
serious. Don was often the messenger when it was something less than
pleasant. It might have had something to do with his being six foot seven,
as I guess everyone figured I couldn't get too mad at someone that big.
On that day of December 10, it was Don who said, "Craig, we've got a
problem." In our business "problems" were commonplace and this was
not unusual.

Don and Cheryll explained that the November revisions of our budget
were in and the deficits were larger than anticipated. Simply put, the
properties needed another $11 million. And if that wasn't enough, they
added that their estimate of the total that day that we would need to loan
the partnerships that year was going to come to about $40 million. In other
words, Hall Financial Group needed to raise the $11 million and pronto!
That meant I had to write another check. Fortunately I had the money,

but I wasn't a printing press. At that point I still thought we were strong enough to handle whatever might come our way, but I decided immediately to investigate fully any potential problem. This still was nothing out of the ordinary for our historical experience or for real estate in general. Cycles and temporary cash needs have always been a regular occurrence in real estate. Our investors knew from our track record and my speeches that this type of thing happened from time to time.

With those simple words from Don and Cheryll—"we've got a problem"—our newest odyssey began. The profits from the First Federal transaction hadn't even been collected but were already spent. It wasn't the fact that the partnerships would require more cash in 1985 that was so alarming, but rather the uncertainty of the coming market. What would the future bring?

Why hadn't we realized our problem earlier and done something to remedy the situation? The nature of the real estate business on a big scale is highly leveraged and highly complex. Leverage simply means borrowings. For instance, if you buy an investment for $10,000 cash, you have no leverage on that investment; but if you borrow $7,500, you have 3 to 1 or 75 percent leverage (i.e., $3.00 of borrowing for every $1.00 of cash equity). And leverage is a double-edged sword—great on the up side and devastating on the down side. Real estate is often bought with high leverage of 8 to 1 or more. The risk in leveraged real estate is that rental income declines when the market softens and expenses go up for advertising and other rental costs, but interest payments remain constant or even go up. What may seem like reserves at one moment can be gone the next. With our annual rent revenue being more than $300 million a year, even an unexpected decline of 5 percent can cause a shortfall of $15 million. The declines that were about to occur in 1986 were more like 10 and 15 percent. Rent was dropping dramatically, but even that we could handle. Downturns like 1985's weren't pleasant but they weren't that unusual. The real problem was 1986: a virtual free-fall in revenues that wouldn't begin to stabilize until late 1988. In late 1985 we never would have believed the situation could turn as bad as it in fact did from 1986 to 1990.

Unlike many businesses, our expenses do not go down with lower revenues but instead increase. Increased costs of advertising and fix-up from more move-ins and move-outs than would occur in a stronger market meant our expenses were actually higher. In 1986 we simply didn't have enough rental income and we were getting squeezed harder financially every day.

The structure of our company and its affiliated entities is somewhat complicated. The Hall Financial Group provides property management, asset management, and other services to the partnerships that own the real estate. It gets paid fees for its services. In total, we have about 350 partnerships (approximately 250 that we had put together and then 100 that we had acquired the general-partner position in) and several service corporations. They depend on one another in many ways, although they are legally separate entities. The partnerships are formed to buy one or more properties. They are set up as limited partnerships with individual general partners—including myself and other members of senior management—and limited-partner investors. The investors want to limit their liability, which is one reason they are limited partners. In turn, they want us to do all of the work and take the risk, which is why we are general partners. This is just like the way we put together the small rooming houses described earlier. Being a limited partner is similar to buying stock in a corporation except that there are tax benefits to being a limited partner. For one thing, in a corporation the profits are taxed twice (i.e., once in the corporation and again when received by the individual). This isn't the case, however, in a limited partnership, where taxes are imposed only on the partners. In a corporation, shareholders have no personal liability for corporate debt. On the other hand, in a limited partnership, the general partners have reasonably controllable personal liability, while the limited partners have none. The general partner's liability is "reasonably controllable" in a real estate limited partnership because the mortgages on their properties are generally nonrecourse debt, which means that the only claims the lenders have are to the collateral on the loans—usually the property itself. In the event of default on the partnership's non-recourse loans, the lenders can foreclose on the property, but in general can't collect any shortfall from the limited partners or the general partners.

Although theoretically, we didn't have many "recourse" (personal) liabilities, we did have some liability in cases where investors were paying money in overtime. In those situations, I would borrow money to pay up-front costs either personally or through one of our corporations or partnerships, but often with my personal guarantee. In many of those cases, we had loans from banks with recourse or personal liabilities. Sometimes we would buy properties before we raised money from limited partners. For that kind of purchase, we had a $100 million line of credit from a consortium of banks, including Bankers Trust. Looking back, I realize that if Bankers Trust and those other banks hadn't thought so highly of us back then, we wouldn't have grown so fast and our problems wouldn't have been so large. I'm only partially kidding when I say that. Indeed, lenders did have a role, a large one, in fueling the boom that ended in the bust in Texas. And we surely weren't the only ones affected.

Generally, when times got tough we were not legally required to pump money back into the properties. Nonetheless, as of mid-1989, together with the Hall Financial Group, we had put more than $145 million back into the properties and, in almost every case, the contributions were voluntary on our part. But if we didn't put the money in, our investors would have lost many, many properties. The investors had investments ranging from $10,000 to $150,000 per investor in the 350 various partnerships. In total over $1 billion of investor money was at stake. The contributions we voluntarily made to help the properties came both from the corporation, which got its cash flow from management and service fees, and from money that I had from other business sources, such as my personal stock market transactions. In the end, I actually liquidated virtually all of my non–real estate holdings from 1986 through 1989 and used all the money to help our limited partners.

It is very difficult with a company the size and complexity of Hall Financial Group to have dependable control and projections of cash flow. If you go back in history, many real estate people are seemingly up one day and dead the next. Unlike almost any other business, real estate is perceived as a steady way to make money, but in reality it is often highly volatile and is a risky business. This has been true throughout history, but especially so in the last decade because the world around us is changing more rapidly than ever. We are living in a time of a major restructuring, going from a manufacturing to an information society and from a national to an international marketplace. The international flow of information and money means financial conditions change very quickly and are, largely, beyond individual control. Both of these phenomena gripped Texas in the 1980s.

Like most other real estate companies in the Southwest, we hung on to our optimism too long. To build a real estate business, you have to be an optimist. In the late seventies and early eighties, we were in a very inflationary period and everyone who wanted to be in the game had to include that inflation in their perspective. It's hard to get out of that mind set, and leaving it behind truly goes against the nature of the entire business of real estate. If you're ultraconservative, you don't do business and you don't grow. If you are projecting on a more optimistic inflationary basis, it's hard to know when you have to change gears. It's hard to realize when the market and the world are changing in a negative way until after it has happened. Usually we don't know of these major trend changes until they are well under way. Hindsight is always the best judge, but it can be a very different view from the perspective in the heat of the moment.

In any real estate business, in any market, there are periods of difficulty. Generally, you don't want to admit to the world that you are in a tight cash squeeze, but in reality most real estate companies of all sizes are often in a modest cash crunch in one way or another. They traditionally get through either by stalling or by finding cash resources in some other area of the business, such as property management. In a sense, that's what we were doing when we took $40 million from the stock market profits I had made and current management company profits to make short-term loans to the Hall real estate partnerships.

In a major downturn like the one Texas and, to a lesser extent, other areas of the country suffered in the last half of the eighties, you eventually back up and say, "We can't look at this one with the same optimistic point of view." We initially thought that 1985 was just the typical market problem you simply outgrow, one that you "fix" by having some good things take care of some bad things. It looked like previous cycles to us; we simply had no idea how bad things were going to get. Quite the contrary, in December of 1985 and even the first quarter of 1986, I was sure our problems would be solved by March or April 1986 through certain debt restructuring. We never could have dreamed of what would actually develop and would be coming down the pike at us.

Between December 10 and 20, 1985, we contacted our largest lenders in California to bring them up to date on our preliminary concerns. After talking to Don and Cheryll, I immediately set those lender meetings up and began making plans to analyze the problems. The difficulty with a large corporate entity, however, is that the entrepreneurs—in the case of Hall Financial, myself and a few key individuals—are less able to put together a quick fix when the corporation has swelled to giant proportions: You can't turn a battleship as fast as a small powerboat.

My first move came the very next day when we called our largest lenders in California and arranged to meet with them to discuss the cash-flow problems we were having. At that time we were not in default on any loan. Our plans were to analyze all the projects in the Southwest, where the problems were most severe, and put together a new conservative projection for the next five years—assuming that the market would get no better and would probably get worse. Then we would test how long those properties could continue to operate at the current levels of required debt service.

It's no simple task to maintain debt in a downturn. Typically, out of every dollar received in rent, roughly fifty cents goes to expenses and the remaining fifty cents pays the mortgage. But if apartment rents decline—as they did rapidly in 1986 and 1987—a property can be left with only ten or twenty cents, and sometimes less, of each income dollar to pay the mortgage. At that point, you must renegotiate loans to keep the debt service manageable or face default.

Many of our properties were purchased in 1982, 1983, and 1984, when interest rates were in the 13 to 17 percent range. But in late 1985, interest rates tumbled. This also made new properties, built at lower interest rates, more competitive, causing all rents to fall further and faster. With both interest rates and rents down, we had double trouble.

One of our biggest lenders, Beverly Hills Savings Association, with whom we had fourteen loans totaling approximately $28 million in debt, was insolvent and, in fact, was being directly controlled by the federal government. We decided that our chief financial officer and our chief outside counsel should both make an initial trip to California to have a preliminary meeting with the Association's officers.

Larry Levey, our financial officer, had been with Hall Financial Group for more than a decade. I had always thought of him as a quiet, capable financial generalist. But in the ensuing struggle, Larry became known as the rhinoceros. He met every challenge head on, charging lenders like a rhinoceros and then letting their barbs roll off a thick skin.

Bill Sechrest, known to us as Cosmic Bill, was our chief legal gladiator, whose optimistic attitude, sense of humor, philosophical and analytical approach kept us going during the hardest of times. Bill was invaluable during our struggle with lenders and the government, but he understood well my general philosophy about legal counsel—it is "counsel." I make an effort to understand the legal process. I think that to win in litigation, you must be a "professional client." While lawyers usually try to do their best for clients, in down times they cry all the way to the bank. The fees can be astronomical. In our litigation with the government, we spent more than $2 million in just two months in the fall of 1986. In total from 1986 through 1989, we would end up spending over $35 million in fees spread among numerous firms, which included both our counsel and counsel for lenders in restructurings, where we were required to pay the lenders' fees as well as our own.

Back to our trip to California that December. In Mission Viejo, at the headquarters of Beverly Hills Savings, Larry and Bill met with an assistant vice president who was completely perplexed about the reason for our visit. He punched our loans up on the computer and, since we were current, he simply couldn't understand why we were there. "Your loans are current, why are we talking now?" he asked.

On this trip as well as the many to follow, as we met with each lender, a very frightening and sad reality began to set in. We realized that of our biggest problem loans, the concentration of our lenders were California savings and loans, and their financial problems were greater than our own. Most of them were already quietly under the direct control of the federal government, and our loans, which were huge, were not yet even in default. We weren't a part of their problems at all at that point; yet they were already broke. Nevertheless, our position greatly affected theirs. In December 1985 we had more than $500 million in loans in California savings and loans alone. We decided to do an unusual and unconventional thing: Instead of hiding from regulators or, for that matter, from the lenders, we confronted the problem straight on, advising our lenders of our belief that a problem had arisen, and instead of merely waiting for that problem to emerge over time, we assembled a broad task force to look at our entire portfolio under a microscope. We thought it was the fair, honorable, and wise thing to do. We asked the savings and loans to help set up a meeting with their government supervisors, which resulted in a December 20, 1985, meeting with officials of the Federal Home Loan Bank of San Francisco. At that meeting we had no financial information and nothing specific to discuss, but wanted to describe our general concerns and plans for a detailed analysis of the situation.

The year was 1985, for many Hall associates and for myself, one with no Christmas. I sent my family ahead to Florida and canceled all vacations for anyone who had not already left for the holidays. We began a holiday work vigil that lasted from December 20 through January 13. Between fifty and one hundred Hall people, along with about seventy-five people from the Arthur Andersen accounting firm, worked in twenty-four-hour shifts, putting together new financial information. We desperately wanted to get our arms around this situation. The cost was enormous and was borne by the corporation, not by the partnerships.

In the real estate industry, this round-the-clock vigilance was both extraordinary and nearly unprecedented. Delay and avoidance are the traditional tactics of many real estate entrepreneurs. In my case, I've always believed in dealing with things in a straightforward and aggressive manner. My plan was to deal with the decision maker. The question of the day was to figure out who that was in each case. At that point, it looked like the government was calling the shots with virtually all of our California lenders. But who in the government made those decisions? Our December 20 meeting was scheduled with the Federal Home Loan Bank Board of San Francisco, which was responsible for the majority of insolvent thrifts where we had loans. Before that meeting, I thought the workout of our loans would happen swiftly. In fact, if someone had asked me on December 19, I would have predicted our loans would have been restructured without fanfare or media interest or attention by the end of January or first of

February 1986. I knew that it was in everyone's best interest. The stronger and less adversely affected we were, the more we could pay on the loans. I was prepared to tell the Federal Home Loan Bank Board that I would put all of the profits I could make back into these deals, to essentially work for them for the next five years to be honorable on those loans even though I had no personal liability to do so. My plan was to pay everything the properties could pay and a whole lot more. The extra money would come from Hall Financial, which was willing to give up its cash profits for the next five years. We just had to have our ducks in a row for that meeting, and I was hopeful that we could work things out quickly. The plan was good for my investors, the lenders, and the government. All we wanted was a chance to face the problems honorably, and a quick and quiet positive resolution seemed in everyone's best interest.

So we worked through the night—night after night—for three weeks. We simply had to be prepared, at whatever cost, to analyze where we were in terms of the properties' future cash-flow projections. To my dismay, the preliminary results which we received on January 13, 1986, were worse than I had ever anticipated, but we immediately disclosed the information on January 15 to all 10,000 of our investors. Yet even then, we didn't realize just how bad things would eventually get. I still thought we could solve problems a lot easier than what later proved to be the case, but the market just got worse and worse throughout 1986 and 1987.

PART THREE

THE
GOVERNMENT,
WESTWOOD,
AND
ME

CHAPTER 6
REARRANGING THE DECK
CHAIRS ON THE *TITANIC*

THE FIRST MEETING WITH the San Francisco Home Loan Bank was on December 20, 1985. It was a very preliminary meeting because we simply had no hard facts, only a general concern. We were trying to act in a very responsible and timely manner in all respects. Our lenders had helped us set up the meeting, but I didn't expect such a large turnout. When we walked into the conference room, we were greeted by fifteen to twenty federal and state regulators. But typical of the government, the upshot of that meeting was merely to set another meeting. They were interested in our approach for working out the loans and wanted to know what was going on, but were totally noncommittal. Basically, they wanted lots and lots of information, and, when it was available, we could all meet again. We agreed that the next meeting would be held on January 14, 1986, and we returned to Dallas to cancel the holidays and began our round-the-clock vigil of preparation. We geared everything we had toward the January 14 meeting.

During those weeks before January 14, we began to take a detailed look at the problem as a whole, at our entire situation, not just looking at the loans with each S&L on an individual basis. We formalized our strategy with what I called "global solutions" and we prepared up-to-date financial information on each property, each loan, in order to give the Federal Home Loan Bank of San Francisco a full look at our company, our problems, and our resources. At that point we were fourteen days late on payments on only eight of a total of 243 loans with all the affiliated partnerships and the company. However, we wanted to determine, face, and solve the problems before they escalated and further hurt our lenders or investors.

Before the January meeting, we sent the San Francisco Federal Home Loan Bank (FHLB) advance copies of the several-hundred-page books of data we prepared. Included in that were three different global solutions and one loan-by-loan solution. For this meeting, we took Bill Sechrest,

Larry Levey, Mark Wiedelman, who was also with Hall Financial, and Bob Kralovitz, head of Arthur Andersen's national savings and loan accounting practice. We felt good about how we had worked so hard to prepare for this situation and had every hope that our approach and solutions would be a model for future government real estate workouts.

Literally, as we left Dallas for San Francisco, we also prepared an extensive letter to our 10,000 investors, disclosing the problems we had discovered, discussing our proposed solutions, and frankly explaining our situation.

We arrived for the meeting at the FHLB offices in San Francisco on time, and while waiting in the lobby, Joe Lenihan, vice president of the FHLB, came out and asked me to come into his office to see him and David Martens privately. Joe and David were both mid-level employees at the San Francisco FHLB. David was then the chief accountant. They told me that earlier that day the bank's attorneys had advised them to cancel our meeting, but feeling that would be impolite, they said we would continue with a meeting of sorts. I suspect going ahead with the meeting was David's idea. He was one of the few individuals we worked with in the government who didn't seem to always follow the bureaucratic flock or be controlled by the ever-present legal oversight. An accountant by profession, David was always courteous to us and avoided the internal regulatory politics. He was motivated by doing what was right for the government, which was fine with us. The FHLB system is composed of twelve banks, with San Francisco being by far the largest and most powerful. Since the FHLB system is owned and controlled by the United States government, bank employees, as a practical matter, work for the government even though they are direct employees of the bank and outside of normal civil-service restrictions.

David and Joe told us they had reviewed the massive amount of information that we had sent and added that they didn't have the authority to deal with our "global solutions," which proposed working with the sum of our lenders as opposed to the individual parts. I had given them choices A, B, C, and D, but they had chosen "None of the Above." We would have to solve the problems on a loan-by-loan basis, they said, and they wanted to work with each savings and loan individually. Then the S&L managers would make recommendations on each loan. When the recommendations came back to them from the savings and loans (since they really controlled the savings and loans), they would then process them one at a time. This was the message in our private session.

The long-awaited formal meeting started an hour and forty-five minutes late because they couldn't find a conference room; apparently too many other problem meetings were taking place at the same time. Only some lower-level analysts for the San Francisco bank attended our meeting, much different from the high-ranking attendance we had back in December. It was clear after the first few minutes that we had spent thousands and thousands of dollars to get out there and countless hours of overtime by our employees and Arthur Andersen for nothing. I had asked employees to give up their Christmas holidays and they had responded loyally. We knew the potential seriousness of the situation at hand; we faced it, and after intense work, in just a few weeks we had devised realistic solutions. Our ideas would help the savings and loans and the government both in our problem loans and as a method to solving a likely bigger industry problem. But there in San Francisco a horrible realization came over me as I discovered we had no audience. We had become too hot to handle and, except for David Martens, no one wanted to take responsibility or face the problem. What we were telling them was that the markets were heading for a severe decline. No one wanted to hear it. We had worked hard to get market data and good projections of the problems ahead, but found the official answer was ignore it till it was an absolute crisis.

What was happening to us, at least in part, was that we were continually being compared to EPIC, a real estate syndication company that was about half of our size, but its earlier default sent tremors throughout the financial system. While the initials originally stood for some longer name, the company had simply come to be known as EPIC. EPIC's problems were highly publicized and very well known to every regulator. In the early eighties, EPIC got into financial trouble and in order to bail itself out bought a state savings and loan in Maryland, then folded itself into it as a subsidiary and began to buy and syndicate pools of single-family home mortgages. In 1985, still running from its problems, EPIC filed for bankruptcy. The company was eventually sued by many for fraud. Its problems at even half our size had a huge negative impact on the financial system for a while. Edwin Gray, the head of the FHLB Board in Washington, had a bad case of EPIC-on-the-brain. He became concerned that each real estate company with loan problems was going to become another EPIC, full of problems and burdened with fraud. Practically every regulator who came in contact with us was afraid of being tagged with dealing with the new hot potato. EPIC seemed to be on everybody's mind.

We saw the volumes of information we had sent—appraisals, financial background, and pictures for each property—clearly untouched, still in the boxes that we had shipped to San Francisco. We later found out that the excuse of having ''no authority'' to deal with this or that permeated the entire regulatory system. Indeed, searching for the ultimate authority became another quest, another obsession of mine as we tried to solve our problems and protect our investors.

Throughout January, we continued our negotiations as requested by the Federal Home Loan Bank of San Francisco with each S&L in California individually. But our problems weren't confined to the West Coast. We had a number of loans with Texas savings and loans and with Texas banks and other financial institutions in different areas of the country. In Dallas, I met with Roy Green, president of the Dallas Federal Home Loan Bank, and made sure he was fully briefed on our activities. He was pleased we were facing and addressing the problems before a default occurred. He reviewed my general approach and agreed we were on the right track. Still, this was the beginning of some very strange times in Texas, an era tied to the unexpected crash of the price of oil.

At the time, the prevailing wisdom was that oil prices had bottomed out, but reality quickly showed 1985 to be the calm before the storm. In early 1986, oil prices were in a free-fall. By the spring of 1986, we had begun to talk to bankruptcy lawyers in reference to May Petroleum as a contingency because the banks were regularly threatening to call our loans. Even though we had paid the loans down by huge amounts, they were saying there weren't enough oil and gas reserves (due to the extreme price declines), according to the formula in the loan agreement. With First City and MBank having liquidity problems of their own, like many borrowers we were adversely affected.

Back in the days of practically handshaking on bank transactions in Texas, bankers valued relationships, knowing they wanted to do business with customers on down the line. But in Texas in 1986, bankers and customers alike took off their gloves and quit thinking long-term. When the banks pulled out a lawsuit and said "pay or die," the borrowers pulled out a lawsuit and sued the banks for "lender liability." What had once been an unthinkable act—to sue your banker—was now commonplace. No one was thinking or cared about what would happen to the relationships when the smoke cleared.

Bankruptcy was a dirty word to me. It meant failure. It meant giving up. But in Texas in 1986, bankruptcy meant, if anything, the opposite. To many people, bankruptcy had simply become the easy way out, and for others, if it were carefully structured, it was the appropriate business decision. Yet I never entirely changed my view, especially as it regarded my personal debts. While I gradually accepted the idea of bankruptcy as necessary for selected partnerships, as I felt a duty to investors to use all legal means available, I steadfastly held to my views of avoiding voluntary bankruptcy as a tool to use against my personal creditors and those of my companies. I learned that bankruptcy was a last-resort tool in the workout game, that we could throw a property partnership into Chapter 11 to protect it from creditors. Indeed, our lawyers informed us that as general partners we had a duty to use all reasonable legal tools—including bankruptcy—in most partnerships to try to save properties for investors.

In our letter dated January 15, 1986, we told our real estate investors just that—that we were prepared to take a stance to protect their property from creditors. I had reservations about the tough-stance wording of the letter and the way it referred to possible bankruptcy of individual partnerships. Although I normally write my own letters, another member of Hall management had written this one because of my time constraints and priorities in dealing with the crisis at hand. I thought we should be more careful about using that volatile language. My instincts were correct. Little did I know at the time what trouble that statement would cause our company. In the meantime, I had planned to announce our problems to the media and explain how we were working on solving them, as well as what we foresaw as an impending industry-wide problem. Having discussed this with several associates and outside counsel, I decided to wait until I returned from an important company sales meeting in Hawaii. Upon my return, I planned to call one respected reporter, Steve Brown, real estate editor of the *Dallas Morning News*, to give him the story. I knew he understood the market and that he would be interested in getting the facts straight.

However, that January 15th investor letter found its way into the hands of another reporter at a weekly business publication. I was extremely busy wrapping things up so that I could get away to the Hawaii meeting, but I advanced my plan to call Steve Brown and he came to my office that evening for an interview, at which time I gave him a copy of the letter. I also returned the call of the other reporter and she interviewed me by phone. In the past, this reporter had not been careful to check facts and had printed some inaccurate stories, but the result of that interview with her was a fair and accurate story the next week.

I expected to see a story the next day in the *Dallas Morning News* business section. What I didn't know was how big the story would be. We were the first of many large real estate companies whose problems with lenders became public. On my way to the airport, I opened my paper to find a picture of me and our story, not in the business section, but on the very front page of the *Dallas Morning News*. A banner headline read "Hall Financial Plans Debt Restructuring." By the time I got to Hawaii, the sales force had a thousand questions. Our story had been picked up by the wire services and broadcast news—"Craig Hall Covering $40 Million in Real Estate Losses . . . Some Partnerships May Go Bankrupt."

It was the first time that word *bankrupt* was used in a headline about us and, although it was far from the last, none of my corporations or I ever filed for bankruptcy.

We had caught the media's attention in a much bigger way than I had anticipated. When times were good and I was making big plays in the stock market, I had been portrayed as a "wunderkind," which is a German word meaning wonder child. Now the press wanted to see how the wunderkind handled the hard times. By the time I got to Hawaii, our story had been distributed coast to coast by the wire services. I had messages to call *The New York Times*, the *Wall Street Journal*, several television and radio stations, and of course, the Dallas papers. They all requested copies of that investor letter and we honored their requests.

Meanwhile, our sales people were reading the articles and had worries of their own. The bad news could be devastating to their business of selling our limited partnerships—a fear we would later watch come true. In 1985, we had been the largest private-placement sponsor in the country. Now we were big news in a bad way.

Laurie Cohen, a young reporter for the *Wall Street Journal*, thought there was a "story behind the story." On February 3, the *Journal* ran the results of her suspicions—"Hall Financial's Loan Problems Could Hit Savings and Loans"—which pitted us against the savings and loans in an adversarial role. Though our problems certainly had a huge effect on those savings and loans, the savings and loan industry in general was in trouble long before our problems surfaced. At this time, everyone knew real estate was soft, but most companies were doing everything possible to hide the bad news as long as they could. The result of all the media attention was that the then California savings and loan commissioner took me to task (also in the media) for threatening the savings and loans with bankruptcy. He didn't know us, or anything about us, but he was reacting to the media coverage. We were simply trying to face our problems openly.

February 4, 1986, may have been the worst day of my life. As part of my efforts with May Petroleum, I was negotiating with Drexel Burnham Lambert on a $50 million debenture for May to raise funds for expansion. During the past months, Drexel was very positive about backing us. But now they told us they probably couldn't sell the debentures because of the negative press. That same day, Continental Insurance called us and said they were canceling our utility bonds because they no longer had confidence that we could pay the utilities on our properties. Again, because of the press. It was a dangerous precedent. If other bonding companies followed suit, we would have to come up with an average of $60,000 to $70,000 in deposits for each of our 243 properties. That added up to more than $15 million that we simply didn't have available for nonproductive purposes!

Then, Bankers Trust called and told us they decided not to extend a loan we had with them. They were the lead bank on the $100 million line of credit on which they said they wanted to be paid immediately (which wasn't possible) or they would demand more collateral. And that wasn't all: one large investor with interests in many of our limited partnerships stopped paying capital installments on ten investment units. And we had calls from tenants in our office buildings wondering about the status of leases if we went bankrupt. Everything was crumbling before our eyes. And it didn't stop.

Two days later, examiners from the Dallas Federal Home Loan Bank began knocking on the doors of Resource Savings Association and Hall Savings Association, both savings and loans that I owned. They wanted to make sure we weren't looting Resource Savings and Hall Savings to save our business. As I knew would be the case, they never found anything wrong.

Banks were walking away from financing arranged for new acquisitions and some of our lenders were calling our loans and washing their hands of us completely. It was almost as if Hall Financial were a bank and all of the depositors (creditors in our case) were lining up for their money. I felt like Jimmy Stewart in *It's a Wonderful Life*. If I could just keep the doors open each day until closing time, maybe I could make it. But the bridge and the cold water underneath it were looking mighty inviting.

Around this time, we turned to Ken Leventhal of Kenneth Leventhal and Company, a man who's been down this troubled road with borrowers and lenders many times. Kenneth Leventhal and Company is one of the largest accounting firms in the country, and among their talents is their specialized ability (primarily in real estate) to restructure complex financial situations. Ken and his firm have been behind many successful restructurings, probably the best known being their resurrection of the Trammell Crow Company from the mid-seventies real estate crash. He told me that as rough as things were now, the publicity was bound to make it even worse. He was very much a realist and reminded me that I might be bankrupt at any minute. But we kept holding meetings, we kept communications open—with our lenders, with our sales people, with investors, with tenants, and with the press. It seemed that since we were being open, many reporters were assuming that we were only admitting to the tip of the collapsing financial iceberg. The constant media coverage was getting to all of us at Hall Financial Group. Finally, for a while I stopped talking to the media, which was even worse; then the negative coverage increased.

By March, we were renegotiating debt on 102 properties. March also brought our first casualty—a small 114-unit apartment complex in Greenville, Texas. We had fought to keep our investors' interests intact, but in the end, the property was lost to the lender. Unfortunately, the press, following the foreclosure, stressed the "pack mentality" of lenders and foretold of other lenders waiting in line to foreclose. No one ever pointed out the fact that a single foreclosure of a $1.8 million property was not necessarily the end of our $3 billion portfolio. After all, each property was structured legally to live or die on its own. That is to say, there were no legal liabilities between properties, and the partnerships were intentionally structured so that one partnership with problems would not affect another. Under these circumstances, it was mind boggling to me that a national paper like the *Wall Street Journal* would make such a big deal about such a small foreclosure.

Our restructuring team had been negotiating with the individual savings and loans since our January 14 meeting in San Francisco, but I also had maintained contact with federal regulators in Washington, San Francisco, and Dallas. I knew that after we cut deals with the savings and loans the feds would have to give final approval. And when that day came, I didn't want any surprises. In late January, there was a flurry of phone conversations and calls for information. I asked to talk to the Federal Home Loan Bank board chairman, Edwin Gray, but was assured he didn't have a major role in my matters. I put in calls to Chairman Gray anyway, but they were not returned. My suspicions, however, were correct. When I received a call from Roy Green on January 29, he told me Chairman Gray had given orders for a special Craig Hall examination at all of the savings and loans that did business with us. I had previously given Roy a list of the Texas savings and loans at my meeting with him in early January, but I never realized then how that list would be used.

The "special examination" was hard on my already ailing reputation. That day and the next, the phones rang incessantly as S&L presidents called me to see what the heck was going on. All this was breaking behind the scenes as the media coverage was breaking across the country. The regulators would go into the savings and loans in which I had done business for years without any defaults and state that they were there to do a special exam on Hall limited-partnership loans. The savings and loans figured we must have really done something wrong. It instantly ended years of credibility and all because we tried to face problems before they occurred and went openly to the regulators.

How did I first find out about the investigation? Again, they came to my savings and loans, too—Hall Savings Association and Resource Savings! Examiners from Puerto Rico to Iowa descended on all of these savings and loans all over the United States at the same time. The expense to the government must have been enormous. And it was all for nothing because they didn't find a thing. Not a number out of line. And they were positive, I'm sure, that at least at Hall Savings and Resource Savings they would find wrongdoing and shut me down for loaning money to myself. Wrong again.

I was on the phone all day on January 29. I called San Francisco. David Martens at the San Francisco Federal Home Loan Bank was very apologetic. He even went so far as to call Washington and try to stop the examination, but his authority didn't reach that far. That day, I wrote the first of many letters to Chairman Gray. I never got an answer. My letter was specific and direct—if Mr. Gray had questions, why waste taxpayers' money? He could at least start with me. I was a phone call away and happy to cooperate. There was nothing to hide.

Shortly after this blitzkrieg, I got a call from Roy Green. He was in New York at a meeting of the presidents of the district banks with Chairman Gray. He said my situation had come up and they were talking about launching another investigation into my business. They had come up empty the first time but were sure they had missed something. Green went on to tell me that Rosemary Stewart, the head of enforcement, had come up with a way the bank board could get subpoena power over me by launching what the Federal Home Loan Bank Board called a 407M Investigation at Resource Savings. This investigation was supposed to look into wrongdoing at savings and loans. It certainly would be unnecessary overkill in this situation and very embarrassing. It was nothing short of harassment. There was no basis for such an investigation. I said we had cooperated and would continue to cooperate, but I didn't like threats. That day I sent Chairman Gray a letter stating as much. I offered continued cooperation but expressed resentment and surprise at his unusual approach. I told him not to threaten us or play games. We were happy to cooperate but tiring of this hard-nosed approach. If I had anything to hide in my life, I couldn't have taken such a tough stand. The fact was that neither Hall Financial nor we were out to fight with the regulators or hide anything. We had always had a great relationship with regulators prior to this. We just wanted to be dealt with openly and straight up—and to address market problems in a responsible way for everyone's best interests. This would become the second letter he didn't answer.

Roy said he would try to stop the Bank Board from launching the trumped-up 407M Investigation to get the subpoena powers. We scheduled a meeting for February 3 in his office with representatives from San Francisco and Washington to discuss the situation yet again. The regulators at that meeting amazed me with their lack of knowledge of real estate limited partnerships. They asked us what a limited-partnership syndication was and how it worked. In that meeting, they asked for permission to see the books for all of our corporations and partnerships. They had no legal right to that, but I gave it to them. "Come on," I was saying. "You can look at anything I have." In February and March, there were between six to eight examiners on the third floor of our building, again at great cost to the government. When they finished, they found absolutely nothing wrong. All the numbers added up. Some of the regulators were surprised again. Others, like David Martens and Roy Green, were not surprised; they had already decided that we were on the up and up. In the end, the regulators never found anything wrong with our savings and loans or our corporate books. There's no doubt that once that credibility was established, it helped us a great deal with the future relationship. But from their standpoint, they had a new animal to face—honest market problems of borrowers, not fraud. We were the first big example, but there were a lot more to come.

During that time, some of the S&Ls were getting restless in California. They didn't know what to do. Worse yet, they didn't know what the regulators truly wanted them to do. Then came another big meeting. While regulators were still going through our financial details and while we were fully cooperating with them, they sent out a mailgram, without our knowledge, to all of the savings and loans that did business with us all over the United States saying that the Federal Home Loan Bank Board was holding a special meeting of all "Craig Hall Creditors." Many of these "invitations" went to lenders with whom we were totally in compliance with all loan terms and likely would never be in default. Other invitations went to lenders we didn't even do business with. We were quickly branded and cut off from the industry. Attendance was required. Again, how did we find out? They sent an invitation to the managing officer of Resource Savings. To this day I'm amazed at the gall of holding a "creditors meeting" like a bankruptcy before any bankruptcy or even default had occurred on the vast proportion of loans. It could easily have led to a self-fulfilling prophecy. We were in a downward spiral of perception more than reality.

The Craig Hall Creditors Meeting, called by Chairman Gray's Federal Home Loan Bank Board, was held March 10, 1986, in the California Ball Room of the Sheraton Plaza La Reina Hotel at the airport in Los Angeles. As if I weren't furious enough, the invitation stated that a representative of the Victor Palmieri Company, a company well known for handling major liquidations in the real estate and oil and gas industries, would be speaking at the meeting. I don't think the regulators really knew what they wanted to do at that point, but certainly the Palmieri Company would benefit if it could be appointed receiver and liquidate the Craig Hall empire. I called David Martens and asked him if he knew about the meeting, and he said John Price in Washington had organized it. In Roy Green's office, in February, I had met John Price, who was the associate director of the Office of Examinations and Supervision for the Federal Home Loan Bank Board, and ultimately responsible to Chairman Gray. At my request, David later called John, who after some deliberation agreed I could make a presentation at "my" creditors' meeting. Ken Leventhal had been working on the numbers and our plans, so we rushed to complete them to take to Los Angeles.

There were actually two meetings set for March 10, one at 10:00 A.M. for the largest lenders or servicers who managed loans for others, and another at 1:00 P.M. for all lenders. Our team flew out the night before. It was a very uncomfortable flight sitting next to Bill Sechrest. At six foot six he was visibly frustrated that we wouldn't pay for the larger, first-class seats. Larry Levey also went with us. Ken Leventhal, head of Kenneth Leventhal and Company, and Ken Townsend, who was in charge of that firm's Dallas office, met us out there. Ken Townsend had coordinated the extensive cash-flow study that had been completed by their accounting firm for the savings and loans and the government. There must have been fifty people from the federal government in attendance. I had breakfast the next morning with John Price and a few other government officials. I tried to find out why Victor Palmieri was invited, but only got a lot of double-talk. Everybody said somebody else invited him. The 10:00 A.M. meeting included about forty people. A lot of them were people I knew from Dallas, people who have since been removed from their savings and loans by the federal government. It actually got started almost two hours late because there were so many small, clandestine meetings going on all over the hotel. Everyone was on eggshells.

After a short while, they allowed me to come in and to talk for about a half hour. I was also invited to address the 1:00 P.M. meeting. Imagine standing in front of about 150 of your favorite creditors as they are being told that in the future they aren't going to be paid. Then they put you on stage. Now that's fright. Everyone was in a feeding frenzy due to all of the publicity in January and February about our "threatening lenders with bankruptcy." Heads of several savings and loans that were friendly to me kept coming in and out of the meeting telling me what was going on. Other than during my speech, I was kept out of the meeting. In fact, there were armed guards at the doors to the ballroom who made sure only those with invitations were allowed in. Meanwhile, David Marshall, then president of Resource (the S&L that I owned), was trying to remember every word said. He had a broken arm at the time, and I had told him I'd break his other arm if he didn't write down every word. He was supposed to learn shorthand before he went to the meeting. He took copious notes, so I know what everyone said.

I know, for instance, what happened in the presentation made by the President of Victor Palmieri Company. We were not going to let anyone take us over and liquidate our investors without one whale of a fight. The funny thing is the S&Ls were smart enough to read through to Palmieri's potential self-interest. Although the Palmieri representative gave his talk on the alternatives, including all the S&Ls moving against us together in an attempt to get a receiver (e.g., Palmieri and Co.), the S&Ls simply didn't buy that approach. They weren't unhappy with our management nor our approach, they were just confused and were trying to figure out what was in their best interest. Of course, there were some exceptions, and some of the executives were pretty emotional, but none bought into the idea of banding together in an attempt to get Palmieri or someone like that appointed as a receiver to take over our properties. However, they might have bought into that nonsense if we hadn't been there to turn the tide.

I also received a report that in my absence Roy Green said some nice things and stood up for us. I know that a lot of savings and loans stood up for me. The regulators constantly walked a fine line. It seemed like nobody wanted to make a step one way or another. Finally, the regulators said the savings and loans could foreclose or work with us. They left it to a vote and the savings and loans voted to work with us. They formed a creditors committee of the bigger players, who were supposed to negotiate a standard type of deal and then go to the regulators with an outline of the forbearances they needed to make the deal work. The regulators appointed one S&L chairman from Texas together with a California S&L chairman to co-chair the creditors' committee. The regulators said that they stood ready to consider forbearances on the Hall loans, or at least that was what was indicated at that meeting. Forbearances are regulatory releases from technical parts of the savings and loan regulations. This was important to S&L owners and represented the only concrete positive action of the regulators at that meeting. It later turned out to be a big negative because the S&Ls were betrayed by the regulators, who didn't grant even the most minor forbearance—despite their leading everyone to believe they would.

Before the meeting began to break up, I evidently must have shown tremendous anxiety and stress, pacing in the hallway while the representatives from the 150 savings and loans sat in the ballroom with probably thirty to fifty regulators. Another twenty or thirty were out in the hallway just pacing the floor. The guards continued to check the ID of everyone who went in.

As the meeting broke up, I saw some of the members of my contingent, and we decided that now was the time to pack up and go to the airport. Then, all of a sudden, some of the savings and loan executives started coming up and talking to me. One of them was one of the leading savings and loan people, a young man who had built an empire that many of us affectionately called "Gunbelt Savings." It had more than $3 billion in assets, but was infamous in its aggressive and flamboyant style and fast growth. He was not a big lender of ours. The four loans that we had with this S&L had been borrowed before 1983, when we had stopped doing business with him because his aggressive style was very different from the way we do business. I hadn't even talked to him in two or three years. He was putting his arm around my shoulder and saying, "Come on, Hall, you've got to have a drink with us." I told him I really didn't feel like a drink and, besides that, I had an airplane to catch. He insisted.

At the Sheraton Hotel bar there were numerous S&L executives and they all became friendly and jovial. One drink after another, people were making jokes and loosening up and enjoying the camaraderie of the day. It had been stressful for me, but now we were in a totally different environment in the bar. I glanced at my watch and again said that we had to leave to catch our plane. What would have been an hour or so sitting around the airport was now going to be just a short, last-minute run to catch the plane. Then our host quickly said, "Absolutely not. There is no way I'm going to let you take a commercial flight back. You're coming with us." He said, "In fact, I'll take Sechrest. His legs are too long for those regular airplanes anyway, but that's all I have room for." I felt bad when he told Larry Levey that he had better get going to the commercial flight because he didn't have room for everyone. We were eager to take him up on the more comfortable seats and so, with Larry's encouragement, we did.

Our lender host apparently had a DC-9 or a 727 on order—seriously! But this was his G-3 plane, which was plenty of luxury for any huge empire or the president of a country, let alone a fast-growing "Gunbelt Savings."

This plane had it all: big swivel seats, lots of room, and a very attractive, full-figured flight attendant to serve drinks and dinner. We had hardly gotten into the air when he broke out the expensive wine—I mean really expensive. There were drinks, there was wine, and then came the food: fine china and a delicious meal. Our host had relegated his savings and loan friends to the back of the plane so that I could sit up front next to him. After we had gone an hour or so he said, "Would you like to watch a movie?" Notwithstanding the glamour of this flamboyant life-style, I wasn't sure if he was kidding, but I said, "Sure." He then had the stewardess bring a box full of video cassettes and gave me my choice.

Shortly thereafter, we were well into *Beverly Hills Cop*. It was a fun movie and it was beginning to take my mind off of the day. A great meal, a couple of drinks, and *Beverly Hills Cop*—who could think that just a short time earlier I had been giving a speech to 150 different financial institutions that were all seething at the information that they might be part of a major default. Nevertheless, at the moment, things could not have been better. But, alas, there was a problem. As the plane came in toward Love Field, *Beverly Hills Cop* had not quite finished. We all wanted to see the end, so our host told the pilots to circle the field a couple of times so that we could see the end of the film and, finally, we landed.

He, like many of the savings and loan owners, had a lot at stake in our situation, but he was not mad at us. On the contrary many, though certainly not all, S&L owners knew of the true market problems and preferred working with borrowers for mutual benefit, along the lines we were proposing. Most smart S&L owners and managers were well aware of our efforts and appreciated them. They were far more concerned with the inconsistent and undependable regulatory environment. In time most of the S&L owners and managers at that March 10, 1986, meeting would lose their savings and loans. Our host who built the once high-flying S&L was no exception; he eventually lost it all. For many of them, fate either has, or will, include criminal indictments as the FBI searches for those who crossed the line.

Life is full of ironies and a strange mix of events. We were safe and sound, back in Dallas, ready for the next part of our own odyssey. No one could have convinced any of us in our wildest imaginations of what lay ahead.

The realities of dealing with lenders and regulators in a world of crisis and chaos were bad enough. But for us matters were far worse in perception than they were even in the worst of our reality. If perceptions could kill, we were sure to be dead. It was only a matter of time.

As I briefly described in the preface, on April 25, 1986, the *Wall*

Street Journal front-page story was titled "Property Damage." Its first subtitle was "Syndicator Craig Hall Struggles to Shore Up Real Estate Empire." The next subtitle was "His Highly Leveraged Deals Suffer as Inflation Ebbs and So Do Some Lenders." The article talked about how my approximately $3 billion "financial empire" was faltering in an attempt to get creditors to "grant extensions of hundreds of millions in debt to avoid bankruptcy courts." It even named such banks as RepublicBank Corp., Bankers Trust, and Michigan National. The stock of those banks were all affected on that day. Ken Leventhal predicted, "If the Hall organization goes into the tank, you'll have major problems with the Federal Savings and Loan Insurance Corporation, savings and loans, and many banks." This particular reporter for the *Wall Street Journal* attempted to get the dirt and the story behind the story, but dirt just wasn't there. We ran an honest and good business, so the reporting basically was more of an exposé of how fast and far one can fall when "inflation ebbs."

Laurie Cohen of the *Wall Street Journal* worked long and hard at trying to get someone to go on the record saying something bad about me or Hall Financial. She and other reporters tried and tried to get one of our competitors to come out with a strong, negative statement. While the credible sources in real estate were either supportive or silent, one small division of a regional brokerage firm in Dallas had a president who, it seems, was looking for opportunities to get his name in print. I've never met him nor, from what I understand, does he really know anything about us. He did, apparently, lose some deals to us in the early eighties and he was more than willing to give the kind of colorful quotes that the reporters were looking for. His famous quote in the *Wall Street Journal* article was as follows: "Craig Hall is only trying to rearrange the deck chairs on the *Titanic*." That same charming quote appeared in numerous magazines and newspapers following the *Wall Street Journal* article.

Ironically, a year or so after the first quote, while I was still mad about it and thinking of suing the brokerage firm of Rauscher, Pierce and Refsnes, Inc., I met with the chairman, David Smith. David offered his apology and said the firm would like to do something for us to make amends. I now look at the quote and laugh. It is kind of clever, but at the time it didn't seem too funny. Perceptions can often be more important than reality. In those days I would say if you took a private poll, most people would have agreed that our fate was all but sealed. To the average reader we were merely rearranging the deck chairs on the *Titanic*, and there was no way we would do anything but sink. With that perception being commonplace, it made turning the reality positive, and avoiding the almost inevitable, self-fulfilling sinking prophecy, all the more difficult.

One of the lessons one learns in tough times is that you have to step back and put life and business in perspective every now and then. Some of my senior executives probably had that in mind when pondering an upcoming interview I had scheduled with a reporter from a major national magazine in the spring of 1986. My associates must have realized how nervous and depressed I was. I was particularly sensitive to what we perceived as the many beatings we had already taken, and this would be just one more bad day.

As I anxiously awaited his arrival, my secretary announced that the reporter was here. In walked a very hairy, short (under five feet) chimpanzee, whom I later came to know as Deena. While I was awaiting the reporter to do my interview, Deena came into my office, gave me a big kiss (a kiss by a chimpanzee is something you don't forget), sat down, took a pad out, and was ready to take notes. Even I couldn't contain my laughter when the real reporter showed up a few minutes later. We were trying to get Deena out of the building without the reporter seeing how, in the middle of all of our problems, we were simply monkeying around.

This was just one of many times that my associates came through with the right medicine for the right situation.

C H A P T E R 7
WHEN THE GOVERNMENT OWNS YOU

AFTER THE MARCH 10 showdown, we got back to one-by-one negotiating. We were now under the spotlight of media attention and regulatory
scrutiny, and savings and loans were being competitive with one another
and worrying because they didn't want to get a worse deal than someone
else. But we made progress. We offered to give half of our general-
partnership ownership in the properties to a pool to benefit the savings and
loans. We were willing to give up our interest to protect the limited partners.
At times, we felt we were giving everything away, but I knew at the time
that we needed to give the savings and loans something significant. The
media coverage was pitting us against the lenders, even though it wasn't
that way in reality. And it became clear that to save face the savings and
loans needed to say publicly that they were getting a great deal from Hall
Financial Group. We were willing to give them a great deal provided they
would say so—it would be helpful to both of us.

The closer we got to some sort of agreement, the stranger things got
with the government representatives. The savings and loans would take
their deals to the regulators and say they needed certain forbearances that
the feds had promised to "consider" at that March 10 meeting. Then the
feds would reject the agreements. In March, we were very close to a deal
with Westwood. And we were planning to use the Westwood deal as a
model for the creditors committee. Westwood was our largest savings and
loan lender, our "bell cow" for the restructuring workout plan. By March
28, we had a letter of intent virtually ready to sign. This deal with Westwood was so important because all of the lenders were saying they wanted
to see what everyone else was doing before they signed a deal. With the
regulators still flip-flopping all over the place, the savings and loan institutions were getting mixed signals—first work it out with Hall, and then
don't. Every day I spent hours on the phone with John Price and the other
regulators trying to get a reading of the situation. We were a hot potato;

if the regulators helped, their concern was that they would encourage more workouts. Moreover, if it came apart, later they would have made a mistake. They needed a policy but were slow to come to grips with the reality of just how bad the markets really were and the fact that we were just an example of a much bigger problem.

On March 27, I was at Commonwealth Savings in Houston trying to work out some loans. I was meeting with Ed Smith, one of my partners in the Cowboys, who was the major shareholder of Commonwealth; Don Norris, Commonwealth's chairman; and with Jamie Jackson, the president, who used to be one of the three members of the Federal Home Loan Bank Board. In time, Commonwealth, one of the respected pillars of the savings and loan community, would, too, find itself broke and in receivership, but on March 27, 1986, Ed Smith, Don Norris, and Jamie Jackson were still very much in charge. I was catching them up on Westwood and Beverly Hills Savings and our meetings in San Francisco. I had a plane to catch that night to go from Houston to California to, finally, sign our letter of intent with Westwood the next day. We had negotiated from mid-January until March 27 the language of the twenty-plus page document and now we were almost there. While I was in the meeting with Ed, Don, and Jamie, I got an emergency call from the Westwood attorney, Paul Walker. The conversation was very mysterious. He said, "Craig, I can't say any more, but don't get on the airplane and call me at 5:01 California time." Ed Smith had invited me to dinner, so I went over to his house and made the call from there at 7:01 Houston time. I had guessed by then what I was going to hear, but I still couldn't or didn't want to believe it.

Paul Walker told me Westwood had been closed by the government and had been taken over by the Federal Savings and Loan Insurance Corporation. Paul said he didn't know how this would affect our negotiated loan modifications, but there were new lawyers for FSLIC now involved in the deal. Paul said he had met with them and thought they would hire his firm to finish the deal with us. Paul estimated that it would be a week at the most before the letter of intent was signed and we were back on track. I was stunned. At first I had trouble speaking, but then I realized that Ed and Molly Smith were looking at me and I tried to recover. I told them what had happened. At the time my hope was that this truly would be a temporary delay. I learned later that when you're dealing with government agencies, lots of lawyers, and new, hot political issues that no one wants to face, there is no such thing as expedient decision making. This was the beginning of that lesson.

The next day I called John Price in Washington. He said he was sorry and hoped this wouldn't hurt us. He knew our deal was close. John said he was going in to meet with Chairman Gray in a matter of minutes and would see what they could work out. But it wasn't just a matter of minutes or a matter of weeks before the deal got rolling again. Weeks turned into months and the delay had a harmful effect on all of the savings and loans involved in our overall restructuring as well as our partnerships. Everyone was waiting to see the government's example with Westwood, but the wait just dragged on and on.

In April, the *Dallas Times Herald* had an article about our first bankruptcy. Though negotiations on the loan were ongoing, and this was one small property out of over 250 properties that we owned, the story's headline read, "Hall Group Files for Bankruptcy." It was devastating. Although Barbara Demick, the reporter, called immediately to apologize (someone else had written the misleading headline), the story—along with that horrible headline—was picked up by the wire services. Whether something is true or not isn't what counts. It's the power of perception, and that's often controlled by the media. The general public began to believe we were broke. Everyone was waiting for our final death certificate and they were all sure it was just around the corner. The subsequent retraction couldn't make up for the confusion, but I know it was an honest error. I respect the way Barbara Demick handled it and I know the paper didn't mean to harm us. Yet its effect greatly compounded our mounting problems.

Throughout the whole ordeal, the media did keep one thing straight: they never accused me or my company of being dishonest. A few reporters told me later that they had been looking for anything bad or wrong they could find on us, and though some reporters exaggerated our difficulties, they never accused us of any wrongdoing. It wasn't because they didn't look, and look hard enough, either. But constantly being in the media with stories more or less predicting an oncoming demise wasn't easy to handle. I heard that a number of people started betting pools on when the Hall companies and I would be in bankruptcy.

Meanwhile, there were constant reassurances for everyone that Paul Walker had been hired to finish our workout restructurings. But throughout April, May, and part of June, there was this unknown law firm that Paul Walker was reporting to. Paul and the lawyers we had dealt with didn't seem to have all the cards anymore. I had been so impressed by how demonstrative they were, how badly they seemed to want to get the deal done back in January and February and March. Now, mysteriously, it seemed like the deal kept getting stalled. I was told it would be done in a week. Then I just knew it would be done before my birthday on April 11. I agonized day by day, phone call by phone call. I was being led on about when it would be done. It was excruciating because so much depended on this deal as a precedent.

Birthdays are usually a time to celebrate, but in 1986 my birthday seemed like anything but a time to rejoice. I wanted, in the worst way, to just have the peace and quiet of solitude, but some of my friends from the company felt differently. I was stopping by the house of John Calandro, one of our senior vice presidents, to drop off some papers that he had requested and, all of a sudden, found that a surprise party had been planned. I was really surprised, which is unique for most surprise parties. The party turned out to have a positive and friendly tone like any party, but also a kind of feeling that perhaps the end for all of us wasn't far away. It was interesting to see who was there and who wasn't. While it was mostly company people, there were also a handful of outsiders. Unfortunately, they were mostly lawyers and accountants involved with the restructuring. I tried hard to smile and be friendly at the party. One of the interesting things that one learns in trying times is that most people keep their distance. You find out who your real friends are. One couple at the party, Ted Strauss and his wife, Annette, who is now mayor of Dallas, made a very big effort to be there. They are good friends and, because I know their schedule is unusually demanding, their mere presence meant a lot to me.

The party did have its lighter moments. The gifts included a specially prepared Monopoly game of getting through the tough times, with everything from government obstacle courses to helmets for doing court battle and more. In looking back at the creative energies that people used to loosen up the tension at the time, I am reminded about how important perspective is. Keeping a sense of humor is critical and this time was, perhaps, the lowest of low points. But while the party was going on around me, my mind couldn't help but think about the Westwood deal. Could we keep it alive or would it die?

I wasn't about to let the deal die, no matter how much it seemed that everyone wanted it to. We had been too close in March to let that happen. On one hand, the regulators were saying it was economically logical to work out something with us, but on the other hand they were saying that if they pushed a workout, they would be taking a risk of being embarrassed and they were worried about how other borrowers or savings and loans would view it. Logically, they were in a tough spot, but by giving mixed signals, they did the worst thing possible. Everyone was on edge because of the media attention—it was days, weeks, and months of going nowhere fast.

Throughout this time we kept working on the restructuring both with the S&Ls individually and with the creditors' committee.

Finally, we got our creditor-committee model finished (this was more or less the standard restructure terms we were proposing), and we literally went door to door to our lenders all over the United States with letters of intent, which were preliminary agreements. We thought it would be easier to at least get a preliminary agreement signed rather than waiting for all final documents. It was like signing a sales agreement on the purchase of a house. Since no one wanted anyone else to get a better deal, we gave them what is called a "Most Favored Nations" clause, which basically said that if other savings and loans got a better deal, we would come back and give them that same provision. The point was, please sign now. Everyone said it could never be done, but in April and May, we finally started to get signers. Virtually everyone felt our situation was hopeless. They all felt reluctant to even try our plan, yet we convinced them, one by one, to come along for their own best interest. Our plan was good for the lenders and, of course, for our investors.

We were further in default. Our employee morale was very low and we were naturally having trouble raising new limited-partnership money. I began to believe the newspaper stories. This period was one of the most depressed of my life. In 1984 and 1985, I had made $65 million and $75 million a year personally. Awesome amounts of money. And now every penny was going back into the business that we were on the verge of losing. All we had wanted to do was honorably face our problems. In the first quarter of 1986, we had put $15 million voluntarily into solving these problems, and yet no one cared what we had done "yesterday." The mood of the creditors was driven by greed, panic, and confusion. Had I thought it would be as bad in the markets as 1986 was turning out to be, I never would have put the $15 million into nonrecourse loans in the first quarter of the year. Nonrecourse loans are loans that have collateral as their sole security for repayment, and if things go wrong, the lender can only take the property. Usually commercial bank lenders have personal liability or corporate liability; this is called recourse. Property mortgage loans are often nonrecourse, as were our partnership loans.

During 1986, in our constant efforts to solve problems, we kept paying so much into nonrecourse debt that we lost huge amounts of money. We didn't expect the markets to continue downward. We just didn't know. I worked hours and hours in a state of absolute mental depression. I would sleep two hours nightly and wake up with the bed wet from perspiration. I never gave up, never threw in the towel, and never worried about my personal finances because I always knew we could make it. My biggest concern was for my investors. In April and May, I felt like I was coming to the end of a marathon. Everything was hard, one inch at a time. We would fly to another little town, day after day, to beg another savings and loan to sign that letter of intent. Knee pads for begging became standard equipment for our restructuring staff, especially me.

In addition to the savings and loans, we, of course, had commercial banks, insurance companies, and others who had extended us one type of credit or another. In our efforts to inform all of our lenders what was going on, as I traveled the country I would stop and see insurance companies and commercial lenders as well as the savings and loans. On one such trip I had a dinner scheduled for March 14, 1986, with our loan officer and her bosses, four of the senior officers from Michigan National Bank. This bank has been one of our longest-standing and strongest relationships. At that time, Michigan National had approximately $30 million in loans to me individually and to the company, virtually all of which were totally unsecured. They believed that my signature was good enough, and we had done business for many years. Michigan National had made large profits from our account. We were one of their largest borrowers, if not the biggest at the time.

The dinner was set up as a late-night meeting, which we made even later with our plane arriving at the small Michigan airport about one hour and ten minutes behind schedule. We had been whistle-stopping the eastern part of the United States and talking to lenders, having already been in New York, Greenwich, Pittsburgh, and now Detroit all in one day. As Don Braun and I met with the five anxious lenders, our descriptions of the nature of the problems certainly didn't help their digestion of the fresh fish that we had for dinner. While perhaps I had lost some of my sense of humor, I couldn't help but play a little game that evening by asking the lenders what their guess would be as to our cash losses over five years based on new projections that we had just run. While they weren't much in the mood to play games they indulged me. First the most senior individual guessed $10 million. Beep—the buzzer went off and I said he was wrong and had lost his prize. Next the group vice president, just below the head guy, guessed $50 million. He had the advantage of knowing from my expression that the $10 million was way too low. Beep—the buzzer went off. He, too, didn't win the prize. Finally, to spare the agony, I told them the number was more than $250 million. At that point and for most of the rest of the dinner, you could hear a pin drop. On the plane on the way back, that event played over and over in my mind. Don and I discussed it and at least we got a bit of a chuckle out of it. Although Don and I both have a lot of respect for Michigan National Bank and the individuals at that dinner, at a certain point the numbers all become academic and the bottom line is: what were we going to do about the problems?

Shortly after that meeting, Michigan National Bank announced the size of their loans to us and took an immediate $3 million reserve for possible collection problems. Their stock that day went down about 10 percent, temporarily lowering the value of the huge bank by far more than our total loans. Michigan National is an excellent, well-managed bank and they worked with us from the beginning in resolving the loan problems. By the time of this book's publication, approximately $25 million will have been paid in principal and all interest throughout the time period will have been kept current. In short, Michigan National will not lose a penny and will continue to make a substantial profit on our accounts. We're proud of that and grateful for their help, as well as the assistance of other banks in extending terms and working with us during the times of difficulty.

Then came a very big wrench in the whole plan. We were basing all of our renegotiations on the Hall Financial Group putting its profits from new business back into the problem properties. We had expected to raise a very minimum level of $100 million in new limited partnerships in each of the next five years. We had made all of our projections based on that. In my heart of hearts, I knew we'd do twice as well, so I wasn't worried at all about meeting the plan. We were voluntarily going to give the savings and loans all of our corporate profits to help our investors for the next five years. In other words, we'd work for the savings and loans and the investors for at least five years, even though we had no liability on the mortgage loans. However, we didn't expect the Packwood Tax Bill, which surfaced in May as part of the Senate Finance Bill. In May, I was at a Young Presidents Organization meeting talking to Don Williams, head of the Trammel Crow Company, about that bill. He thought it would pass, and it began to sink in that this could really happen. It did pass and that meant the business as we had known it was dead. Values would decline overnight and there would be a three- to five-year severe adjustment period before a new real estate investment world could sort out the huge amount of change. My plan was dead. I didn't have time for lots of accountants to work on new numbers. Decisions needed to be made or we were history, and with our demise, many investors and savings and loans and banks would suffer huge losses.

The tax bill lengthened depreciation, eliminated the favorable capital-gains differential from ordinary income, and worst of all you could no longer deduct partnership losses against salary or ordinary income. The bill suddenly eliminated the whole essence of historically built-in economics in real estate. Clearly, it would have a devastating effect on our plans.

For the next forty-eight hours I worked on the numbers. The profits from $100 million a year of new limited partnerships had to come from some place other than private placements. We were really in desperate shape and I knew it.

I also knew that if we went back to the lenders and tried to start over with a new plan based on after-the-new-tax-law realities, we would be slaughtered. We couldn't ask the lenders to take less than promised, and Hall Financial couldn't voluntarily pay as much as planned. So I came up with the idea of capital calls. I would go back to the investors for the first time in our history and ask them to put more money into their partnerships (this was a capital call). It would be strictly voluntary, but for the capital calls to be successful, I needed to go around the country personally to explain it to investors—which I later did—and, much to the surprise of a lot of critics, it worked. With capital calls, too, we were at the forefront of the industry. Many limited partnerships since have saved properties on the format we developed. In the end there was sacrifice by everyone (i.e., Hall Financial Group, limited partners, and the lenders) in the short run, all for long-term gain. It is gratifying to learn, as we did, that people will pull together in times of trouble when there is leadership, a good reason, and a reasonable plan.

We were finally close on Westwood again. This time, it was really more than a letter of intent. It was a very extensive agreement and, as a part of the contract, we were going to pay about a million dollars in consideration of their signing this agreement. It had been an exhausting, rough six months. But finally, after almost having an agreement and then having the savings and loan taken over, we were again close to signing Westwood.

The first week in June, Paul Walker, Westwood's chief counsel, called and said we had a meeting set for June 10, 1986, in Los Angeles to negotiate the final details of the agreement. This was the same meeting that was supposed to have taken place back in March, but postponed because Westwood had been taken over by the government. In the interim, a crew of new people entered into the process, including Scott, an employee of the San Francisco Home Loan Bank, who was appointed the special representative for FSLIC, the conservator. Though Scott wouldn't be at this meeting on June 10 and had kept himself totally aloof working through Paul Walker, he was really the new decision maker. He had merely delegated the negotiations to Paul Walker.

The June 10 meeting was the breakthrough we had been waiting for. If we could get Westwood signed up, that would mean 90 percent of our renegotiations were out of the way in at least a preliminary manner and, hopefully, everyone else would fall in line.

The negotiations on June 10 were of a technical nature, mostly rather minor things, it seemed. I was ecstatic to find no deal killers at the table. There were a few items left open when the meeting concluded. I returned to Dallas in good spirits. On June 12, Paul Walker called and said the Westwood board had refused the deal. We had many phone conversations over the next few days about a couple of issues, but we finally came to a compromise. On Tuesday, June 17, Paul Walker called me and said that we now had a deal on our workout. I was to wire the one-million-dollar up-front cash payment to Westwood that day to seal the agreement on the renegotiation and he would telecopy the signed document. It was finally done!

It was like New Year's Eve at our offices in Dallas that evening. With Westwood's permission, we put out a press release that Westwood had signed the letter of intent. Then we held a champagne celebration for our 300 employees in the office. The positive publicity would be key to the capital calls. Everyone had worked hard for this, and finally things were falling into place. The next week I was to start a whistle-stop tour around the country explaining the Westwood transaction to investors and get them to support the capital calls necessary to fund the Westwood agreement.

What I didn't know was that a regulator whom I had met briefly before was heading right for me. He seemed a rather minor participant at the time, but Scott, the regulator, would soon figure very largely in our future.

I was optimistic. On July 15, I had been on the road for the better part of a week, flying from stop to stop to tell registered reps, broker-dealers, and investors about our intentions to make capital calls a part of the restructuring with Westwood. I was pleased with the meetings so far.

The capital-call payments investors were asked to make were in addition to their regular investment payments and were to help cover cash shortfalls. They were an essential part of the workout with Westwood. In return for renegotiated mortgages at lower interest rates, I would, in many instances, assign half of my ownership share in the property to the lender. We would also make a commitment to lend more corporate money to the partnerships and to defer the fees that were owed to us by many partnerships. Now, with the capital calls, the investors would be asked to make additional payments. It was this sort of three-way cooperation (us, the investors, and the lenders) that could solve some very substantial problems. The parties involved were not giving something for nothing. With the properties saved, in the future, when the cycle turned up, each party would benefit. It was a win-win result, which is the way we always try to have negotiations end up.

Everything still hinged on Westwood, though. With a signed letter of intent agreement, the capital calls would clinch the deal. I was determined to make sure the investors saw the benefits of the plan and I believed they would start writing checks. We hoped other lenders would see the Westwood transaction completed and then fall into place. Most of the lenders had already signed letters of intent but were waiting on Westwood to put their final loan restructuring in place.

Though we had gotten the signed letter of intent from Westwood, the entire Westwood loan package was far from being finished. Westwood had participated our loans out to six different lenders; this meant that they had sold part of their ownership of the loans to other lenders. This was not unusual but it sure complicated matters. Now we had to go to each of these participating lenders and help Westwood negotiate agreements with them. It was really Westwood's obligation to handle the participants, but we were happy to help. Paul Walker, the Westwood counsel, had told me before my capital-call tour that three of the six savings and loans had to be brought into line. One of those, Cal America, was apparently a shoo-in. If Cal America didn't agree to a mortgage workout, Westwood had a buy-back agreement they would exercise, and Paul had told me Westwood would buy back the loans if they had to and then the deal would be off. Later I would find out that you can't rely on everything you are told. If this buy-back existed it would never be acted on, and all of what I relied on would turn out to be wrong.

Another of the participants, Long Beach Savings, was a source of real problems. According to Paul, their chairman was not getting along with the Federal Home Loan Bank of San Francisco, and Paul told me then that he had threatened him with litigation if they didn't agree to workouts by the deadline.

On June 23 and 24, I was in a meeting with Howard Schweitzer, Paul's partner, and various savings and loan participants of Westwood. It was during this meeting that I first heard a supposed deadline mentioned for all of the savings and loan participants to be brought into line. I hadn't heard about this before, and when I did, I assumed it was a self-imposed negotiating deadline, as Westwood and Hall were working together to get the participants' agreement. Howard had explained to the savings and loans that Scott, as a special representative of the conservator, FSLIC, had set July 15 as a deadline for all of the savings and loans in the Westwood deal to agree with Westwood on their parts of the workout. We had never spoken of it as a "drop dead" date. In fact, it was not in our documents and had never been discussed with us. It seemed like a good idea, something to shoot for, a deadline to push the participants. By now, we had been working on these deals for more than six months. In my wildest dreams, I couldn't imagine Scott—whom I had met only very briefly at the December 20, 1985, meeting—unilaterally, without even informing us, imposing a ridiculous limitation now. I didn't think the comments Howard made to the savings and loans were really a true deadline but instead his way of negotiating with the savings and loans.

Paul had asked for my help with Long Beach. I had gotten to know the chairman of Long Beach, Roland Arnelle, so before I started the capital-call tour, I had several phone conversations with him. The problem was that he felt misled by Westwood from the start and thought they were being more than greedy in the workout. But he said he had no hard feelings with Hall Financial and felt the deal could be done despite his problems with Westwood. Before I left on the tour, I had called Paul with that good news.

A busy schedule awaited me in Atlanta on July 15. After I got to the hotel, I was to address the seventy-five employees of our Atlanta office. Following that there would be a private dinner meeting with broker-dealers and registered reps, then an evening speech to about 250 of our investors from the Southeast, and a late-night flight to Michigan. A similar schedule awaited me in Southfield, Michigan, the next day.

When I arrived at the hotel, several messages from Paul Walker were there waiting for me, each marked URGENT. I called Paul immediately and he abruptly told me today was the "deadline" to get the participating savings and loans signed. I asked him about Long Beach and he said Long Beach was fine. Now the problem was with Capital Federal, and Paul asked me to call them and straighten things out ASAP. He told me the whole deal was off if they didn't come on board.

I was confused. Since when had this whole deal balanced on this new deadline created by Scott? In all our negotiations, we never had expected to get all of the participant savings and loans on board. It had never been treated as an issue before. It wasn't in the documents. It wasn't in my notes. It made no sense at all. What was going on? Paul explained that FSLIC had ordered him to begin foreclosures by 1:30 P.M. if all six savings and loans weren't signed. He was frustrated and embarrassed, but dead serious.

I had employees waiting for me to give them reassurance, to boost them on in our task of capital calls, and now I was faced with this. To come this far only to find ourselves stalled—perhaps permanently—by some arbitrary deadline was crushing. I gave a quick speech to our employees and then was on the line with Mike Freed, Capital Federal's attorney. Like Long Beach, Capital Federal was at odds with the way

Westwood had handled its loans. I asked Mike about this "deadline" and he said he felt that FSLIC was playing some kind of game. He had worked with them in the past and this sounded familiar to him. The phone call with Mike and his associates was long and intense, but I had to break for the meeting with the broker-dealers and reps. After the meeting, I was back on the phone with Mike and Paul. I got away for just a few minutes to dash to the dinner meeting and make a few comments. After another hour on the phone, Paul, Mike, and I reached an agreement that was acceptable to all of us. Paul said the Westwood board would meet on July 16, the next day, and he expected the board would approve the deal.

Finally, I thought I could relax. But awhile later, I called Paul again to fill him in on some details. He had awful news—Scott had authorized foreclosure on all of the Westwood properties.

I couldn't believe what I was hearing. We had just spent hours on the phone getting Capital Federal in line and Long Beach settled. What was the problem now?

Paul said that Capital Federal had missed the "deadline" by a couple of hours and that Cal America hadn't agreed to anything. I asked him about the Cal America buy-back option that had supposedly made Cal America such a shoo-in, but Paul couldn't offer any explanation or help. He said he couldn't believe it either, but there was nothing he could do. He said Scott was acting on his own and I would have to take it up with the powers that be in Washington—Scott's bosses at the Federal Home Loan Bank Board.

It was a nightmare as I continued to listen to Paul tell me that the foreclosure procedures had not gone forward yet on properties in Texas because they had to be posted. The laws for how to foreclose on properties vary by state. For instance, in Texas you post a legal notice three weeks before the first Tuesday in any month, and that Tuesday it's foreclosed by a public bidding process on the courthouse steps. In Michigan and most other states the process is more complicated and takes months. He said that also it was too late to be calling Michigan, so the only foreclosures that had actually begun that day were in Colorado. Some consolation. I would soon learn that the Colorado foreclosures had actually begun a few days earlier while we were frantically going through this ludicrous fire drill. Scott had started foreclosures while we were diligently raising money pursuant to our agreement. I think it was expected that we would fail and, to the surprise of the regulators, we were succeeding at everything we promised.

This new development was a disaster. If Westwood started foreclosure, I would have to put sixteen properties into bankruptcy to protect them. Despite our progress with other lenders, they would inevitably follow suit in the ensuing panic. I could see all of our troubled properties—half of our portfolio—lined up like dominoes all falling toward bankruptcy. Trying to raise funds through new offerings or capital calls under those conditions would be ridiculous. Who would buy investments from a sponsor with half of its portfolio in bankruptcy? Ironically, the biggest loser would be Westwood and the other savings and loans. If we fell, so would at least thirty savings and loans, ending up insolvent.

That night in Detroit was sleepless and full of questions. If the deadline was so important, why hadn't Paul Walker or Howard Schweitzer stressed that on June 23 and 24? Why hadn't they told me personally about it? More to the point, why wasn't this deadline described in documents—especially the letter of intent agreement? The agreement had all of the material contingencies but no mention of this supposed deadline. With Westwood under conservatorship of FSLIC, wasn't it in everyone's interest to agree to the workouts instead of ending up with sixteen additional troubled properties to dispose of? What was going on and why?

I think Paul Walker believed without a doubt that Scott would never go through with the foreclosures on July 15. Was this all just an amazing power play for Scott? Were the bureaucrats enjoying running over a young and large real estate borrower like me? Were the lawyers just caught up in the idea of litigating this mammoth deal instead of making the nonjudicial workout happen?

This young fellow Scott didn't know me, nor did he know anything about the properties or the workouts. Did that just make it easier for him to play these games with people's lives? There we were dealing with a company that employed over three thousand people, had ten thousand investors, maintained the properties well, managed them well—and he was starting a disastrous avalanche. Lying in bed awake that night, I could see the chain reaction starting—other savings and loans would not work out their loans with us. They knew Westwood was the government and they would follow that lead. It was not my only nightmare. Didn't Scott realize that this transaction could be disastrous for the entire banking system? Scott was playing with dynamite. And now I know that Washington knew it. Washington apparently didn't want to, overtly, tell Scott what to do. Legally, there is a separation between FSLIC corporate in Washington and FSLIC as conservator of each separate failed savings and loan. But that was just Washington's excuse. The easy decision was to start the foreclosure process. No one wanted to take responsibility for trying something that might not work. They had never before done a workout this massive with so many different lenders. Foreclosure was economically a loss for the government, but no one would get into that kind of detailed analysis. It was the safe decision.

No matter how hard I tried to rationalize it, I couldn't get this deadline and Scott out of my mind. How could FSLIC expect total agreement when these savings and loans were at odds with Westwood regardless of us? Earlier in March, it had been decided that it was Westwood's responsibility to bring those savings and loans into line. Now, with the workouts all but done, the rules had been changed—now it seemed like we were expected to bring those savings and loans into the deal. FSLIC was foreclosing and it didn't make sense. It was as if Scott never wanted the deal to work and had set it up to fail. But not before Westwood got our million dollars! In less than a month, we had been totally double-crossed and defrauded of our money. It was terribly bad faith. If a private company had treated an agreement with such callous arrogance, there would have been great legal ramifications, but the government representatives seemed to act above the law.

I had to continue my investor meetings. This was ludicrous. I began a fact-finding mission. I called John Price in Washington. He was in charge of all of the field offices, including San Francisco Federal Home Loan Bank, where Scott worked. I explained to John what was going on, but he didn't know how much he could do to stop Scott's actions since Scott's obligation was to Westwood alone, whereas his concerns were for the system. This had to do with technical separations between FSLIC as a corporate entity and FSLIC in its capacity as conservator of Westwood— the latter being supposedly a separate entity, not under John's control. John said he would check things out and get back to me. He was concerned about what was going on, but he was giving me a lot of political double-talk as well. He started out saying he didn't know anything about the foreclosures; then he said he had been out of town and some of his assistants must know about it. But I found out later, in a deposition, that John had sat in on the meeting with Scott when foreclosure was discussed.

To my shock, we found out later from Scott's own deposition that that meeting was actually on June 17. That was the very day that we signed the preliminary agreement (letter of intent) and paid one million dollars as a good faith payment. Scott admitted in his deposition that he had called the Washington meeting to get permission to foreclose a month later, even at the very same time as we were being misled to sign the agreement and pay the million dollars. On July 11, Scott received a memo from Washington granting permission to start foreclosing, as he had requested at the June 17 meeting. The permission didn't come from John, who had refused to grant it, but from his boss. In the June 17 meeting, John Price had spoken up against foreclosing on us. One of the only fun things about lawsuits is you can find out a lot of things that you couldn't find out otherwise.

In my phone conversation of July 16, John Price dismissed the situation as last-minute maneuvering to bring the participating savings and loans into line. He also said that Scott had simply had enough of the entire situation and had decided to foreclose on a whim. Frankly, no one really believed Scott would go through with it, apparently including Washington. Everyone thought it was crazy. They felt pressured into granting the memo authorizing foreclosure but had hopes he would give the restructuring a better chance to work.

I also called David Martens at the San Francisco Federal Home Loan Bank that day. David had already heard about it and had called Washington to delay the foreclosure; he said he would continue to help. He knew it was a mistake for the system, and the S&Ls would needlessly suffer. He was one person who understood what a needless mess was about to unfold.

I got a very interesting picture from Joan Williams, a senior vice president and loan administrator at Westwood. She was as shocked and confused by the foreclosure order as I was. She had been a part of the long months of negotiations and couldn't believe how arbitrary the fore-closures seemed.

Next I called Jim Cirona, president of the Federal Home Loan Bank of San Francisco. He said he didn't know about the foreclosures at all, and when I told him that Long Beach and Capital Federal had come aboard and that Paul Walker had told me that the Westwood board had not ap-proved the foreclosure, he seemed a bit uneasy. Cirona seemed upset that Scott had acted on his own and said he would talk to him and call me back. Throughout my entire "fact-finding mission," I kept detailed notes of every conversation, as is my nature. Later, in the lawsuit that would come soon, these notes would prove to my advantage. I also called Roy Green in the Dallas Federal Home Loan Bank that day. He said the whole mess was political and he didn't know if he could help but would try.

By mid-afternoon on July 16 I had some answers. The problem was allegedly Cal America, which wouldn't agree to the mortgage workout plan. So I got on the phone with Cal America and was appalled to find they didn't even have the facts of the deal! I did as much explaining to as many people as I could and by late that afternoon Joan Williams called to tell me Cal America had accepted the deal.

Things were surely back on course again, I thought, and I had twenty minutes to prepare a speech for the eight hundred Michigan investors. This was truly unbelievable!

Then, I got a call from Paul Walker. He was upset. He asked me what I or my attorney had said to Jim Cirona and said that someone was quoting him as saying that Scott was a madman acting alone. Now, Paul told me, he had received a summons to see someone he referred to as the "almighty Roger Ferree." I didn't even know who Roger Ferree was, but I was soon to find out. Paul asked if I would be available later to talk to this "almighty Roger Ferree" and clear up just what had been said. Roger Ferree, I would later learn, was the head outside lawyer who had been calling all the shots since the March 28 conservatorship. I agreed, but that call never came. The next day I learned from one of my attorneys that Paul Walker had retired from the case.

The mid-July massacre had begun. Cal America had again changed its mind and was not agreeing to the restructuring. And this whole situation was getting more bizarre and more political as each day passed.

In sum and substance, we had been given mixed signals by the S&L regulators for over seven months. In their defense, this was a new problem and they were without any guidelines as to how to handle it. One minute they wanted to work with us to solve problems and the next they were attempting to sneak behind our backs and hold huge meetings with our creditors or launch investigations against us to try to prove we did something wrong. It was inconsistent, illogical, and seemingly impossible to get someone to face the facts of our situation, let alone the coming S&L crisis (of which we were merely a large example of real estate problems to come). If the problems had been dealt with earlier, it could have saved the taxpayers a lot of money.

Now in July we were finding some individuals within the regulatory system who were not only unwilling to meet and face important issues but, in fact, had devious plans. They had taken a million dollars of our money and signed an agreement they apparently had no intention of keeping. We may never know why, but the power and big egos of people can cause outlandish behavior. Many people in the same condition as we were would not have had the will to fight back. Our spirits were dampened, but we knew this wasn't the way our government is supposed to work. We still believed that if we could get to the right people in government, who had high integrity and cared about the system, we would be able to solve the problems. We were determined to press on and find out how we could save our investors and work with the lenders and avoid foreclosures.

CHAPTER 8
BEATING THE SYSTEM WITH THE SYSTEM

AT THE BEGINNING of this next phase of our battle with the government, we thought our mission was clear: get Cal America back on track and Scott would call off the dogs. In retrospect, it's funny that I thought it would ever be that simple.

I got the Cal America people to agree to a meeting in Dallas on July 21 to go over the whole deal again.

Larry Levey and I pursued Cal America with a vengeance. Joan Williams at Westwood and Vicki Neemeyer, Westwood's general counsel, had told me that they felt we had until Tuesday, July 22, to get the whole deal done. Tuesday was the next Westwood board meeting. On Thursday, we were scheduled for a preliminary court hearing in Texas. FSLIC was seeking a temporary restraining order to keep us from collecting August rents on properties and to have a receiver appointed over the Texas properties with Westwood loans. This was an unusually aggressive action for a Texas foreclosure suit. Things were starting to heat up.

We met with Dave Harmon from Cal America at 7:00 A.M. Monday, July 21, in Dallas. Dave told us that he had been at the Federal Home Loan Bank in San Francisco on Thursday and Friday of the previous week. He said that his supervisory agent asked him on Thursday why he wasn't working with us. Then, on Friday, she told him not to even try to work with us. He said the Federal Home Loan Bank of San Francisco seemed very hostile regarding Hall Financial. I still don't know the reason for the change of attitude, but I suspect it has to do with my calls to John Price and others in Washington.

We proposed a deal to Dave Harmon for Cal America anyway. He wanted some modifications and so we spent the day going back and forth between Dave and his accountants and lawyers, to get everything precisely documented to best help Cal America. Joan Williams continued to emphasize that we needed to finish up before the 11:00 A.M. board meeting on Tuesday. She said that Scott or Greg Mitchell from the San Francisco Federal Home Loan Bank would probably attend that meeting. She also told me that the Westwood foreclosure was still scheduled for July 24 in Colorado. Joan was being very helpful and clearly trying to do what she thought was best for Westwood.

Dave kept pushing us for more and more. Although we didn't give up anything for Westwood, we made modifications and concessions out of our own pocket to make the deal work. Finally, late in the evening, we telecopied documents back and forth, and by midnight, the deal was signed and done. I talked to Joan Williams the next morning and she was thrilled to hear we'd solved Cal America. She said Scott was in Costa Mesa, but she would try to reach him to let him know. Then she told me that she and Vicki had been told that Westwood was not to take any more of my calls and that Tom Roberts, an FSLIC outside lawyer, would now be the contact.

We had telecopied the signed letter of intent from Cal America to everyone concerned. But as the day wore on, I didn't hear from anyone. I talked to Roy Green, the head of the Dallas Federal Home Loan Bank, and he was concerned about the lack of communication. He suggested I go to California and attempt to meet with Jim Cirona, president of the San Francisco Federal Home Loan Bank. He told me things were getting very political. He implied we were a pawn in a bureaucratic power struggle between Washington and San Francisco about who could make which decisions.

The next day I called Jim Cirona, who agreed to meet and set up a time, but just as I was leaving for the airport, heading for our meeting, his secretary called and canceled the meeting. Jim never took my calls or answered any more letters after that. I called John Price and he said that Washington and the bank board, meaning Chairman Edwin Gray, were now involved. I told him we had gotten Cal America to agree. He then said that might not be enough. Once again, I couldn't believe what I was hearing. The government was now moving in full force.

But we pressed on. Thursday was our first day in court. Uncle Sam, on behalf of Westwood, was trying to take away the Texas properties that Westwood had signed the June 17 agreement on. Our hearing started at 1:30. The courtroom was reasonably full with lawyers and witnesses on both sides. The suit was first to seek possession of the August rents, then a receiver, and finally to foreclose on us. The testimony, all in all, was rather calm—other than a few emotional outbursts from me as I tried to make some points that really went beyond the scope of this initial hearing.

The other side didn't seem to score any points and at the end of the day, the federal judge said that surely, if all of those things that were supposed to be done by this deadline of July 15 were done now, then that should be good enough. He said something to the effect of, "Why can't the differences be resolved now?" The lawyer for the government shocked us all with this response: "My client (Westwood) has changed its mind. We don't want to go forward with this deal." Regardless, the judge urged us to attempt to reconcile the differences. I took that as a very positive sign.

We were beginning to learn that FSLIC at that time was, indeed, lawsuit happy. A prominent Dallas law firm had been hired to sue me, but soon after our hearing in the judge's court, the firm was fired. Then FSLIC turned around and sued for $150 million the law firm they had hired. One of the firm's partners was involved in a deal with an S&L that FSLIC didn't like. It was amazing. FSLIC never sued us for anything but foreclosure and related issues. The government knew they could find no wrongdoing to accuse us of committing. Of course, along with this lawsuit, we made newspaper headlines again.

On July 25, the judge's decision came: the temporary restraining order had been denied. We had won! We were encouraged by this victory. Over the weekend, we strategized plans to try to settle and we tried to schedule a meeting with "the other party." We had a court date for a related case on July 30 in Colorado, but thought probably it would be put off, since it appeared we were so close to getting this wrapped up. Once again, we were wrong. On Tuesday afternoon, Rodney Acker, the then outside attorney for FSLIC, called and said there would be no settlement discussion and the hearing in Colorado would not be put off.

So Larry Levey, our chief financial officer, Jeff Hage, one of our outside attorneys, and I boarded a plane for Colorado. We stayed at the Antler Hotel in Colorado Springs, the closest place to the courthouse. We were to meet our Colorado attorney there, with whom we had talked by phone but had never met in person. Previously, he had won a temporary restraining order battle in Colorado for us. This hearing was for a preliminary injunction—in other words, more legal maneuvering—but we knew we should win, so we weren't too worried.

Our Colorado attorney was supposed to meet us at 8:00 P.M. As we waited in the lobby, we watched two people in blue jeans check into the hotel. One was a fellow with red curly hair down to his shoulders and a long red curly beard. The young lady with him looked a little less like a hippie from the sixties, but definitely not a lawyerlike sort of person. Our lawyer was late and we joked about these folks being our attorneys. Well, guess what, that *was* our attorney and his associate. The three of us were a little shocked when our less-than-establishment-looking lawyer came over and introduced himself and his young assistant.

After our meeting started, though, we were encouraged. I was convinced that this team was hardworking and would be successful. There was one thing that bothered me. That night, the Colorado attorney had said that one benefit at the temporary restraining order hearing had been that the judge was kind of a hippie like himself. But tomorrow, we would have a different judge—a more establishment judge.

The government had lost the first round in Texas to us. Still stinging from the slap in Colorado, FSLIC came in loaded for bear. They had their trial lawyer from Denver, Bob Conley; the San Francisco attorney for the Federal Home Loan Bank, Rob Grow; the head litigator and strategist, Roger Ferree; the litigation counsel from the Federal Home Loan Bank Board of Washington, Jose Ceppi; and a rare honor—Scott Schultz, who was there to testify or just to observe, we'll never know which; and others I didn't know. I had been trying to meet Scott Schultz and had written and called him for months without ever getting a response. The closest I had ever gotten to him was a returned phone call from his lawyer to my lawyer.

A well-dressed smooth lawyer from Denver, Bob Conley, stood up at the beginning of the proceedings and told the very conservative-looking judge that this case was a repeat of one held recently in Dallas that his client won. I thought to myself that we had won that one, and as he continued, I couldn't believe what I was hearing. Bob Conley went on about the government's victory in Dallas and as the judge listened, his eyes swept the courtroom, filled with government officials. Conley brought up the standstill agreement that had extended the Westwood letter of intent past the July 15 deadline. The judge in Texas had said the standstill agreement was valid, but I kept thinking that wasn't what this hearing was about—that wasn't what we had stayed up the night before past 2:00 A.M. preparing for. Conley was urging the judge to establish that collateral estoppel applied to find in favor of the federal government. Collateral estoppel is a legal doctrine that basically means if a legal case has been decided by one court, then the same case can't be brought in another court. It may seem simple, but it is not always clear how similar one case is to another. My attorney kept trying to get a word in, but Conley was in control and we were clearly outnumbered by the very obvious presence of government folks. After listening to five or ten minutes of Conley's opening statements, the judge immediately found in favor of the FSLIC.

It was over. We hadn't even gotten to the point of testimony. Much has been written about the difficulties of fighting the U.S. government in court. After all, federal judges are on Uncle Sam's payroll, too. But here in state court in Colorado, the inequities were hitting me like bricks. There was no question that we would appeal this, but all it did was force us to put the Colorado properties into bankruptcy. The government already had appointed receivers. Whether we would have beat them on appeal or not, the government was winning. It looked like they were going to break us up piece by piece through foreclosure, leaving us a weakened force against their huge, endless budget for lawyers.

I tried to regain composure and then went over to congratulate the other side. I started toward Scott and he, literally, began to run in the other direction. It was comical. I chased him down the hall with my hand extended, telling him, "Congratulations." He rushed off after a brief hello, then he just ran out of sight. As I was walking back to the courtroom I heard loud voices. Roger Ferree, the head outside counsel for the government, was yelling at one of our attorneys, Jeff Hage. Mr. Ferree was heatedly shouting at this young lawyer, "If your client doesn't stop sending letters to Chairman Gray, there will never be any meeting and there will be no settlement ever." He said that it was "unethical" for me to contact Chairman Gray. As he was walking away from Jeff, I approached Mr. Ferree to introduce myself and told him that his statement confused me. Mr. Ferree shook my hand but barked that he couldn't talk to me if my lawyer wasn't there. So I motioned for Jeff to come over and continued my questions. I said that all I wanted to do was sit down and meet with someone of authority and to understand what had been going on. He told me to stop writing letters to Ed Gray and threatened that if I didn't, there never would be a chance of anyone talking. He said that I could not deal directly with his client, that everything had to come through him, that he was in charge. "I am in control," Roger Ferree said. We tried for a while to play Mr. Ferree's game. From then on, all settlement proposals went through Roger Ferree. We telecopied proposal after proposal through Mr. Ferree, all in an effort to get someone to talk with us. We played his little games of formal lines of communication via the telecopy machine. Finally it became obvious that he had no serious intent to resolve the problems or allow anyone of authority from the government to meet with us. He seemed to be calling the shots for Scott and, indeed, the government. It was a tragedy for the taxpayers and us that this man had such power. It truly seemed as though an outside lawyer, whose firm received hundreds of thousand dollars per month so that the fight continued, was calling the shots for the U.S. Government. That was unbelievable.

Right after the "mid-July massacre" of foreclosures started in Colorado, I had begun a campaign to meet with Chairman Gray. I had called him, but neither he nor his secretary nor anyone else on his executive staff ever returned my calls. So, typically, I began to write everyone: Chairman Gray; Jim Cirona in San Francisco; my contact in Washington, John Price; and Roy Green in Dallas. "I am totally baffled and would like to know if Chairman Gray or others at the bank board could be available to discuss this matter in the immediate future," I wrote. "We have made incredible progress toward resolutions that are mutually beneficial, and tremendous losses can be avoided if we simply continue to work together on the course that we have been working on over the last several months." I received no response to that letter, ever.

I wrote subsequent letters on July 22 and July 25 after the hearing in Dallas where we won the temporary restraining order battle. I emphasized that if we didn't work things out, FSLIC would have at least a billion dollars worth of real estate in its lap unnecessarily costing taxpayers big dollars. We also had $450 million in investor payments left to collect, money that would be lost if this whole deal toppled. This would hurt many commercial banks. Futilely, I continued to ask who was in charge. Was anyone really running the Federal Home Loan Bank Board at that time, or was it an agency out of control with outside law firms (some good and some bad) having inordinate power? Who was in charge?

A clearer picture of Chairman Edwin Gray eventually began to emerge. He seemed to be a man who was in over his head, in charge of an agency running wildly out of control. He probably meant well and thought he was doing what was right, but it seemed to be overwhelming his ability to control the situation. These were unprecedented times. The situation was moving fast and had very negative political implications if it became known to the public too soon. The whole government agency seemed to be on the attack, reacting rather than planning. So much was in the hands of outside lawyers litigating with unlimited budgets. Because of the deep pockets and the added benefit of government immunity (wherein senior government officials are not subject to depositions like the rest of us), the attorneys for FSLIC generally could win lawsuits against any opponent. And I certainly wasn't the only Texan feeling the wrath of Chairman Gray and the expensive outside legal firms with a mission to destroy. His apparent "get Texas" attitude was very well known. But we couldn't just lie down and die. That would have hurt many innocent investors, not to mention the FSLIC and my company. We couldn't and weren't about to let that happen.

In a deposition, a potential witness in a lawsuit is asked questions with a court reporter present who is recording the questioning under oath.

Lawyers of both sides are present and the answers can be used in the trial. Meanwhile, depositions were proceeding on the Texas lawsuit. Scott's deposition was quite an eye-opener. He had entered college in 1971. He went to the University of Wisconsin and then to Oregon State University for graduate work. He had been with the San Francisco Federal Home Loan Bank for six and a half years. He had no private sector experience. His description of those to whom he reported was like a Chinese puzzle. My God, this fellow had the ultimate authority over Westwood, yet he wasn't very high on the totem pole. He was essentially an assistant vice president of a big bank. His answers to our questions were the ultimate bureaucratic double-talk. We counted no less than 167 times, according to the court reporter documents, when Scott answered "I don't know" or "I can't remember." Scott, the man who held the key to a possible default of as much as $2.5 billion dollars of loans, sat there and expressed his absolute ignorance of the situation. As he was the decision maker, it was pathetic and sad.

When asked about the so-called deadline for foreclosure and when that was first set, he said it had been decided at a board meeting on June 13. That was outrageous. If they had discussed foreclosure among themselves in mid-June, why hadn't they put that deadline in the letter of intent agreement? Why hadn't they at least discussed it with us before signing that letter and accepting our million dollars in cash. We were aghast. I was there and couldn't believe my ears.

When asked why they decided to foreclose, Scott said simply that "things were deteriorating." He couldn't be more specific than "things."

Scott admitted that he "never looked at" the two volumes of information we had sent to him in San Francisco, which had been prepared by Kenneth Leventhal and Company originally at the request of John Price and Roy Green on February 4, 1986. It cost us several hundred thousand dollars. He vaguely remembered seeing some red binders, but he couldn't be sure. The binders were gray. We moved on to the restructuring plan and asked Scott what he thought about the plan itself. He said that "no analysis was performed as to the overall acceptability of the plan." About the only thing he knew was that he had seen drafts of the Westwood agreement. He said he simply had no knowledge of the plan; he hadn't reviewed it. In other words, he had had one of his agents, Fred Stemmler, president of Westwood, sign an agreement calling for a million-dollar payment, then accept the million dollars from us, and after all this, he had not even reviewed the plan at all for feasibility. Now he had decided that what he hadn't reviewed wasn't good enough and so he'd foreclose. The more he answered, the more bizarre and confused it became to all involved.

Scott did say at one point, when his attorney, Roger Ferree, was out of the room and his testimony was flowing a little better, that on June 17 he had held a meeting in Washington to seek approval for the foreclosure in mid-July. This was unbelievable. June 17 was the very day that Scott's attorney, Paul Walker, had called me to say the transaction with Westwood was complete and I was to wire the money. The agreement letter, coupled with the cash, was a contract that was the result of months and months of negotiation. True, it had lots of contingencies, but common law would imply a good-faith effort by both parties to work out the details. Now we were being told that on the very same day that we wired the government that money, a meeting was going on in Washington, at Scott's request, to approve foreclosure. While we at Hall had been in the lobby of our Dallas headquarters celebrating the signed letter of agreement with champagne toasts, Scott had been getting permission to kill the deal.

As Scott droned on, it became increasingly clear that we had to find the true ultimate authority. Since the mid-July massacre, I had continued to get mixed signals from Washington. It seemed as if someone was telling Scott to settle with me because I was continually encouraged to make another offer, to make a better offer. We tried and tried. Then each offer would be rejected, I would pursue my sources in Washington, and they would tell me to try again. I was on a merry-go-round and was getting nowhere. I had to get to the man with his hands on the controls of the FSLIC. I just had to get to Chairman Edwin Gray.

Hall Financial Group was now at war with the U.S. government, a war I never wanted, but my sense of right and wrong wouldn't allow me to walk away. The war had many fronts. On the one front I was determined not to let this become an infinite legal battle, and believing truth to be the ultimate weapon, I kept up my direct letter-writing approach. I appealed time and again but seemed to be getting nowhere. In hindsight, the letters probably helped, and my instinctive and direct-from-the-heart-and-soul approach is one that I still think is honest and right and wouldn't change.

Meanwhile, on the second front, the legal battlefield continued. It seemed futile at best. Our resources couldn't begin to compare with the endless pocketbook and status of the U.S. government, but we continued to fight foreclosure every step of the way. We had some victories, particularly with a courageous and thorough Federal District Judge in Michigan, Julian Cook. If necessary, I was determined to continue the fight all the way to the Supreme Court of the United States.

The third front was in the press. By this time, the summer and fall of 1986, the problems in the S&L industry were becoming front-page news almost daily. We continued to attract attention because of our size and the fact that our problems were the first reported. I continued to try to get my message across to the press, that I was simply trying to solve a problem, to save my investors and company associates of nineteen years and, quite frankly, to do what was truly in the savings and loans' best interest as well. Meanwhile, Chairman Gray was continually coming out with new regulations. He was working overtime but, in my view, not facing the reality of the marketplace. He was trying to reregulate when it was far too late; he was fighting yesterday's war, at a large, unfortunate cost to tax-payers.

The last and final front was the political front. I found that the best way to fight the government was to go to the government for help. The S&L regulatory bureaucracy was obviously out of control. I had observed it, been a part of it, and it was frightening. So now I turned to the essence of democracy in this country, our elected officials. Not being particularly involved politically myself, it was investors who suggested contacts in Washington, senators and congressmen who might be able to help.

I started with the head of the Senate Banking Committee majority staff, Danny Wall, the man who, months later, would replace Ed Gray as head of the Federal Home Loan Bank Board. Still later he resigned under pressure. My first contact with Mr. Wall was on August 4. Shortly after-ward, I contacted some influential senators and congressmen, both Dem-ocrats and Republicans. Then I contacted some high-ranking administrative officials. I continued to campaign aggressively for a meeting with Chairman Gray through the help of these contacts and others. All I wanted was help in reopening communication. I was not asking for any assistance in any way regarding the agreement or any transaction—just to reopen commu-nication. But we continued to hit a brick wall. When many of these officials saw excerpts of Scott's deposition, they were amazed and very concerned. Everyone tried to help, but Chairman Gray dug the hole deeper and deeper, continuing to stonewall any communication.

Communication after July 20 had broken down completely as we continued to fight the FSLIC foreclosures through the court. FSLIC's lawyer, Roger Ferree, was our only link. He continued to tell my attorneys that there would be no dialogue with anyone but him. He said I should stop my personal pursuit of a meeting with Chairman Gray. Chairman Gray apparently wasn't willing to confront me under any circumstance.

In mid-August, I began to formulate, privately, my "ultimate strike." This would be virtually my last resort. Rather than wither away piece by piece, we would divide the company into two areas: properties that were breaking even or making money and those with negative cash-flow problems. We would scale down the operations into these two parts, the "good" and the "bad." Part of the key was not to let the good be slowly dragged down by the lengthy one-by-one fight to save the problem properties. We were prepared to default on as much as $1.5 billion in loans and file mass bankruptcy, and we set October 5 as our deadline. By defaulting on everything at once and carrying out the rest of our plan, we thought we could best help our investors in the bad as well as the good properties. I began in mid-August to work daily on the "ultimate strike" and to unfold parts of this plan to the senators and congressmen with whom I was working as I continued to appeal for a meeting with Chairman Gray. The plan was not a vengeful threat, just reality. It included a major lawsuit against those involved for acting in bad faith, gross negligence, and fraud over the handling of the Westwood agreement and the overall workout. Also, I was prepared to release to the media my letters to Chairman Gray and others in his administration at the FHLBB. I would go public with the whole mess and let the chips fall as they may.

What we were after—a restructuring workout of our loans rather than bankruptcy and foreclosure—wasn't something new and different or unheard of. It was no different than what Chrysler had accomplished nearly ten years before us. The government should have honored the June 17 Westwood agreement. As we saw it, working out the loans had incredible advantages for the government. As the savings and loan crisis unfolded, it became obvious that FSLIC would be left with more real estate than it could ever hope to unload in a fire sale. Foreclosure and liquidation were not going to be the answer this time around. Dumping properties on the market would only make the avalanche of failing savings and loans worse. We were willing to work out our loans, pay back our debts over time, and, in the meantime, keep millions of square feet of property out of FSLIC's hands. We were putting millions of dollars of new additional money into the system that would not be available if they foreclosed. I just couldn't understand why the regulators couldn't see the logic of letting us finish the workouts. We had made so much progress. It didn't make sense, and the man with the answers, I was convinced, was Chairman Gray.

There were a number of key elected officials, staff members, and senior-level administration individuals who saved us from ever having to use the ultimate strike—both Republicans and Democrats. One very influential Republican Congressman, for instance, initially wasn't interested and considered this just a constituent issue. But as he learned more, he saw that it was far greater than the problems of one Dallas businessman. He realized that there were many public policy issues in question and that perhaps the S&L system as a whole was at stake. He worked hard to help.

I had not been a contributor of his and didn't know him before this situation. He is a first-class gentleman and a great Congressman.

A number of the elected officials I talked to were Texans. My hope was that they would understand the issues and see that we were a representation of bigger public policy questions of how to deal with the depression in Texas real estate and savings and loans rather than just an individual company in trouble. Our hopes worked to a great extent, but a unity between Republicans and Democrats is tough even with a good, common cause. For the most part, we found individual officials who cared, tried hard, but couldn't motivate Chairman Gray even to meet with me. This, to some extent, polarized the situation more, but at the same time Ed Gray was feeling the interest of many Republicans and Democrats in the issue.

On September 3, 1986, a close friend, Dr. Martin Cohen, and I made a trip to Fort Worth to meet with then Majority Leader Jim Wright. I had never met Mr. Wright and I had never made any contribution to him. In the past, I had contributed to the Democratic Congressional Candidates Committee in a general manner, but never to Mr. Wright or his campaign. Contributions weren't the issue here anyway. The Cohen family members were not big contributors either. They had requested the meeting because Marty and his uncle, Dr. Frank Cohen of Fort Worth, had been friends with Mr. Wright for forty years and they had asked if he would be willing to listen briefly to my problems as I was a neighboring constituent. The then Majority Leader of the House had told them that he would be glad to schedule a fifteen-minute meeting, and I was pleased to get that much time.

We walked into Mr. Wright's office in the old Federal building in downtown Fort Worth at 5:00 P.M. Nothing fancy, just down-to-earth government-issue. When our fifteen minutes were up, we were still talking. As I described the series of events and our ultimate dilemma, Jim Wright was appalled. After more than an hour of meeting, I guess I had caught Jim Wright's attention. He thought our whole situation was outrageous. He made no promises but said he was very upset about the matter and that he would look into it and do what he could.

On September 11, I was in the law offices of Winstead McGuire in downtown Dallas being deposed as part of numerous lawsuits. It was just another one of those days I spent on bankruptcy hearings and depositions. My secretary called with a message for me to call John Price in Washington. This was the breakthrough we had been waiting for. John had been asked to call on behalf of Chairman Gray to indicate their potential willingness for a meeting. He said a letter would be forthcoming and that I was to respond with a formal proposed agenda for the meeting. I got the letter and responded that day, but I didn't get a response to my agenda until five days later. Finally, this "emergency" meeting was set for September 24.

On September 18, I was in Washington to see a number of people who had been helpful to us behind the scenes. I thanked a few Congressmen and Senators and Majority Leader Wright's staff, among others. By now a number of members of Congress had an earnest concern about not only our situation, but the future of savings and loans and Texas real estate in general. The FSLIC was quickly becoming insolvent and Congress was now considering a huge recapitalization bill. Of the ten to fifteen Congressmen with whom we met at different times, most were concerned that Chairman Edwin Gray's out-of-control administration would not only waste the money, but would do more damage with it. Their concerns were not based on our story alone but other information they already had prior to ever hearing about us. When we first approached them, Congressmen or their staffs often would say, "Oh no, not another Ed Gray story."

In the meantime, executives with the California savings and loans were trying to help us by pursuing their own Congressmen and Senators in order to get things rolling again. They wanted to help despite their fear of regulatory retaliation. They were trying, as we were, to get the situation back together and were in favor of a workout. They saw the stonewalling process that Chairman Gray and attorney Roger Ferree were perpetuating as unnecessary and damaging to them and potentially to the economy.

On September 24, the date of the "emergency meeting," Bill Sechrest and Larry Levey, as well as a Washington attorney we had retained, and I met with representatives of the Federal Home Loan Bank Board. The Federal Home Loan Bank Board was then the controlling agency that oversaw the twelve Federal Home Loan district banks and the Federal Savings and Loan Insurance Corporation. The bank board had its own staff but also worked closely with FSLIC and regional bank staffs. The new President Bush 1989 S&L bailout law has completely restructured the system even to the point of eliminating the Federal Home Loan Bank Board itself. But in 1986 the Federal Home Loan Bank Board under Chairman Gray was the authority. Representing them was Sam Canell, head of FSLIC; John Price; Roy Green; Shannon Fairbanks, chief of staff of the bank board; Harry Quillian, general counsel; and a couple of other bank board attorneys. No Chairman Edwin Gray. When we were being led into the "chairman's" conference room, I saw Edwin Gray in the hallway; when he saw us coming, he immediately went into his office, avoiding any opportunity for a formal introduction.

Shannon Fairbanks, chief of staff, quickly took control of the meeting. She was very competent and it became obvious that she was well respected. In her straightforward style, she made it clear that the bank board could not compel or instruct the conservator or tell any S&L what to do or not to do. As the meeting went on, our specific requests were directly denied. Shannon suggested we go back to the savings and loans and attempt to restructure what had already been built. She went on to say that the bank board would be willing to help in that process. At one point she and Harry Quillian left the room and talked privately in Chairman Gray's adjoining office, presumably with Mr. Gray.

When Mrs. Fairbanks came back, she told us the bank board would informally encourage everyone to go back to the table and that she would issue a press release encouraging communication. We weren't sure later if we had heard her correctly about the press release because we had never seen the bank board do anything like this; indeed it hadn't. But it was important that she offered the presence of a bank board member at future meetings with the savings and loans.

Two days later, on Friday, September 26, we had planned a meeting with all of the California savings and loans. We were going to announce our ultimate-strike bankruptcy plans for October 5. We told the representatives at the bank board meeting about that plan. We explained to the bank board representatives that the bankruptcy of $1.5 billion of loans and massive litigation would hurt the savings and loans needlessly but that the chain reaction of the government's Westwood decisions had unraveled the restructuring plan. They began to see what was really going on. They said they would send a representative to the meeting in California. Mrs. Fairbanks indicated she might even try to go herself.

The September 26 meeting proved to be excellent in many ways. First, all of the California savings and loans plus some of the Texas savings and loans attended, and Shannon Fairbanks was there. The press release had been a big help attitude-wise, though so much momentum had been lost earlier through Scott's, Gray's, and Ferree's stonewalling. We were moving ahead; the breakthrough, believe it or not, had truly begun.

The irony of the September 26 meeting was that the roles had oddly changed. I ended up defending Mrs. Fairbanks, who was attacked by the S&L executives for the bank board's mishandling of the situation. When she addressed the legal separation between FSLIC corporate and FSLIC as conservator of Westwood (alleging Scott had sole authority), they almost booed her out of the room. It was an eye-opener for her and I must say she handled it with great dignity. Over time I came to have great respect for Shannon Fairbanks, who is a very strong and competent individual. She served the Federal Home Loan Bank Board very well.

After the meeting on September 26, as we headed for the airport,

Larry Levey told me that during the meeting, he had taken a special phone message for me. It was from one of our Washington attorneys, who indicated that Jim Wright had decided to hold up the FSLIC recapitalization bill pending further assurances that our situation and other public policy issues in Texas would be properly addressed. This meant the entire $15 billion of legislation was being brought to a complete halt until Chairman Gray or his agency's representatives reopened communication with us to deal with the issues of our situation and give reasonable policy assurances that more thought and care would go into the resolution of the Texas S&L crisis. The House banking committee staff had requested that a representative from Hall and our attorneys meet first thing Monday morning to discuss it.

Mr. Wright later took a lot of criticism about holding up that bill. The delay of the bill by then Majority Leader Wright was a major part of the House Ethics investigation that occurred in 1988. In fact, I testified before the House Ethics Committee about this matter in what was described to me as a "closed-door hearing" on October 5, 1988. At that time, I was told that if I talked about the substance of my testimony to anyone other than my attorney, I could be fined $5,000 at a minimum. To put it mildly, confidentiality seemed to be important to the House Ethics Committee and its special counsel.

However, contrary to this required confidentiality, the special counsel released a report dated February 21, 1989, on a semipublic basis, regarding their investigation. The 279-page report contained 17 pages excerpted from my testimony. Unfortunately, the report contained 22 factual errors in just the 17 pages dealing with my testimony. Because the report took portions of my testimony out of context, the resulting perception differed considerably from the reality. Actually, the substance of the report bore only partial resemblance to my full statement on the record because very pertinent, important parts of my testimony were omitted. For a document of this importance to contain even one inaccuracy or misrepresentation, whether all of this was intentional or inadvertent, would be unfortunate indeed from a standpoint of national interest, let alone in fairness to Speaker Wright.

When I was contacted in the fall of 1988 to testify before the House Ethics Committee, I was truly pleased and excited. In fact, I spent an entire week beforehand preparing detailed documents and backup information, all of which I voluntarily delivered to the committee. I exceeded every request the committee made of me and gave them what they said was a very coherent, organized, and detailed approach to the subject matter.

The subject was Speaker Wright's effort to assist me in getting the government to reopen communications with me. In fact, my only request of the committee was for a copy of the court reporter's transcript of my testimony. It was fortunate that I made that request because it was the comparison of that transcript to the counsel's report that verified the twenty-two inaccuracies.

I testified without an attorney, which is unusual and certainly surprised the special counsel and congressmen who were members of the committee. Since I had every desire, willingness, and interest to tell the truth, I felt it was unnecessary to have a lawyer. The truth was really very simple. I had gone to the Speaker as a constituent to ask his help with my situation of having been abruptly stonewalled by the FSLIC administration. As previously mentioned, I had never met Mr. Wright, nor had I made any contribution to him. From what I knew of Speaker Wright and his efforts in the savings and loan area, particularly those in which I was involved, he was highly ethical and concerned solely with the public interest.

It seems inconsistent and unfair to me for the House Ethics Committee to require witnesses to refrain from talking about their testimonies and then for the Committee to release incomplete and misleading versions of those same testimonies. This was extremely frustrating but a learning experience in many ways. Of course, our government is not 100 percent perfect and that is frustrating, even infuriating sometimes in situations like this, because those of us who are patriotic citizens and believe in the system want—and rather expect—it to be perfect. However, even with its share of flaws, I believe our governmental system is still, undoubtedly, the best in the world.

Speaker Wright never asked me for any contribution of any nature. He recognized that if $15 billion were given to FSLIC without proper accountability, it could do more harm than good. Mr. Wright also knew, from his own investigation, that what had happened to us and others was a strong indication that the bank board was, indeed, out of control and dealing poorly with this situation. Wright's holdup of that bill was a strong, demonstrative action, and we were astounded. We were grateful, but we knew that Jim Wright's concerns went much further than our company, to the state of Texas and the S&L system as a whole. We never asked for his intervention in the merits of the matter itself, only to encourage communication to proceed.

The next Monday after the bill was held up on September 29, following a lengthy conversation with me, Shannon Fairbanks and the bank board decided it was in everyone's best interest to fire Scott as special representative of the conservator of Westwood. The bank board appointed Angelo Vigna, who formerly headed FSLIC, in his place. Over a period of time, we worked with Shannon Fairbanks, Angelo Vigna, and Rosalyn Payne. They were each bright, hardworking, and did a great job for the government. It was very refreshing. I have great respect for them, as I have for many individuals within the Federal Home Loan Bank system.

In essence, we were starting again with a whole new team of negotiators. We still had a lot to accomplish—the Westwood loans wouldn't be restructured until December 31, 1986. The regulators felt they were under extra scrutiny with our deals. They wanted to give us a chance, but there was extreme pressure to make our restructuring tough to avoid criticism. It was actually a very tough deal but thoughtful and fair for both sides. The October deadline I had set inevitably had to be extended. The workout was slow going. But this time around we thought there were no deal killers at the table.

Finally, this time, we were right.

Looking back, I absolutely understand and respect the problems the regulators had in those days and, frankly, I have a great sense of empathy for them. It's a difficult job even in normal times to be a regulator. In the mid-1980s times were anything but normal and the pressures on the regulators, including and especially Chairman Gray, were intense. Chairman Gray probably meant well. Most regulators I know are good, hardworking people, but the system was in crisis and the policies and structures didn't work, making their jobs very difficult.

In our case, I am convinced at this point that part of the problem came about because we were the first large problem that had crossed district lines in the Federal Home Loan Bank system. Also, the Westwood loans were complicated with many subparticipants (other savings and loans owning part interests in Westwood's loans). These complications made the government's decision to foreclose not only the safest way but also the easiest.

Another part of the problem was the difficulty in trying to deal with Chairman Gray. In many ways, I don't blame him. I don't think he was out to get us. I just suspect he was overwhelmed and maybe didn't know which way to turn. His background, as a public relations executive and friend of Nancy and Ronald Reagan, hardly prepared him for these complex system-wide financial matters. It was unfortunate, in my view, that he was appointed to, and stayed in, that position. But in fairness, this was a time when unprecedented problems in the S&L industry were unfolding, and being chairman of the Federal Home Loan Bank Board was a very, very tough job for anyone. I am sure Edwin Gray had good intentions and did his best in an exceedingly difficult situation.

Businesspeople often make the mistake of judging the government by their own rules. But the government is very different. It is not logical or profit motivated like the private sector. It's complex, political, and while mostly well intended, often slow and ineffective in many respects.

I came away more impressed with the people who work in government than I ever would have expected after my experience. The overall system is totally different and must be judged from a different perspective than normal business. There are reasons in my view why the government should stay out of private industry to every extent possible. No matter how well intended and good the people are, the system seems to breed many reasons for nondecisions that only add to the ineffectiveness. The government is not a risk-taking system, whereas the private sector needs to be a risk-taking system to succeed.

In the past, large corporations had started to become more and more bureaucratic and more like the government. More recently, however, that has proven to be ineffective, and in order to compete worldwide, even big companies have changed their philosophies in this regard.

It is important to understand that most bureaucrats are strangled by the system. My perception of government workers prior to being more directly involved was that they watched the clock, worked nine to five, and took long breaks. I assumed they didn't kill themselves worrying about their jobs. I admit at that time I held a sort of prejudice against government workers, and I thought they were people who didn't have the aggressiveness to be in the private sector. I know now that I had a very unfair and inaccurate picture. In characterizing any large group, generalizations can be dangerous; people vary a great deal. I found that for the most part government workers are very dedicated and hardworking. They are often working for a lot less money than they could command in the private sector, and a number of them are there because they genuinely believe in what they are doing.

But the people really aren't the problem; the problem in the system is "the structure" of the system itself. One on one, most people are caring and professional, but when they have to deal with a structure of the bureaucracy, at least in the case of the Federal Home Loan Bank system, difficult situations often boil down to paranoia and placing blame. Concern over job preservation, overall frustrations, and general tensions may create unproductive stress and turn good, hardworking, well-intentioned people into ineffective managers.

There is too much emphasis on being strict and not enough emphasis on the practical view of "let's get the job done." It's interesting to watch good people make good, intelligent decisions in meetings, acting like they want to get things done; then when it comes to putting it in writing, they worry about how their report or correspondence will look weeks or months later in a file.

Another problem in a bureaucratic system is that the middle management people are often overworked and it's easy for them to become callous toward the "outside." The easy approach is to generalize and put people into boxes, avoid looking at specifics, then make quick, tough, and usually negative decisions. The failure of the power structure of middle management becomes all the more critical during a time of crisis.

In a crisis, time is important. Decision making, taking risks, and taking action to solve problems are critical. To do nothing is to make a decision in and of itself. If you do nothing, the events of the moment will control you, but it's a decision to allow that to be the case. Outmoded, antiquated solutions of doing nothing go on far longer than is appropriate because the system simply doesn't delegate the authority. Middle management relies on old-line policies such as "foreclose first, think about it later."

Perhaps one of the most important observations I can make is that lawyers inside and outside government agencies have too much power. Unlike the private sector where, at the end of the day, the economics of staying in business and making a profit rule, in government, politics and not making embarrassing mistakes rule. Lawyers try to take control wherever they are, but when you have a paranoid environment it's easier for them to take over completely. In the private sector, businesspeople take risks and make decisions. In the bureaucratic environment of the Federal Home Loan Bank system, the businesspeople don't tend to be strong enough alone to take the risk of disagreeing with their lawyers. Once a situation gets into a legal environment, the lawyers have a strong, more absolute control. This is dangerous, expensive, wasteful, and leads to very uneconomic and unproductive conclusions.

I am not saying there isn't a role for lawyers and that lawyers aren't important, but in Chairman Gray's administration, the use of lawyers seemed to go way overboard. There was a lack of accountability—how do you measure a good job from the standpoint of lawyers? Huge dollars were spent by the government—more than $83 million in 1986—on outside legal fees. It's just simply a terribly difficult thing to control. Who is overseeing and controlling how much lawyers are spending? The government workers are not regarded as controlling the process once lawyers get involved. This is totally contrary to the effective way that private industry works where one has to look at survival in the world as being true to profit and loss and the economics of cash flow.

Under the Chairman Gray regime in particular, lawyers seemed to become totally litigation crazy. Lawsuits against law firms, lawsuits against borrowers, lawsuits against past S&L directors and owners, all created a paranoid atmosphere. There is no question that there are individuals and companies who should be sued. But in a depression, the problem is not exclusively a matter of fraud. Criminals certainly account for a percentage of the failures of institutions, but the economic situation accounts for the majority of them. The question is not only "Who did it and why?" but even more importantly for the rest of us, "How do we fix it?" Too much time has been spent on placing blame and not enough time on solving problems.

It's unfortunate that people, especially bureaucrats, are often too intimidated by lawyers to control the legal process. When the legal process is left to its own devices, unbelievable waste and ineffective expenditures cost the whole system and, eventually, the taxpayers many valuable dollars.

Our situation is a good example. It is my understanding, from records and talking to people, that the government was paying an outside law firm $300,000 to $500,000 a month to deal with our loans at Westwood. That's ludicrous when the whole problem could have been solved with a few hours of meetings with anybody of reasonable intelligence who was a decision maker. Indeed, the earlier lawyers who had tried to solve the problems were later stripped of their power by a new law firm. That new law firm constantly played games, pretending to be interested in solving the problem. The firm, it appears, really was motivated to keep the litigation going and eventually tried to bankrupt us. Why not? They were making money at it and nobody was controlling them. The young man in charge was, from what I could see, heavily influenced by the lawyers. He wasn't the person responsible; the system put him in charge and an outside law firm was firmly in control. The firm would advise him in a very narrow manner from strictly a legal perspective rather than with a legal and a logical and businesslike perspective to help in solving the big-picture problem. The result was waste. Had we not opted to stay in there and fight, potentially hundreds of millions of dollars could have been lost.

My experience and observations of Congress might be surprising; my experiences surprised me. I expected more questions like "What is your political party?" "How much have you given in contributions?" and similar self-interest oriented inquiries. The representatives I approached did not ask me those questions. Instead of self-interest, I found smart, hardworking people who truly care about the system. But it is hard to get their attention. Everything in Washington must be condensed to one page to be effective. However, once someone's listening, they know how to cut to the chase, and if they believe it is a real meaty issue and the facts are right, most Congressmen and many staffers will go out of their way to do what they believe in.

No matter what my difficulties were and the intensity of my frustrations at the time, I thank God I'm an American. I'm grateful to our elected representatives and so many others who worked to achieve in government what they believe is right. But I believe more than ever that it is the responsibility of each of us to fight, if and when necessary, for fairness and justice. If we don't, we will lose our system. In the end, I learned that my faith in our government and my perseverance to get through the setbacks worked not just to solve our problem, but to make a difference for others. This great country does belong to us, the people.

PART FOUR

THE DEPRESSION GRINDS ON

CHAPTER 9
HOME RUNS THAT STRIKE OUT

NEW YEAR'S EVE 1986 was quite an evening at the Hall home. MaryAnna was sick in bed with a bad cold, and my four daughters were pushing me to stay up late enough so that we could ring in 1987 together. The truth is, I fell asleep at 9:30, again at 10:15, then at 11:05. . . . Each time the girls would wake me up, I would try again to fight off my exhaustion. The kids made more food than an army could have eaten. The next day I was greeted by the smell of stale pizza, shrimp, and a few other things that didn't get put away. I did manage to be awake at midnight though. But at 12:01, I went up to bed, knowing that I hadn't been a total party pooper, but still sure my kids weren't going to nominate me for "Fun Dad of the Year."

As I was going to sleep that New Year's Eve, I thought with a sigh of relief that we, as a company, Hall Financial Group, had done what almost everyone thought we couldn't do in 1986—we had survived! We had outlived what had seemed like an eternity of bad times. So much had happened so fast in 1986. But with that pain behind me, I looked forward to 1987 and was again feeling optimistic. Not only had 1986 been a year that we survived many business attacks, but personally, our family had come through some very difficult times together. The year 1987 would be a new start and it held a new future for all of us.

Business-wise, the Hall Financial Group was lean and mean and ready to go. Our first order of business was to improve our image, which had taken a beating in 1986. We figured a public victory statement would help. After all, why not let the world know the facts? So we did. We sent press releases to the media on the current status of our workouts, which were 85 percent complete on more than $1 billion of debt restructuring. In addition to the $125 million that, individually and through the company, I had at that time put in to make this happen, our investors came through with an additional $50 million. As of the completion of this book, I've now put in more than $145 million to help the partnerships. We had stood up to our problems and we were moving ahead.

I had bounced back to my old optimistic self too soon. As 1987 began to unwind, it became more and more evident that the real estate markets were simply not getting any better. They were actually getting worse. While our property-management business continued to collect fees every month, rents were down and the fees were lower than expected. That hurt us at the corporate level. Worse yet, the properties were not doing as well as expected. The market was sliding further and further, making the workouts that we had just done extremely difficult to maintain. By the end of 1987, we would have to write off or reserve more than $60 million of our own loans to properties as uncollectible debts.

Even though we had cut overhead on our properties, our revenues were still nose-diving. We were operating the entire Hall Financial Group on the property-management fee revenue, since the investment business had almost ground to a halt in 1986. Where our revenues in 1984 or 1985 had been 60 percent related to limited-partnership front-end fees, by 1987 and 1988 this was less than 10 percent. While property-management fees were falling, the other fees fell much faster and it was the property-management fees that we depended on during the last half of the 1980s. The one-two punch of the real estate market crash and the very untimely, and worse yet, retroactive change in the tax laws were starting to make 1987 a horrible year. We had come through rough waters in 1986, frequently in the spotlight with negative news. Now, the press coverage was better. We were being given credit for surviving, and we had, but some of our problems were far from being solved. For many in the industry, the years 1987, 1988, and 1989 continued to be even worse than 1986; for us it was bad, but the nightmare of 1986 would be a low that was hard to beat.

The remaining restructurings and the new ones that became necessary were more difficult in 1987, and new problems kept surfacing. Our victory statement had been a psychological boost for a month or so, but the problems persisted.

The whole process of restructurings continued into 1987, and with it continued my personal obsession not to give up. Many of the Hall Financial associates have great stories about what we went through in those very difficult times, in the restructurings in 1986 and 1987 in particular. Patrice Binkley, who had been an acquisition officer with the company, became one of our many ombudsmen (our title for restructuring workout officers). As an ombudsman, she had the unfortunate position of being on call virtually twenty-four hours a day and sometimes feeling the rage of

Craig Hall. Patrice, who is now back as an acquisition officer, recently reminded me that in 1987 while she was expecting her first baby, I had, as I often did, put out an "all points bulletin" to find Patrice. It wasn't uncommon for me, in those days, to turn to my secretary, Tricia, and order the immediate location of a missing executive or associate so that I could find out what was happening on one deal or another.

Patrice reminded me that on one particular day in 1987 she was in the middle of an examination at her obstetrician's office when the doctor's nurse came running in and said, "You have an urgent call from Craig Hall." Craig Hall was a rather common name in those days as our press filled the papers daily, and immediately the obstetrician, at midpoint in the exam, figured out a way to get Patrice a phone. Tricia finally connected me to Patrice, who was still in the examination room with no clothing on. Patrice remembers feeling anxious and worried about what could be so important and has never let me forget the fact that I merely wanted an update on all of her workout restructurings. Perhaps my overanxiety in that particular instance was a bit misplaced. Nevertheless, my secretary had the ability to find anyone at any time on a twenty-four-hour-a-day basis.

Thinking about the restructurings, I remember some of the earliest court cases. We didn't always get our way by sitting back and being a wallflower. Sometimes things came down to legal confrontations, and that included court testimony by many of our executives and associates. While I spent days and days in testimony and depositions, some of the people like Patrice and others learned over time to become professional witnesses. Jeff Kelly, the regional vice president of property management for Houston, and Patrice Binkley were working on restructuring one of the loans assigned to Patrice when we learned that things weren't going well and they would both have to testify in court. This was a new, alarming experience at that time, because neither one of them had ever seen the inside of a courtroom. As they prepared the day before testimony, both of them became more and more nervous and couldn't sleep that night. Then when the actual hearing started, our lawyer embarrassed and roughed up the witnesses for the lender so badly that both Jeff and Patrice were looking at each other scared to death. They were wondering what would happen when we got called to the stand.

Finally it was our turn, and when our lawyer looked at his two babes-in-the-woods witnesses, he, too, became nervous. Patrice quickly said, "Call Jeff first." Our lawyer called Jeff and his testimony was calm and brilliant and we were clearly winning the case. As the lawyer saw that the opposition wasn't laying a finger on Jeff in the cross-examination, he turned to Patrice and whispered to her, "Go hide out in the women's room so they can't call you as a witness—Jeff's doing a great job and we won't need you to win the case." Patrice quickly obliged.

Fifteen or twenty minutes later, the case was over and we had won. The odd thing was it took an hour and a half before Patrice came out of the bathroom. She apparently had hidden in one of the stalls, figuring a bailiff or somebody might come in looking for her. They couldn't call her to the stand if she wasn't present in court, and she wasn't about to be seen anywhere. After her first experience as a potential witness and hiding out in the bathroom for an hour and a half, Patrice has been a witness in many other legal cases and, like others in the company, rose to the occasion. She and many others have developed skills as good witnesses and competent, professional legal clients.

We realized in mid-1987 that we needed some kind of new business. While cash flow was still critical, we had to get some momentum going in a positive new direction. We decided to follow our instincts and go with the old saying "If life hands you lemons, make lemonade." In examining ourselves in 1987, we clearly saw that the lemon was the difficult economy and the fact that we had been labeled a company with severe debt problems. The lemonade was that we had achieved a high level of skill in doing workouts, and that was a needed commodity. Many companies were trying quietly to face what we had faced publicly. Real estate developers and limited-partnership sponsors across the country, particularly in the Southwest, were going broke at an alarming rate. We had fine-tuned our skill at turning around difficult times, perhaps better than anyone else in the country. So, we set up a growth plan based on adding other people's problems to our workout activities. The plan was to acquire the general-partner position of troubled syndication companies for little or no money, and then do as much as possible to save properties and partnerships. We would receive fees and increase our economy of scale by keeping overhead at almost the same level as we had before the new business.

With our new growth plan, we led a dual existence in 1987 and 1988. We were a successful growth company, but we were also still struggling with our old problems. It was a Dr. Jekyll and Mr. Hyde existence. Although we were growing, our growth cost us some investment capital—capital we didn't really have to spend. Even though each deal was legally separate and we didn't have absolute legal funding obligations, there were still cash strains put on our business. At the same time, our own properties were draining us of our limited resources. At this rate, our budget was not going to balance. We decided to start selling some of our best properties to raise cash and increase our overall corporate strength. Likewise, I personally made a commitment to sell all of my personal assets

I hadn't already sold in 1986 to raise cash and increase liquidity. Finally, as part of our long-term corporate restructuring, we planned to do a debenture for the corporation, a long-term debt issue in the $50 million to $75 million range. We felt that having come through our restructuring—even though we still had some cash-flow problems—we did have positive momentum. The debenture in our view was to meet temporary capital expenditures to continue growth. The problem was to find investors sophisticated enough to believe in what we believed.

The Judiciary Center in Washington, D.C., was a property we had purchased in the spring of 1986. It helped the company in 1986 with fees and profits totaling more than $6 million. Now, in 1987, less than a year later, we found that this property would again be a big profit maker. Many of the investors that had originally invested in Judiciary Center before the tax laws changed would be very happy to get out now if we could only find a way to sell the property. While that wasn't possible with many of our properties, an opportunity arose with Judiciary Center. A Japanese investor group purchased the property from us for $86.9 million. That meant a large real estate commission for Hall Financial Group and substantial profit for our investors. With that sale and others, our liquidity was returning by the beginning of the third quarter of 1987.

When we were first introduced to the Japanese family that would eventually be the buyers of the Judiciary Center, we scheduled our initial negotiation. Our management met with their management to negotiate at an early morning meeting. Since the Japanese had interpreters, the meeting was lengthy and there were a number of issues that were complicated by the cultural differences and styles. That first negotiation lasted three days. Our people were exhausted. They would leave the large room in the law firm in which we were negotiating to go to one of the little side offices and grab fifteen or twenty minutes of sleep in one of the chairs, only to wake up and go back to the negotiating table. While we were able to resolve everything after our three-day marathon and make great progress, this whole ritual would be repeated again about a month later. Finally, several weeks later at the closing party that the Japanese were hosting at the Waldorf Astoria, we asked one of the Japanese interpreters why the Japanese always negotiated around the clock in such an exhausting manner. The reports I had gotten were that we thought they were simply trying to wear us down. We were shocked and chagrined when the interpreter told us that the Japanese, too, were wondering why we negotiated in that manner. Everyone was too polite to call off the negotiations for an evening of sleep, thinking that the other side was encouraging the long marathon meetings. Had either side known that the other was merely trying to accommodate and work through the cultural differences, we all would have been a lot more rested.

The transaction itself was well structured for both sides. We did develop, and still have, a very deep respect for and rapport with the Japanese family. They are fine people to do business with and we have enjoyed many of their customs. One of the things that the Japanese often do is exchange gifts as part of business meetings. We have exchanged many interesting, lovely gifts with the Japanese and enjoyed the enriching relationship greatly. We have become personal friends with these very honorable people.

At the closing, I wanted to make sure that we had some outstanding gifts for our Japanese friends. We started with beautiful books on Texas and some other local Texas items to encourage them to come to visit us in our neck of the woods. But then we thought a memento of the closing itself also would be appropriate. So, we thought of the beautiful and expensive Mont Blanc pens. But I decided this was a large transaction and we should show proper respect, so we bought three sterling silver Mont Blanc pens, one for each of the Japanese principals involved in the transaction. At the closing, when we presented the pens the Japanese were most gracious and thankful. When they each were poised to sign the papers with their new pens, the pens didn't write! We realized that we had forgotten to put ink in the pens and, of course, we were very embarrassed. At that moment, the head of the Japanese family making the purchase pulled out his regular pen to sign the papers. It was a stunning solid-gold pen!

To this day we manage the Judiciary Center for that same Japanese family and have developed a good, positive relationship. We have put together joint-venture investments with them in Texas and look forward to a long and mutually enjoyable relationship. Some people in the United States feel quite upset about foreign investment here; it is a complex issue. The reality, however, is that the world is becoming one large marketplace, and capital flows cannot and indeed should not be held by nationalistic boundaries. Careful thought must be given to fair and open trade for all sides, with sensitive and diplomatic negotiations.

With the situation finally looking better, we began to move forward with the idea of finding long-term financing (in the form of a debenture) for the Hall Financial Group. We had retained the investment brokerage firm of Bear Stearns and Company, which spent months performing the due diligence required prior to the planned offering. The firm was hesitant about our financing and wanted to make sure that the transaction was squeaky clean from every angle and put together in a manner that no one could criticize. This took an inordinate amount of time, but it was necessary. After all, we had a lot to overcome, and it hadn't been that long since the suggestion of bankruptcy was on the front pages of the newspapers. To be asking institutions a year later to give us a $50 million fifteen-year loan demanded a full explanation. Bear Stearns, as a part of its due diligence, actually had gone to many of our properties all over the country and had become intimately familiar with our financial information. They were impressed with our management and pleased with the quality of the properties. Once again the solid principles of management came through for us.

Meanwhile, May Petroleum had been following a separate but similar course of action to that of our real estate division. In late 1986, we had been continually reviewing the various opportunities to buy troubled oil and gas companies. It was my firm hope and belief that the opportunity to make lemons into lemonade also existed in the oil and gas industry. But in the case of May Petroleum, we were finding one disappointment after another. During the last quarter of 1986 and the first quarter of 1987, we looked at dozens of companies and made offers on several with no results. May's weakened financial condition and the constant pressure by its lenders gave us very little capital to expand. Our competitors with more cash continued to beat us on deals.

In the spring of 1987, the May board decided to change direction. We would stay in the oil and gas business, but only through a small amount of exploration, which had always been the heart of the company. Additionally, we would liquidate our oil- and gas-producing property reserves if we could get a good price. Our change of heart came with the experience of bidding for other companies' reserves. We also realized we should be the sellers, not the buyers. By early July, we had sold the operating reserves of the company, which yielded enough money to pay all of the May debt in full and have $38 million in cash left over. We kept our leases and continued exploration. Now the board was looking for a service company to acquire in order to diversify into industries other than oil and gas.

By late summer 1987, things were looking good for an overall economic turnaround. The question that remained was why were the real estate markets continuing their downward spiral? We were successful in acquiring general-partner real estate interests, and by the end of the summer had added 17,000 new apartment units to our inventory—almost 30 percent growth from the beginning of the year. The debenture was looking better and better every day. Bear Stearns was actually surprised at how well our real estate was doing. May Petroleum was liquid, and my personal financial position was turning around. I was finally able to focus my attention on the stock market again, an area that I had always enjoyed. In 1984 and 1985, I had made more than $60 million personally in the market.

While I did make some money in the market in 1987, I never could focus the attention on it that I had in 1985. The year I sat out—1986— was the year the bull ran wild. I had missed a lot of opportunities and lost momentum. As I started to re-evaluate in 1987, I became convinced in August that the market was headed for a significant setback.

I started to sell short the Standard & Poor's Index of 500 stocks (S&P 500), a broad measure of common stocks. Through the futures market, investors can bet on whether the index and, in turn, the market will go up or down. I was betting the stocks were headed down. If they went up, I would lose big. If, on the other hand, they went down, I would win in a very big way and I would be back in the game. This gambling institution people call the futures market is every bit as fast moving as a craps table in a casino. I admit that a certain part of me enjoys the risk and excitement of the market. I hope and believe that I don't let that feeling carry me to an overextended position, but in 1987, I came closer than ever to betting it all. I was, in short, going for the home run.

In retrospect, it's clear now that I was hurting so badly from the setbacks of 1986 that instead of looking at the phenomenal success we had made in recovering our position and continuing to whittle away at the debts, I wanted to hit a home run and clear everything up with one shot. If I were right and the market crashed, we would have made as much as $50 to $100 million very quickly. This would truly put me back in business and on my feet. But as time went on, the market continued to climb and instead of making money, I lost a significant amount of money.

Smith Barney, in the summer of 1987, was one of the firms handling many of my accounts. They had a futures trader who convinced my in-house trader, Allen Moore, that he and I were two of the most out-of-step, stupid people in the universe. After talking to the Smith Barney representatives a few times, I decided he was right: Allen and I *were* dumb. Everybody knew the market was going to 3,000 at a minimum and probably 3,500. Here I was, stupidly shorting the market at 2,600. I should have been ashamed of my contrarian logic.

I no longer had the courage to follow my own instinct, so instead I started betting the other way with the help of the Smith Barney experts. In September and October, I was betting the market would soar. Not only was my personal money in the market, but money that I controlled in a partnership raised in 1985 for stock investing, as well as money approved to invest by the May board of directors. While the only futures investments were with my money, the partnership and May were buying stocks on margin. As luck would have it, the biggest week of investment for May Petroleum was the week prior to the October 19 crash, now known as Black Monday.

In addition to the futures investments and the stocks that the partnership and May were buying, I also decided in the summer and early fall of 1987 to invest in a special fund being set up by Paul Bilzerian. Paul Bilzerian was hot. It seemed he could do no wrong. He had great investor credibility with billionaire shopping center owner Ed DeBartolo; successful real estate entrepreneur from New York Arthur G. Cohen; and the successful real estate entrepreneur from California, Alex Spanos, who owned the San Diego Chargers. From what I read in the newspapers and heard from Paul, it seemed like he had made more than $200 million for his investors, as well as a few others and himself.

If it were not enough to look at the credibility of those with whom Paul associated and how much money he had made in considering an investment with him, I considered our own direct experience. Paul attempted to get me to join him in the Cluett Peabody transaction as a partner. We did not. At the end, however, we did work with Paul in optioning our stock to him and providing a loan to give him the ability to go forward with the Cluett Peabody tender offer. When his bid for the company was topped by Westpoint Pepperill, Paul sold out his interest and turned our option over to Westpoint Pepperill for us to be bought out. At the closing, there was a disagreement over the interpretation of part of our option, and I was impressed with the way Paul stood up for us. Later, in 1986, when he turned over our $3 million investment in the Hammermill transaction into $4.3 million in little more than sixty days, his credibility again was high with me. For all of these reasons, when he approached us to be part of a select group with Ed De Bartolo, Arthur Cohen, and Alex Spanos to invest in the same type of takeover investments that had previously made multimillions for himself and the others, we felt it was a great opportunity.

Paul had approached us in the spring of 1987 to make the investment in his new fund. One weekend in May, I talked with Paul about his SEC compliance and Paul assured me he did everything by the book. Once he told me that, I decided that this was indeed an opportunity we should take advantage of. Had he told me his interpretation of SEC compliance, I never would have gone any further with the deal. In fact, that discussion was critical to my decision to invest in the fund. This fund ultimately purchased the Singer Company. T. Boone Pickens (who, ironically, is now my Dallas neighbor) also helped Paul Bilzerian complete the Singer Company transaction. We didn't actually invest until summer and early fall of 1987. One of the major points of our negotiation was that we would have the right once a year to sell our interest back to Paul at the then-fair market value. This was critical to us because we knew that while we would be able to part with the $20 million investment that he had asked for on a temporary basis, we would certainly need the money back in the next couple of years.

During late spring and early summer in 1988, Paul had told us that our limited-partnership interest would be worth $60 to $80 million by Labor Day. Paul knew we needed the money and that we had always planned on our investment being short-term. That was why we had negotiated the written agreement that included the provision that, at a minimum of once a year, we would be able upon request to sell our interest to Paul personally. We had discussed the buy-back numerous times in the summer of 1988. That money would have made a major difference to us then and he knew it.

Labor Day came and went. In September we negotiated an exact price to finalize the buy-out. Several times Paul stalled with one story or another. He had seemed to be very inconsistent in his stories throughout the summer, one moment telling us that he would buy us out, the next minute saying Arthur Cohen and Alex Spanos would buy us out, and the next minute saying The Singer Company would buy us out. He controlled The Singer Company, and we felt comfortable being able to rely on his representation on behalf of the company. But it was beginning to confuse and disturb me, and I worried that perhaps, for whatever reason, Paul was playing games with us. I wanted to get away from him and the whole Singer transaction in the worst way.

In mid-September, a buy-out at $40 million was agreed upon, effective the first week of October. The $40 million would go to HSSM#7, our joint venture, and in turn would be divided 40 percent to the Hall Financial Group, 40 percent to Hall Venture Investment Fund, and 20 percent to me individually. While it went to three different pockets, it was all related money and all cash that we needed. It would be enough, particularly at that point in time, to really help us rebuild important areas of the business, such as acquisitions. The closing date, initially, was to be October; then, after several extensions, it was the end of February 1989. The deal was that he would rather agree on the number and have us formally bought out after he settled with Mesa and Shearson on buying out their interest, than to have us attempt to sell to a third party at a price that he felt would hurt his negotiations with Mesa and Shearson. Moreover, he didn't want new partners. We agreed to the supposed short delay.

During this time we continued to lose property and face extreme pressures from lenders on a daily basis. To say the least, this was almost beginning to feel like 1986 all over again. At this point in time, we could have done so much good toward saving properties with just a little more cash, plus we could have bought some great new bargains.

In late 1988, we continued to press to close the transaction agreed to in September. Then, on December 21, Paul was indicted on twelve counts of criminal fraud. While none of the issues involved The Singer Company, they had a tremendous spillover effect. Singer couldn't get the financing, and Paul's personal ability to finance a buy-out of our interest overnight became much more difficult. Paul, nevertheless, assured us that by the end of February the company would finish the buy-out as previously agreed.

February and March of 1989 passed with no payment. In late March and April, we filed suit against Paul and then Singer. In June, Paul was convicted. After the judge dismissed or consolidated three counts, he was found guilty on every one of the remaining nine counts. We won some important initial motions in our lawsuit, and that brought Paul to the table to negotiate. But after negotiating almost all of August and September 1989, Paul was unable to deliver on many attempted settlements. On September 27, Paul was sentenced to four years in prison, but he remains free pending an appeal he's filed in the case. Our lawsuit continues.

In 1987 we, of course, had no idea that Paul would have the criminal indictments and, later, convictions and other SEC-related difficulties that would dramatically change his ability or willingness to meet his business agreements. And in 1987, the investment with Paul was far from our only stock market–related problem.

Believe it or not, on Friday, October 16, 1987, MaryAnna and I were scheduled to leave on a trip to Africa with the Young Presidents Organization. Our trip had been planned for many months, and it was really our first chance since the business problems had hit for us to get away together. We were really looking forward to it, since we both needed a change and a rest. As October 16 approached, and as fate would have it, the market started to fall hard. There had been a couple of what seemed then like huge drops—down 90 points one day, then 95. I was certain it couldn't get worse. After all, my stock experts and all the other smart guys were convinced we were continuing to go up, up, and away.

By noon on October 16, when we were supposed to be heading for the airport, the market didn't look good. We decided to head for Houston, then check the market again there before flying to Amsterdam. In the car on the way to the airport, I listened to the market reports and talked to my trader at the office. The market was down 60 points, then 65, then back up 20 points, only to go down 40. It was bouncing all around. Part of me kept hoping things would improve, but I was filled with dread.

By the time I got to Houston, fifty minutes later, the market was twenty minutes from closing. I called Allen Moore to ask how it was doing. I was in shock. The market was down 90 points, 95, 96, 97, 100, 102, and on and on. The Standard & Poor's that I traded were doing even worse than the frequently quoted Dow Jones Industrial averages. On a day with a huge swing, the S&Ps might trade 300, 400, or 500 points. But on this day all records had been broken. They were trading on so-called computer-sell programs down 1,000 and 1,100 points. It was unbelievable!

While we were talking, the phone went dead—we were cut off. I suddenly felt like I was losing control of everything. I quickly called Allen back. It was two minutes until closing and he had the floor trader in the future exchange on his other phone and I had to make a quick decision. The market was down 1,800 on the Standard & Poor's. Each second that was ticking away I had to decide whether to take my loss and get out or stay with it. My desire was to tough it out, but I knew I couldn't afford to be wrong. Before 1986, I would have gutted it out and stayed with it, knowing the market would come back, but this time, in an instant, I knew I had been beaten. I knew that my cash position would just barely be sufficient to pay off the margin call from the losses of that day. It was an historic loss for me. I finally said, "Get me out."

In hindsight, while I frequently feel frustrated with myself whenever I lose, like in this situation, we all need to know when to back off. It's fortunate I faced the reality in the stock market, because had I put my head in the sand and not made a tough decision to get out, the next Monday's real crash would have been so devastating that my loss would have been five times greater. Similarly, the whole way Hall Financial faced its problems by being decisive and realistic certainly ended up giving us some short-term headaches, but long-term it probably was the only salvation to surviving the depression. The lessons of the benefit in facing realities even when they are extremely unpleasant cannot be overemphasized in importance.

Thirty seconds later, it was all over. I was out of the futures market. I had lost a huge amount of money that day with a total loss of virtually all of my personal liquidity. I was shocked, mortified, and very ashamed. The numbers were extremely high. My first reaction was to head back to Dallas, if for no other reason than to punish myself. As the first boarding was being called for the plane for Amsterdam, I was still on the phone. Ron Berlin and Don Braun got on the speaker phone and tried to convince me to go on to Africa. They said they would take care of everything. At that point, I felt that this had to be the bottom. How could things possibly get worse? Besides I was out of the risky part—the futures market.

Ron and Don finally convinced me that everything was going to be all right, and as they were about to close the door long after the final call, I finally boarded the evening flight for Amsterdam. While most of the other passengers slept, I thrashed through my mistakes again and again. I started analyzing what I would do in the future. Clearly, I had been trying to get back too much too fast. It hadn't been right to try to hit home runs. I could pay my banks back over time. To do it the fast way, or to try to, had really cost me. There is no such thing as easy money. I was depressed and angry at myself during the entire nine-and-a-half-hour flight. I felt like a caged animal wanting to be anywhere but on that plane.

When we got to Amsterdam at 3:30 A.M. Dallas time, I had convinced myself to turn around and go right back to Dallas. The Dallas flight from Amsterdam and our scheduled flight to Nairobi were both three or four hours away. I wanted to do something now. I finally called Ron Berlin and woke him up at 4:00 A.M. After about twenty minutes, he had again convinced me that things were under control. He went over all the numbers and told me that the bottom line was I needed to get my head back together and then come back and dig into the real estate business again. We both agreed that the stocks May Petroleum and the stock partnership still owned, although both on margin, were at no great risk.

We arrived in Kenya and found our suite at the Nairobi Safari Club luxurious compared to my visions of Africa. We were exhausted from our trip, but we had a lot to do the next morning, so our rest was short. We had a meeting scheduled and then a small group of us had a private tea with the president of Kenya. This was a thank-you for some charitable donations we and others from the Young Presidents Organization had made to some children's charities in Kenya recommended by the president of Kenya. By midday, following the tea, I couldn't stand the suspense any longer. The market would be just about to open and I had to call Dallas and see what it was doing. Lo and behold, when I called, Allen's news was not good. The market was down over 200 points. It was unprecedented and beyond comprehension. During the next several hours, I stayed on the phone while we went through each stock portfolio and evaluated the situation. Throughout that Black Monday, the news became more and more ominous as the stock market went through its worst crash ever, exceeding the 1929 crash.

It was then that I decided I had to get back to Dallas.

When this decision was made it was nightfall in Nairobi. MaryAnna and I were due at a formal dinner party with a number of ambassadors and other dignitaries. It was very impolite of me not to go, but I just couldn't. MaryAnna went ahead to offer my apologies. As I walked her down to the lobby during a short intermission from phone calls, I told her I would probably catch the next flight back to the United States. She agreed and said she would stay in Africa and follow me later.

I went back upstairs, where my first phone call was to the airport. I found out that making travel plans in Africa is not quite as easy as it is in the United States. Unable to get through, I finally decided to take a taxi to the airport and try to buy my way back to the United States with credit cards with the hope that I could find phones at each stage of the trip. Before leaving the hotel, I reorganized and packed and left several notes for MaryAnna. Then I took a shower, made one more call to my office in Dallas, and was on my way.

Sweat was pouring down my body at practically the same rate the shower had a few minutes earlier. I had dressed in such a hurry that without thinking, I had thrown on the safari outfit I had bought to wear in the bush country. But instead of our planned photo safari, I was heading home fast. The taxi, a late-model Mercedes, made its way through the dark streets of Nairobi, carrying me in my state of panic back to a world of financial chaos.

The taxi finally dropped me at the airport. Here I was, this naive American, dressed in a safari outfit complete with pith helmet, safari jacket, pants, and boots. I was sweating through my clothes like I'd been out in the bush for years. I no doubt looked stark raving mad. Most of the ticket agents just gave me blank looks when I said I wanted to get to Dallas and fast. I might as well have been trying to go to Mars. It seemed impossible to find anyone to help me get a plane anywhere, but finally I booked a flight to London.

After confirming my flight, I started looking for a phone. The market would be just about to close, as it was moving closer to midnight. I had to call to see where we were. It took me much longer than I expected to get through the security checks and to the area where the various airline clubs would be. When I finally got there, they were not only closed, but the entire area was under construction. In short, there were no airline clubs. I figured I could make a collect call or get enough change to call through the local phone system. Wrong again. I was quickly told the airport pay phones didn't make long-distance calls. They just didn't do it, no way. That meant I had to find someone in the airport who would let me use a business phone. After a fifty-dollar discussion, I finally found one.

By the time I got my call through, the market was five minutes from closing. As it had been down some 300 points just before I left the hotel,

I stayed on the phone to hear the close of the day. Tick by tick, Allen described the close, then he said, "That's it. Down 508 points." Here I was in a Nairobi airport, the confusion of construction all around me, and after a two-year struggle just to keep my business alive, I had just been wiped out again by an unprecedented drop in the stock market. Black Monday to me was an understatement.

As I walked back to the airline gates, several people stopped to ask me if I needed medical help. Boy, did I. I must have looked like hell. I spent the next thirty hours back to Dallas beating myself up for the failures that occurred. Even though not logically fair, emotionally I blamed myself for allowing the losses to be so substantial. I was frustrated, ashamed, and lonely, and yet part of me was also thinking positively—what can I do now?

When I got to London, I was cool enough to call Allen Moore and talk to him about buying bonds. If the world was turning to deflation, bonds would surely go up. At least we could make some money in the wake of this disaster. As it turned out, we made $5 million on that plan.

Thinking back on the trip from London to Dallas, I am still amazed that I was functioning at all. Instead of sleeping, I got out a yellow legal pad and I started to work. I started making a list . . . If we are going into a recession/depression nationally, here's what we'll do . . . If this is just a stock market crash and then things turn up, we'll do this . . . I started planning one strategy after another, looking for new opportunity. We had already bought $50 million in bonds over the phone and we could continue to buy more. We would hold stocks where we could, make margin calls, conserve cash everywhere, and then go through and re-evaluate each and every part of the business in light of these new difficulties. I was logical, panicky, knee-jerk nervous, and calm all at the same time.

When the plane neared Dallas, I was feeling better. I had more than forty-five pages of notes and I was ready to go to work. When I called my office from my car, I started setting up meetings. At about 3:30 in the afternoon, I was at my desk working away. By 10:00 that evening I was absolutely drained. It had been forty-plus hours with little more than a few short naps on the planes. I went home frustrated and depressed, but a little more in control of things, and crashed.

After my Africa trip, if you can call it that, I buckled down to damage control and started really focusing on the idea of merging the private Hall corporations (my then real estate group) and May Petroleum. The May directors were enthusiastic earlier when we had just discussed the possibility prior to the market crash, and now the merger seemed to be all the more beneficial for everyone. Even though May had just lost a lot of money in the market, it still had more than $25 million in cash reserves—a meaningful number to the Hall real estate corporations. Within days of my coming back from Africa, the May board hired Bear Stearns and due diligence (the homework that investment bankers do) was in process. Bear Stearns was chosen because of their intimate knowledge of Hall from the debenture underwriting. Negotiations were underway to consider a merger even before the crash, and now it seemed particularly beneficial to everyone. From my perspective, there was added incentive: Hall Real Estate's chances of doing a debenture, at least in the immediate future, had fallen by the wayside with the market crash. The market uncertainty had put a temporary end to the type of debenture offering we had planned.

The merger in simple terms combined a company that had some cash and a desire to diversify with a company that had great market opportunities and good management but lacked the liquidity to move forward. If we were right about our market assumptions and real estate was at or near the bottom, then we could use the new capital from May to build a real base for the future. It was one of those simple one-plus-one-equals-three programs that looked good for everyone involved.

Mergers are financial transactions that occur with a good degree of regularity in the stock market these days, but that doesn't, by any means, mean that they are simply or easily accomplished. Typically, a merger involves lots of legal and accounting work to put together a prospectus type of document, a proxy. The companies' shareholders then vote, based on the proxy information, whether or not to finalize the merger in accordance with the proposed terms as negotiated by management and the board of directors of both companies. Many things can go wrong in the process. It is fairly normal to end up with one or more lawsuits.

Throughout the last part of 1987 and into the beginning of 1988, my time was almost entirely taken up with the merger. At the end of 1987, I received a greenmail threat by an individual who bought May shares and threatened to sue and stall the merger if I didn't pay him a big premium to get him out of the stock. Not being one who compromises principles, I wouldn't consider his plan. Instead of paying him that premium, I spent far more money to try to work around him. That was just one of my several roadblocks. Getting the merger done became one more set of difficulties on the long course to recovery. Chapter 10 describes the details of the merger more fully.

Throughout late 1987 and 1988, we continued to work on improving our property-management ability, and we acquired some more general-partner positions throughout 1987. During the post-crash period, momentum seemed to go up and down in an irregular manner. But while we were facing a new and additional crisis, our emotions were anything but defeatist. We had learned some lessons and coping skills in our 1986 survival and after the crash we needed to draw on all of the inner strengths we could muster to make it day by day.

Typically, I announced my market losses earlier than most. I announced May's losses almost immediately in a letter to all shareholders. The announcements got me in hot water. All of our banks naturally were not happy with our stock market losses. Had I made the $50 million and paid them off, I would have been brilliant and they would have been trying to lend us more money. But that isn't what happened; I was wrong and made a mistake committing so much to the stock market.

From the stock market crash I have learned a lot of lessons. One is not to overspeculate and bet the farm. Too many times greed tempts us to overinvest—don't do it. I also learned that turnarounds don't occur with home runs, but happen slowly, one step at a time, and with the help of a solid, well-concieved plan. That plan takes much fine tuning and adjusting along the way. You can't rebuild from a financial crisis with easy short-cuts, no matter how tempting.

The real fight that we all struggle with in tough times is really the war within ourselves. When I think of tough times, it is almost impossible to try to describe them, actually write them in a book, or tell anyone about them. A lot of my closer friends think I'm completely crazy to bare my soul in this book. But if my lessons can be learned earlier by other people struggling to survive in business, then it's worth it. Most people go through some kind of crisis, business or personal, sometime in their lives. There are ways to turn these crises in a positive direction. I am convinced that a carefully planned, one-step-at-a-time, no-home-run approach ultimately leads to victory. I'm also convinced that the experience of adversity can be a great time to learn a lot about the world around you as well as the inner world of what's important to you.

C H A P T E R   1 0
THE MERGER AND MORE TOUGH TIMES

EXHAUSTED, I LOOKED AT the clock in my hotel room on the afternoon of March 18, 1988, in Wilmington, Delaware, and leaned back. I seemed to have just enough strength to pull the bedcovers completely over my head. As I lay down for a short afternoon nap I fell into a deep sleep—like a state of suspended animation. Throughout this period of sleep, my subconscious seemed to mull over the curious odyssey that had led to our presentation in the Chancery Court of Delaware just a couple of hours earlier. The judge had not announced a decision but instead stated, "No one is to do anything in terms of this merger until I make a decision," and then he left the bench. The open-endedness of his statement left all of our lawyers guessing what would happen next.

As I was leaving the courtroom, deep down inside I knew we had lost. This would mean the merger would be stopped by a court injunction. Let down and very tired, I had a feeling of great emptiness. Win or lose, there was the sense of "where is justice?" The amount of money, effort, and energy that had gone into mounting the big campaign for what could still be derailed seemed like a highly wasteful and unproductive activity. Yet this was the way the American judicial system works sometimes.

The circumstance that had brought me to Delaware on March 18 and to that feeling of utter frustration and emptiness, as I reflected on the day's brief legal hearing, was a curious set of events. Our merger made great sense to the outside directors of the company and, for that matter, to the shareholders. The election by the shareholders for the merger had been held on March 11. The results were overwhelmingly in favor of the merger, with 94.5 percent of the shareholders present, in person or by proxy, voting for the merger. Quite frankly, we hadn't expected as great a turnout as we had, nor for the vote to be as overwhelmingly in favor as it was. Ironically, therein lies the problem.

It is a long and complicated story. May Petroleum had a very strange clause in its charter which required that 80 percent of the shareholders of the company be present at a meeting considering a merger and 66⅔ vote in favor. This type of clause is often referred to as a poison pill. It also required that two-thirds of the nonaffiliated shareholders vote favorably for the merger if it involved merging into a company that was controlled by someone who already owned 30 percent of May Petroleum. In short, the purpose of this was to stop a hostile takeover. John May, one of the two founders of the company, had had this provision put in to help keep his position solid as chairman of the company. Meanwhile, the shareholders had continued to dilute his ownership in a series of offerings. It made sense to the directors at that time, including David Florence, the co-founder who is still on the board. But sometimes what makes sense at one time changes with time and circumstances.

The provision was very complicated and very difficult in that if a shareholder bought enough shares, he or she could have veto power over any merger. In December, shortly after the merger was proposed, a shareholder who indicated that he controlled 350,000 shares called me requesting a meeting. I agreed to a dinner meeting. He said that if I didn't take the actions he proposed regarding the merger, he would buy more shares and block the merger and/or file a lawsuit against us. In other words, he was threatening me with greenmail in his effort to take advantage of the merger transaction.

I certainly don't condone such unethical behavior and it irritated and frustrated us at the time. We didn't realize quite how much trouble this fellow could be. However, as we researched his background in the next few days, it began to become clear that this was a serious situation. In fact, this particular individual and his wife, whose small law firm specialized in aggressive, takeover-oriented litigation, had greenmailed (made trouble for companies' managements until they were bought out of their stock at a premium over market) approximately forty companies. They specialized in making trouble for smaller and medium-sized companies by blocking mergers or, in other ways, throwing a monkey wrench into corporate plans, ultimately in order to be bought out. This individual tried first to interest me in using May Petroleum's money to participate in his greenmail schemes. When I didn't go along with that, he later tried to get me to buy out his stock at a $500,000 premium. Sometimes principle is expensive, but I have always been one to try to do what is right, not what is easy.

When we didn't meet the demands of the greenmailer in late December, he threatened in January to sue and try to stop the merger. Because I owned more than 30 percent, we were subject to this "poison pill" provision, and unless we figured out a way to solve our problem, the greenmailer could probably have stopped our merger. In order to comply with the legal technicalities of the May Petroleum charter and not be subject to the demands of the greenmailer, we came up with a plan. Our lawyers worked out all of the details for me to transfer enough shares of my stock so that I owned less than 30 percent. My initial plan was to give the shares to charity, but that would have caused tremendous tax problems for the company's net operating-loss carry forward. At the time, I was in the middle of some estate planning and several advisors came up with the idea that I could give the shares to my children without causing a tax problem for the company. I realized that the recommended solution to the problem of owning more than 30 percent of the shares was to transfer shares to a trust for my children. The shares would be entirely out of my control and would meet the definition for the purpose of the poison pill.

Part of the key to making this transaction meet all the necessary requirements was to have the control of the trusts in the hands of outside independent trustees who would make all of the trusts' decisions, including how to vote the stock shares. I needed to choose people with whom I did not do business, but to whom I could entrust an irrevocable right to manage a substantial amount of wealth for my children. This was no easy assignment since so many of the people I was close to also had interwoven themselves into my business life. Finally, I decided that a young lawyer in Florida whom I respect, Steven Greenspan, would be one part of the equation, but I really wanted two people. Then it occurred to me that an orthodox rabbi with whom I had studied, Rabbi Mendel Dubrawsky, would provide the independence of adding an extra layer of integrity and the spiritual concern for doing what was right. What an excellent choice.

Both of the proposed trustees accepted my proposal and the documents were completed. I explained carefully to each of the new trustees that there might be litigation involved if this greenmailer group pursued matters. Both of the new trustees had not informed me as to how they would vote their shares on the merger and, indeed, I never asked them. Although the rabbi had sought and received permission from his superiors to become a trustee, he still felt it would be more appropriate for him to use his personal name and, therefore, the documents did not include his rabbinical title.

Unfortunately, the greenmailers did sue. They insisted—which I had hoped wouldn't occur—that both the trustees go through a deposition. The suit was filed shortly before the merger would have taken place and the depositions were scheduled. The rabbi was extremely nervous about his deposition. He had never been deposed nor even involved in legal controversy. I suddenly felt terrible about having put the rabbi in this position. Afterwards he told me that the night before his deposition was to be taken, he didn't sleep a wink. I didn't go to his deposition, although I wish I could have been a fly on the wall. According to several lawyers who were present, the young Jewish lawyer who worked for the corporate raiders practically dropped his jaw to the floor when he saw the man he was about to depose. Complete with long beard, curly hair, and formal dark rabbinical clothing, Rabbi Dubrawsky looked like he could have walked off the set of *Fiddler on the Roof.* The young attorney appeared to lose his concentration several times during his questioning of the rabbi. The whole point of the effort by their side was to try to prove that the trustees really wore two hats and that the rabbi and the other trustee were not independent in their management of my children's trust. In other words, were they really working for me and my children's trust (i.e., wearing two hats) or just working for the trusts as we had represented?

It got hot in the room and the rabbi decided to take off his top hat. The joke between the lawyers afterward was that the rabbi truly did wear two hats. He had his top hat and, below it, his yarmulke, which was always worn for religious purposes. Needless to say, the rabbi was, and is still, an excellent, independent trustee. After the deposition was over, he remarked that he actually enjoyed it and, even today, he talks about his "legal experience and expertise."

It was agreed by all the lawyers that we could go ahead and get the vote on the merger at a meeting on March 11, but not finish the merger until we had had the court hearing, which was to be March 18. In the meantime, what they really wanted was a big legal fee and a big settlement. Although it was against our principles, and because of our fear of what the court might do and to be practical, we started negotiating a settlement. The board strongly believed the merger was in the best interests of May's shareholders and was concerned that the lawsuit would be harmful to the shareholders. At first, everyone was in favor of giving this greenmailer whatever he wanted to get the merger done and get rid of the lawsuit. We negotiated to give away more and more and it got to the point that it would have cost a few million dollars for something we all believed was a worthless claim. Ironically, the only reason that we didn't settle is that the greenmailer and his wife kept getting greedier. I was getting more and more frustrated with the pressures of the merger's being stalled and with the lawsuit's having upset the board. Tensions were high and we felt like there were no good answers to the mess.

With all that on my mind and after a day of negotiation, I went to a formal wedding reception for a lawyer and business executive friend in

Dallas. It's strange how some things happen. At the reception, the chairman of an oil company came up to me and told me he had to talk to me privately. He said that he had been greenmailed by the same people a year and a half earlier. He went on to tell me how his negotiations had gone and warned me that these were unscrupulous people who wouldn't be honorable even in settlement negotiations. He talked of their excessive greed and total lack of ethics. After I listened to what he had to say, I decided on moral grounds that it would be wrong to settle with them. I also decided to recommend strongly to the board that we take a stand and stop these people from doing what they were doing. That night, I went home about midnight from the reception seriously pondering the chance meeting that lead to that decision.

From midnight until seven in the morning, I worked on drafting a countersuit and strategies for what we should do next to fight back and fight back hard. I knew I was risking the timely completion—and maybe even the completion itself—of our merger, but right was right. That next morning on Sunday at 7:30, we had a previously scheduled meeting with all of our lawyers to take up the discussion of settlement again. As I entered the meeting and started to tell the lawyers of my new plans, I learned that what I had heard the night before was absolutely true. Our head lawyer had talked to the lawyer wife of the greenmail team the night before, and she had reneged on various points of the settlement negotiations that everyone had thought were previously agreed. The greenmailers were getting even more greedy. In a short time, we all agreed we would aggressively fight the matter through the court system.

After the unexpected vote, we met all of the criteria of that special-article poison-pill provision. In other words, the vote was so overwhelmingly in favor of the merger that even without the trust and my being under a 30 percent stock level, we had complied with the provisions of the poison pill. We felt elated and thought that our March 18 hearing would be a moot point. Yet, despite a huge amount of preparation and unbelievable cost, the hearing simply didn't go well. We had two lawyers make the actual presentation, and the second one simply didn't get enough time and it didn't come off well. I could tell, as I sat there in the hour-long hearing, that we were losing.

We finally did get the results, which came several days after the hearing. We had lost. My instincts in that particular situation were, unfortunately, correct. I had seen that we were going to lose and it was a major setback for me not only in the merger, but also in the momentum of all of our business plans. The question from there was: what do we do next? Probably a dozen lawyers were involved and the advice varied greatly. The primary lawyers were saying not to appeal but to just restructure the merger, refile, and do a new vote. An appeal seemed to be an expensive, time-consuming, and aggressive posture because it was not an easy thing to overturn the Chancery Court in these types of matters. After a lot of conflicting legal advice, I recommended to our board, which concurred, that we appeal because it was the right thing to do. The law was still in our favor, and we believed we would win in the end.

There were really two issues involved. The first was whether we, in fact, did meet the voting requirements of that special article. The voting requirements of the special article required that 80 percent of the shareholders be present in person or by a proxy and that two-thirds of the noncontrol vote be in favor for a transaction to pass. We felt we met those criteria. The second issue was a little more exotic and complicated. It related to how votes are counted and certain technical aspects of voting rights that could have a far-reaching impact on all corporations. Since Delaware is a state in which many of the larger companies are incorporated, and its court system has been widely regarded for years as the leading, cutting edge of law in these matters, it seemed important to see it through to get the law clarified on these issues that would affect other companies as well as ours. It was important to make the Delaware voting procedures clear, and this court case would set certain precedents for the future on similar issues.

Our appeal on May 31 was an hour hearing, one half hour for each side, before the three-judge panel of the Supreme Court of Delaware. The appeal had required briefing and lots of back-and-forth paperwork like all other legal matters, but the hearing itself would be only an hour. It is so ironic to see that each side would get only thirty minutes after what, by that time, already had been more than a million dollars of legal costs to get to the courtroom. It was putting a lot on the line.

The Chancery Court had been frustrating. We were left without any decision for a few days and then, finally, got a negative decision. At the end of the Supreme Court appeal, there again was frustration, again no answer. A significant number of days, then weeks, went by, and finally over a month; then the result came out. It was a split decision. In the Supreme Court, in a hearing of this nature, if not all of the judges agreed, then they could call for an enbanc hearing. (Enbanc means that all of the judges hear the case.) An enbanc hearing, in this case, would mean that all five of the Supreme Court justices of Delaware (the most respected corporate court in the country) would rehear the case. That was an unusual circumstance, but occasionally, when something was an important issue and there was not a unanimous agreement by the panel of judges, such a hearing was required. Therefore, in essence, we didn't win or lose and we were, again, in the limbo position of having our merger further delayed.

We were now well into the end of July, and the decision had to be made to abandon the merger or go forward with the enbanc hearing of the entire Supreme Court of Delaware. The first such occasion that a hearing could be scheduled was August 15. The reason it took so long was because of the time it would take to get everybody's schedules coordinated. Ironically, this was supposed to be an emergency, expedited hearing from the March 18 hearing. Between March 18 and now, late June, we had been in limbo such that neither company could do what it might otherwise do because of the pending merger. We would have to wait until August 15.

We decided to go for it. A lot of lawyers and other people said we were fools and that we wouldn't win. I spent most of the rest of that summer working with the lawyers, the chief operating officer of May Petroleum, and others from the Hall companies preparing our legal position.

Before leaving for the second Supreme Court hearing, I was preoccupied, as I had been most of the summer, thinking of every detailed area and legal intricacy of the all-important argument that would occur on August 15. Again, we had the unusual circumstance of having a very short time to present our case. A total of one half hour for each side would be allotted. As I was getting ready to leave Dallas to go to Delaware, some of the people in the office almost physically grabbed me to insist that I stop by a happy-hour party that the company was holding at Caliente's, a terrific local Mexican restaurant that had been the scene of more than one get-together for the company. When I got to the restaurant, it seemed like the Hall people had taken over. When I saw my wife, whom I had just tried to reach by phone having thought it strange she wasn't home, I realized that the party was more like a pep rally. The pep rally came complete with good luck charms and, most important, a hand-painted T-shirt, made by Clarence from our mailroom, that read "Delaware Dazzler." Superman, watch out. That was the T-shirt that I wore underneath my more traditional conservative business suit the day of the hearing, thinking who knows, it may be the charm that will turn our luck around.

On August 15, our head lawyer spoke. I felt every bone in my body hanging on his every word. I was blessed by a lot of company at that hearing. All the directors were there and we all watched as our lawyer gave a brilliant presentation and argument of our position. At the end of the argument, the five very distinguished justices got up and left, but they indicated that they would come back to let the audience know when they would make a decision and what the details would be on the next stages in this case. While they were out, a few of us went downstairs to the basement cafeteria for some coffee. We were there for twenty to thirty minutes when all of a sudden I had the feeling it was time for us to go back up. We got to the third-floor courtroom just as the justices were coming in and sitting down. Two minutes later it was announced that we had won: five to zero on one issue and four to one on the other issue. The merger could go forward immediately.

I had asked the lawyers to prepare all the papers for the merger before the hearing, believing that the decision would come from the bench, as it had, and that it would be favorable. However, the lawyers had not done it. They thought it would be impossible and unprecedented for the Supreme Court to rule that day. Immediately, we had to scurry around communicating between lawyers in several different cities and states, but within an hour and a half, all of the right documentation was done and our merger was completed. The period from March to August had been a long odyssey.

Reflecting on the events of the merger, which had just occurred, I realized how fragile everything in business can be. Business, like life itself, is a matter of razor-sharp decisions and events that can cut either way. Failure and success often depend on how tenacious you are. If you won't accept failure, then eventually you will succeed. Finally, after two times before the Supreme Court, we had done it. We had completed the merger. Perhaps it was our tenacity that kept the deal going. Most of our lawyers told us a number of times to give up and not to keep pursuing the appeal. The lesson that the merger reminds me of is the fact that persistence and not accepting failure are the key elements of success. Sometimes when something doesn't work, you just have to try and try and try again and again until some new method puts the last piece together and turns failure into success. That was true for our merger and it is true for many business and personal things that affect everyone's lives.

We were feeling really good for a brief moment in time, and then back to reality. Even with the merger, our liquidity was not very good. More to the point, we had lost all of our momentum from the positive things we were doing in 1987, that is, before the stock market crashed. The long delay in the merger and the resulting uncertainty had hurt both May Petroleum and the Hall Real Estate corporations. We were still limited in our capital even with the merger. We were also limited on momentum, and morale needed a lift throughout the company. The merger, newly renamed Hall Financial Group, Inc., was an important step forward, but many problems still loomed.

We had lost a number of properties through foreclosure during 1988 and had gained no new properties. Our new investment business was almost at a standstill. We were doing everything we could day and night to help existing limited partners. The year 1988 had been rough. There were numerous and unpleasant day-to-day fights to keep each partnership alive. The investors generally remained very supportive, but they would never be able to truly understand how much pressure we were under and how hard we worked for their best interests.

In 1988, prior to the merger, we had very little liquidity. In 1986 and 1987 and even through much of 1988, people never knew from payday to payday who would be laid off. The grapevine usually ran wild and layoffs were continuous. Even though we kept trying to put the worst behind us, it seemed that it would never end.

The one good thing about the whole crash period of 1986, 1987, and 1988 was that the parking spaces in the building became far more available. In early 1986, if you didn't get to the office before 7:45 A.M., you simply couldn't get a space in the underground garage. By 1987, it wasn't too tough to find a space, and in 1988, there were ample parking spaces for more than everyone in the whole building.

In late 1988 and throughout 1989, we knew we were in for another trying period of time. The properties were doing better in Texas, but worse in Arizona. In fact, Arizona looked like the next Texas. Atlanta and other markets were also softening as the overall inflation to deflation was beginning to show up in other places. Truly, the Texas experience, while more severe than other areas of the country, was not unique. Many areas of the country were experiencing to some degree the phenomena of deflation in real estate values, in great part because of the 1986 tax law and over-building.

During much of 1989, particularly in the first half of the year, I continued to spend most of my time on old problems. New, fun, and creative projects were now so far back in our history that it was hard having nice days at the office. It was hard, very hard, for all of us, from support staff to management. The year 1989 was a further grinding out of the depression in Texas. Large real estate firms like the ten-billion-dollar-plus Southmark real estate conglomerate were throwing in the towel and declaring bankruptcy. Even well-respected real estate and financial firms like Lomas and Nettleton, a multibillion-dollar mortgage and real estate company, were now in the news with their problems. Lomas Financial Corporation also ended up in bankruptcy and the shake-out of the depression was far from over. In the end, very few real estate companies would be left standing in Texas. Fortunately the news about us was positive, even though we still had lots of headaches. We were one of the very few local companies to start buying new properties. As to our problems, we knew one way or another we would, one step at a time, turn the situation around.

C H A P T E R   1 1
THE CRASH OF OIL, REAL ESTATE, BANKING, AND SAVINGS AND LOANS

I WAS FAR FROM ALONE in feeling the effects of the tax depression. It is extremely difficult for people who aren't living in the middle of a disaster to grasp exactly how devastating one really can be. We all learn from history. If I'm able to convey, even in part, the dramatic impact on Texas and the Southwest and the inherent suffering of many people as a result of the real estate and financial depression that struck the state in the last half of the 1980s, then all of the effort in writing this book will have had value. In seemingly domino succession, real estate values plummeted, the price of oil dropped, and then the entire financial industry stronghold began to fall apart in Texas.

At the time of this writing, one of the brand-new bankers in Texas is John McCoy, Chairman of Bank One. His Ohio-based Bank One in mid-1989 became the successful bidder to take over MBank, then the largest Texas-owned bank holding company, which had failed and was put out for bids by the FDIC. After John had been in Texas for a little over a month working with MBank, I had an opportunity to have breakfast with him. At that breakfast, he expressed how truly surprised he was at the amount of devastation that had occurred in the Texas depression and how little those in the Midwest and other areas of the country really could understand about what had happened in Texas. A few weeks later, I attended a dinner at which John spoke and he made a similar observation, but in even a more pointed manner. He recalled how he had described Texas to his board of directors at a recent board meeting.

John indicated that he had been trying to tell his fifteen directors just how bad things were in Texas and he was having very little luck in describing it. He said his directors were the cream of the crop of the business community of the Midwest. They were all doing well in their businesses and were strong financially. At one point during the meeting he looked at them and said, "Three of you by now would have filed personal and corporate bankruptcy, three more of you would have been in severe financial trouble, and most of the rest of you would have had major economic problems if you and your businesses had been located in Texas, and you're the cream of the crop. The rest of the business community would be in far worse shape.'' That is a very good observation, especially coming from someone with John's experience and perception of many markets. The Texas depression truly is a hard-to-describe, long-lasting disaster that has been the ruin of many a good, long-term, well-established business person.

In late 1987, the headlines read "First Republic Bank Broke." The unthinkable was beginning to happen. First Republic, the $40 billion regional bank, a monument to the strength of banking in Texas, was going broke. It all started with whispers and rumors, but by the end of 1987 the drumbeat of the press was louder and louder each day. By the beginning of 1988, it was clear that a modern-day run on the bank was occurring. Unlike Continental Bank in Chicago, which had major exposure to European deposits in 1984, First Republic was relatively more diversified in its retail deposit base. It was believed to be too diverse in its deposit base and too strong to suffer a run on the bank. Nevertheless, with the relentless pounding of the press, First Republic was suffering the same pains that afflicted the Hall Financial Group in the spring of 1986. While we escaped the perception becoming a reality, as in the case of First Republic, their fate eventually was sealed by the attacks on their credibility. It happened fast. First Republic, the pillar of strength itself, was gone. Today it is as though it had been a natural event, though at the time it certainly was not.

In 1986, our investors stayed with us and we avoided the dreaded run on our bank. If our investors had stopped paying their notes, which totaled $525 million on January 1, 1986, we would have been exactly like a bank with a big run on deposits. Unfortunately, First Republic by early 1988 did not find the same confidence from their depositors. On March 18, 1988, a short couple of months after the negative press had started, the FDIC announced a $1 billion emergency infusion. After that, it was downhill quickly, and on July 29, 1988, North Carolina National Bank became the new owner of First Republic. The bank that had been built over a period of sixty years on a solid Texas foundation had practically disintegrated almost overnight. First Republic Bank was a bank that Fred Florence had built from a small country bank into a major regional institution, a strong pillar of the international banking community. Now it was to become a regional branch of a "North Carolina" bank.

As First Republic went, so, too, did many other commercial banks. In 1987, 63 banks were declared insolvent in Texas compared to 203 in the country. In 1988, things simply got worse with 79 banks being declared insolvent in Texas. In fact, of all of the major banks with assets of more than $1 billion in Texas, it appears that only one, Cullen Frost, will survive not having been forced into a merger, buy-out, or FDIC assistance. This 1980s depression has been different than the 1930s but in some ways worse for commercial banks and savings and loans in this area of the country. For instance, in the 1980s, Texas had to work with the fact that there was no national consensus to help solve the problem; rather, the regulators were at times complicating industry efforts at improving things. At least in the 1930s it was a national crisis with a greater sense of unity and understanding throughout the country. Just a few short years earlier Republic and MBank had been hailed as examples of strong, well-run regional banks. The depression of the last half of the 1980s had suddenly ruined these banks financially and wiped out their venerable reputations.

While the marble columns that represent the underpinning of the financial world of commercial banks were crumbling, the savings and loans were in even worse shape yet. In Texas alone in 1988, through mid-year on a fiscal, twelve-month basis, losses amid the $100 billion Texas thrift industry exceeded $11 billion. Absent regulator intervention, the industry was headed for a $20-billion-a-year annual loss or 20 percent of beginning 1988 capital.

By the end of 1988, virtually all of the savings and loans with assets of more than $500 million had failed. Most would either be merged through the regulators' Southwest Plan or, in some cases, liquidated. The massive industry restructure has become the biggest financial crash and scandal of modern times. In 1986 the press seemed totally uninterested in the savings and loan industry. By comparison, in 1987, 1988, and 1989, the savings and loans seemed to be front-page news on a daily basis.

For all of the visible devastation of the financial institutions, particularly in Texas, the depression of Texas didn't spawn long bread lines. Oddly, even as the depression has deepened in its personal impact on individuals' lives, unemployment continues statistically at a respectable, modest level. Yet the statistics of unemployment tell a distorted story. Texans also filed more personal bankruptcies every month for months and months, peaking in 1987. In 1986, 15,157 bankruptcies were filed in the state of Texas; in 1987, they increased to 24,584; in 1988 to 22,350; and to approximately 12,037 as of May 1989. These records are unique geographically and part of the isolated regional depression. Unemployment rose to 7.3 percent at the high point in 1988, which was far less than the 1930s and, for that matter, even far less than 15.5 percent in Michigan in 1982. This depression started as a "depression of the rich." This is a phrase I coined in 1986 in an effort to explain what we foresaw as happening in this very unique time period. Texas wealth was built during the last several decades on oil and gas, real estate, banking, and savings and loans—in short, on leverage or borrowing. The traditional Texas rich were big debtors. When the inflationary seventies swelled the pockets of the likes of the Hunt family, true to the Texas spirit, they didn't cash in, but instead kept growing. Leverage is a wonderful thing, but what goes up can come down even faster.

Looking back, the cracks in the system really started in 1982 and 1983, but at the time, none of us paid much attention. Oil prices, which hit a high of $35 in 1980, were headed down in late 1982. Houston was the first market to feel the effects. By 1985, the Texas optimists (which all of us Texans are by birth or naturalization) were convinced that the economic blip had passed. The bumpy times of the recession from 1982 to 1985 were bad enough for any area. In 1985, the view was that the tide was more likely to turn for the better than for worse.

Instead of being at the bottom as many of us thought, the end of 1985 was more of a rest period. Oil, which we all thought was very low at twenty dollars a barrel at year end 1985, by June of 1986 sank to nine dollars a barrel, and our Texas depression picked up steam.

What is unique about this slice of economic history is that its backdrop was the fourth, fifth, and sixth years of unprecedented national prosperity. The Reagan years rolled on with lower interest rates, higher manufacturing, and a comeback for the traditional Eastern establishment. The declining oil prices were good for most of the United States. The arrogant Texas "Freeze a Yankee" bumper stickers of the 1970s were fresh in East Coast establishment minds. During 1986, 1987, or even 1988, in Washington, D.C., or New York City, there were not many people interested in lending a helping hand to the Texas depression. In 1989, the John Tower nomination defeat followed by Jim Wright's being railroaded out of office were both in part representative of the anti-Texas climate in Washington. Counterbalancing the Texas bashing in Washington is the fact that President Bush, who took office in 1989, is a Texan. Many of his senior appointments are Texans, and politically Texas is enjoying an increasing Washington clout.

The basis of the Texas depression was inflation turning to deflation. The value of oil and real estate has declined in value by 50 percent or more in a very, very short period of time. This market dislocation occurred on assets that were 80 and 90 percent financed. If the lenders are broke, it is only logical that the borrowers are as well. The problems of the Hunts, John Connally, Clint Murchison, and many of the other historic pillars of

Texas society are evidence that this truly has been the depression of the rich. But as time has dragged on, day after day, month after month, and even year after year, it has become a depression that has hurt many good, hardworking people, leaving scars that will be there for life.

As time dragged on and on, the depression steam rolled through 1986, the era of "the depression of the rich," to a slow, grinding depression in 1987, 1988, and 1989, further deepening from the lack of liquidity in the financial system. Business depends on liquidity (the availability of money), whether it is investment equity or borrowings from banks in Texas. Money for business in the late 1980s was very scarce. In the real estate field, like oil and gas before it, only a very few companies will survive the ultimate devastation. Markets in this time were extremely illiquid with few new transactions being completed. Very little was being done in the way of purchases, sales, or refinancings of real estate. Many people simply continue to grind on and on trying to restructure debt. We were fortunate, being an exception to what most were going through in 1989. While we still had some problems, since we had faced our problems early we were through with the worst of the restructuring and were turning our efforts to the opportunities. For many others the road to recovery was a long way off.

The whole area of restructuring of debt is a very demeaning, illogical, and unfair process. There are no absolutes or standards of fair conduct. Too much of it is a personality game and at the whim of sometimes capricious and arbitrary decision making. There are no real policy guidelines. The numerous decision makers are often middle managers from either a Southwest Plan savings and loan to a liquidating "bad bank" (as the commercial banks call them) to conservatorships, receiverships, or FSLIC directly, or the FDIC directly. The fact is that their decision makers are highly inconsistent in their approach and results. Since in the end the taxpayer is footing the bill, it seems unfortunate for everyone involved, borrower and lender alike, that there are no guidelines or policies so that there would be consistency and some confidence as to the general approach and direction of restructuring. Obviously, the inconsistent approaches are by their very nature, in many cases, diametrically different from one to another. Some are right and some are wrong. The taxpayers lose again.

The real human suffering of a depression can never be quantified in statistics. People's lives are turned upside-down, for the most part by no fault of their own. One of the saddest aspects for Texans is the regional and geographic isolation of the depression. Worse yet is to see the number of oil companies, real estate companies, banks, savings and loans, and other types of businesses that are multigeneration family operations in which the daddies of daddies had built the family fortune end up in liquidation. Those family fortunes and those established companies that survived the 1930s depression are going bust today. This is not a readjustment, this is not a recession, this is a unique, severe depression. It is, for many people, a very, very tough and unique time.

In 1987 and 1988, every time the market seemed to stabilize and get better, things turned around and actually got worse. In 1988, with the mighty First Republic falling, everyone assumed that this action might be the bottom of the down cycle and times would turn up. However, there was the savings and loan bill still to be passed in 1989 and the FDIC taking control of the savings and loans yet to occur. The overall illiquidity in the market and the government control and involvement was awesome. Not since the 1930s had the government been so involved in the financial system. The government, in one form or another in the late 1980s, has been behind almost every major financial decision, right down to whose loans were called and whose were restructured.

The FDIC and various regulatory committees spent extensive amounts of time negotiating with the "Who's Who" of the Texas business and social scene—negotiations with big names who, on the surface, seemed rich but, behind the scenes, were at the mercy of the regulators to stay out of personal bankruptcy. Many people continued to be what was once thought of as honorable and continued to put money in to keep the mortgage payments current as long as they could. As the depression ground on further and further and longer and longer, people eventually ran out of liquidity. People had no cash and no ability to borrow. This was not the downturn these people had thought it would be. It was a deflationary spiral that continued far longer than anyone could imagine during the process.

Part of the reason for the length and depth of decline related to the government involvement itself. The government involvement delayed the natural market forces and dried up lending and any form of market liquidity. Because of the illiquidity and lack of new capital, there was very little to keep prices from continuing in a free fall. Value, after all, depends on a market of buyers with money. Because everyone feared the bottom and the overhang of properties that had been foreclosed by government-related institutions, the buyers with new capital sat on the sidelines until late 1989, when the market started to see money come in, which will lend to the comeback. In a seemingly endless cycle of a self-fulfilling prophecy, the situation continued to get worse and worse, far beyond what the economic consumer demand would have caused if the financial markets hadn't collapsed. The recovery has finally started, but from a very low level.

The oil and gas problems from 1982 to 1985 certainly got the ball rolling. But the steep decline of oil in 1986 was the major debacle for the banks. The real estate community, which depended upon the overall health of the economy in Texas, could not help but follow in severe decline. As the oil industry declined, the overbuilding was still upon us and there was way too much real estate available. Real estate would have been a problem even if demand had continued on a strong basis. But, unfortunately, the two problems of oil and gas declining and real estate being overbuilt collided. The FDIC, the FSLIC, and all of the other related banking agencies were also facing totally uncharted waters. The size and scope of the problem and the uncertainty of how to deal with the liquidations without making it worse were all new and difficult problems for the regulators.

The deflation was caused by many factors. The economic excesses of inflation in the late 1970s led to the deflation in real estate. Oversupply of money and optimism that inflation would cause values to go up even if there was not rental demand caused an oversupply of unneeded real estate to be built. The decline was inevitable, but the 1986 tax law made it a far worse deflation. The tax law change put a halt to a major equity capital source. This mess has been caused by many sources.

Every taxpayer in this country will unfortunately pay part of the bill for the mess by virtue of the savings and loans bail-out law. Yet the biggest costs are to the individuals who have been directly and humanly affected by the overwhelming pressures of the depression. These are pressures that cause many people to crack. I knew a few individuals who committed suicide and some who came close as a result, in great part, of their lack of self-esteem resulting from the loss of their careers. Many others changed and became dishonorable or showed their worst side. Some have survived by working hard, staying honest, and having faith. It really changed the fiber of people, individually and collectively as a society, throughout the entire state of Texas.

With all of the sadness and damage, I believe a certain inner strength has shown through—not only on an individual basis but also as a community. Texas has grown stronger from the survival of its depression. A sense of overcoming the odds and surviving whatever is thrown against a society brings people closer. Texans had been arrogant, but the maturation at the hands of the depression has changed that. Texans had been unrealistically optimistic about many things. The depression has brought new perspective and wisdom, but the positives of the old Texas spirit are happily also alive and well.

CHAPTER 12
ETHICS AND MORALITY IN A DEPRESSION

APRIL 2, 1986, began like most of my days that year—with a 6:30 A.M. meeting, followed by another at 9:30, another at 10:30—a day crammed full of trying to meet with more people than I care to remember. The 10:30 meeting was with MBank, one of the oldest banks in Dallas and one of Hall Financial's main lenders. If I had to make a list of whom we could count on to help us, MBank would be one of the few lenders we thought would surely help. It seems MBank's advice on the May Petroleum merger was more for the bank's benefit and was far less objective counsel than I expected, but personally I still believed that Jim, the president, probably did not know of May's problems. Jim and I at that time had remained friends. We still served together on the board of Back Systems, Inc., a venture-capital company. Given the long-term relationship, I figured MBank might be the first lender to step up to the line and help us solve problems with some East Coast banks that didn't know us well.

Both MBank and various East Coast banks—including Bankers Trust of New York—were part of a banking group that had extended us a $100 million line of credit. The loans went up and down at different times. We borrowed money when we needed it for acquisitions and paid it back to the banks after investors had paid in their capital to a newly formed limited partnership. At this point, MBank's piece of the loan was down to only $1.9 million, far lower than normal.

The meeting with MBank on April 2, 1986, was less than successful. It was a meeting that would start a process that indicated just how ethics were sinking, even with people in the institutions, at the time. Jim had recently chaired our meetings with MBank. But this one was unexpectedly led by a new fellow—Roy. At the meeting, Roy blended in with the rest of the bankers in typical dark conservative suits and white shirts. But from the start, Roy was different from any banker I had ever met before. His act began with the line: "I'm just a country boy from Tennessee, but I have some ideas on how to rework loans.'' He started the meeting by explaining that from now on I would deal with him and only him. He was the recently appointed chairman of the "special loans division"—in other words, as I later learned, he had been hired as a strong-arm to collect loans.

Roy had a new plan, but I didn't like the sound of it one bit. In addition to the joint credit agreement, MBank had an $11 million loan to us on Judiciary Center, a high-rise office building in Washington, D.C. That loan was up for renewal. Roy wanted us to violate all of the terms of the joint credit agreement with the other banks and fold the $1.9 million into a new loan on Judiciary Center. He also wanted us to keep it a secret from the other banks. Then he would give us, for $100,000, an option to buy out that portion of the bank group credit. In essence, we would become a participant with the other banks. This was all a complex ruse by MBank to take advantage of the other banks and get its $1.9 million out of the more risky group credit, which was virtually unsecured. The new first mortgage on Judiciary Center would be ninety days in duration. Then that was it. End of relationship. It was also probably the end of us because in ninety days MBank would foreclose on our best asset, the Judiciary Center, and start an avalanche of other foreclosures. Roy said that we had to take it or leave it. If I left it, Roy said MBank would call our loans and begin foreclosure on Judiciary Center immediately. Judiciary Center was our best asset, and by doing this, MBank would start an avalanche of other banks calling our loans. His plan was: Heads we lose and tails we lose. While Roy wanted to keep his workout plan from the other banks if he truly did start foreclosure, it would have been front-page news and the banks would be afraid to be the last one trying to get a piece of us. It would have been a disaster and Roy knew it. Of course, by then Roy would have gotten his loans out first.

The whole deal turned my stomach. Roy said it would have to be done totally without the other banks in the banking group knowing. When they found out, we all knew they would be furious and, according to Roy's plan, I would take the fall. His plan hurt everyone concerned—except for MBank, of course.

The meeting didn't last long—only about an hour. Roy said he'd call me in a couple of hours for my decision. As if he hadn't been obnoxiously tough enough in the meeting, Roy took me aside from my lawyer and the others in the room and sent me on my way with this farewell: "Boy, you've screwed things up so bad, you can't afford a good bankruptcy." I didn't laugh. It didn't take a couple of hours for Roy to call. By the time I was back to my office, a few miles north of downtown

Dallas, he was already calling and demanding that I meet him for lunch and give him a decision. I told him I couldn't, that I was booked solid through a late dinner meeting. So he told me to meet him for a drink after dinner at the Doubletree Inn, not far from my office on Central Expressway, Dallas's main north-south artery.

It was 11:30 P.M. when I drove up to the Doubletree Inn, a high-rise hotel in Dallas. I was expecting a dark, quiet bar where I could at least hear Roy hammer at me some more, but when I got off of the elevator on the twenty-second floor, I was greeted with a pounding disco beat, flashing lights, and a punk-rock sexy-looking little girl—the hostess. This had been some day, and now I was in the disco Twilight Zone. I was still in a daze when Roy greeted me a few moments later.

"Hello, Hall, I've been waiting for you. I've got a booth over here, come on over here."

The voice was Roy's all right. He really enjoyed calling me "boy" and "Hall," but the source of the voice was a completely different man. No more conservative blue suit and white shirt. Roy had transformed himself into a middle-aged disco John Travolta. Just like in *Saturday Night Fever*, he was decked out for the disco complete with a shiny polyester shirt unbuttoned practically down to his navel, and he had several gold chains around his neck.

Roy ordered himself another Campari and soda, and I ordered a beer. He was really friendly and started talking about everything under the sun—except the loan. I kept wondering when the kill was going to come. Finally, after about forty-five minutes, four beers, and many Campari and sodas, Roy leaned over and grabbed my shirt, pulling me closer to him, and said: "Hall, you've been talking to Bankers Trust, and I told you not to."

He was right. I had talked to Bankers Trust and to RepublicBank that day, but I told him that it would certainly be unethical—and probably illegal—for me to carry out his plan without Bankers Trust and the other banks in the banking group on the joint credit agreement knowing about it. He leaned over even further and said, "Hall, I'm telling you that if you ever talk to the Bankers Trust people again about this transaction we are going to do, your voice will be several octaves higher than the Vienna Boys Choir when I get through with you." Then he leaned back in the booth, and in his polyester shirt and gold disco chains, he reached into his pocket, took out a pocketknife and a piece of wood, and started whittling. He repeated his words from earlier this morning: "Hall, I'm just a poor country boy from Tennessee."

I couldn't believe it. If this dialogue was a movie script, it wouldn't even have made the B movie list. I kept thinking, who is this guy? And why is he working for one of the more conservative banks in town, a respected, multibillion-dollar organization like MBank? It was just too weird. And if this is how Roy started a business relationship, where could it possibly go from here? What had happened to the rules? As we left the disco in the elevator and walked out together into the parking lot, Roy gave me some more unsolicited advice on the bankruptcy that he knew I was sure to be filing soon. He added, "Don't do it for ninety days, boy, because our lien on the $1.9 million won't be valid if you go under too soon."

Despite my later unanswered calls to the president of the bank, the end of the story is that I retained my deep voice and didn't become a choir boy. Eventually, we did do a much-improved version of the deal that Roy had pushed, but every step of the way, the plan was fully disclosed to Bankers Trust and the other banks in the banking group. Months later, I was told that MBank had fired Roy. This story is important as an illustration of those violent, bizarre times in the last half of the 1980s when borrowers and lenders resorted to measures that were unthought of not so long ago. Regardless, I always tried to maintain consistent ethics, to block out all of the craziness around me, and to do what I thought was right and fair.

There's no doubt that the world of business can be a brutal one. But I firmly believe that to be successful in business, you need not claw your way to the top, taking advantage of people along the way. Since my early days as a rooming-house owner, I have always believed that people could be of the highest moral and ethical standards and still be successful.

In fact, I've come to believe strongly that being ethical, straightforward, and honest—a "good guy," if you will—is the best way to get ahead and be successful in business. When people can trust you, and you them, it promotes a continuing business relationship that can be profitable for both parties.

Difficult times put this "good ethics is good business" theory to the test. During the hardest times in the last half of the 1980s, I began to doubt my business philosophy. It is naturally harder to achieve your ideals in tough times than it is when your business is prospering. Tough times change many people. When even basically good people are pushed into a corner, many of them will lie, cheat, and steal—they'll do anything. In those times it seems easier to relax moral standards, to rationalize what is right and wrong or change your standards altogether to fit the current market conditions. In the long run, unethical behavior will catch up with you.

Desperate people will often justify reduced standards in a depressed market. Many real estate firms have stolen money from their good properties and partnerships to pump it into the bad properties or to use it to meet overhead expenses. When you can't make payroll and the money is there, held in trust for a different property, it's hard to avoid "just taking a little." But like a childhood fable, taking a little leads to more and more until the money is gone. It's stealing, pure and simple. In real estate and financial fields, particularly where numerous limited partnerships are involved, it is very easy to take money from one partnership and give to another. But there's no Robin Hood justification here. The result is an erosion of right and wrong that will eventually lead only to disaster.

I know a man in the Southeast who had been a sponsor of limited-partnership offerings for eighteen years when the downturn hit. He always seemed like an honest person. He always treated his investors fairly. He made a point of always disclosing his fees. But when times got tough he was emotionally drained. He saw his business and his life crumbling. He had some good partnerships and some bad ones. Owning a total of approximately six thousand apartment units, he had approximately fifty partnerships. A few of those partnerships had a lot of cash. The rest were losing money. He was dependent upon new business for cash flow, but with the market downturn and the tax-law change, that business dried up. His overhead was killing him. That's when he started to "borrow" from the good partnerships, which was not legally permissible.

After just six months, he had "borrowed" $800,000. But the problems were still there, and his situation got only worse. That borrowing, otherwise known as commingling of funds, compromised his ability to deal with the problem in an up-front manner. Now he had something worse than bad properties to hide from his investors and lenders. He fell into a trap that caught and killed many real estate firms that we, at the time, had looked into acquiring. He rationalized a way to solve a temporary problem, which was his demise. Most heartbreaking of all, in the end he had compromised his otherwise honorable career of eighteen years. Even more unfortunate is that his story was more the norm than an exception.

Through the worst of times in 1986, I am grateful to say that our properties and partnerships that were doing well prospered and those funds were never touched. Other properties, of course, did not do well and we lost some to foreclosure, but we didn't let the good suffer with the bad. Most importantly, we never had anything to hide from our investors, from the government, or from our lenders.

As my daughters were growing up, whenever they would come to me complaining about one thing or another, I used to tell them that "life isn't fair." Eventually, all I would have to say to them is the word "life," and they would respond in unison, sarcastically chiming in the "isn't fair."

They learned that it was one of my favorite sayings, and it is because it's true. The point is that "unfairness" is not a reasonable excuse for altering your values—whether it is on the schoolground or in the business arena. While in the short run I believe life often doesn't seem fair, in the longer run I truly believe there is a great sense of fairness.

When times got bad in the Southwest and we were in the midst of renegotiating debt because of the downturn, Congress threw us one more burden to tote: the first retroactive tax-law change in history. Of course, they came in 1986 and hit our business like a freight train in a time when we really didn't need to take another hit. While Congress was merely looking for revenues needed to bring the tax brackets down to 28 percent, from the perspective of a taxpayer who based multiyear investment commitments on tax laws in 1985 or earlier, it lacked morality and proper ethics to retroactively change the law.

I was then, and am now, in favor of a broader-based, simplified tax. But in the case of the 1986 tax reform, while the ideas and philosophies were right, the execution and transition were horrible. It all but destroyed many people in the real estate industry. In the end, the consumer of real estate product will pay with higher rent. No doubt, the main targets of the tax-law changes were real estate investments and individuals who had been taking large tax deductions through them. Those deductions translated into lower rents for apartment users. The new tax law all but eliminated the deductions claimed by real estate investors in limited partnerships by calling them passive losses and by requiring that they could only be used to offset "passive income." This, for the most part, eliminated our future business and put our present business in a much more precarious position.

The real "unfairness" of the tax law was its retroactive nature. In 1985, Hall Financial Group was the largest private-placement sponsor in the United States. Then in May 1986, while we were restructuring more than $1 billion in debt, we were faced with a wrongful retroactive tax-law change that might make $525 million in payments already committed by investors impossible to collect. Those investors depended on tax deductions for their partnership payments, which were allowed under the law when they invested, but in 1986 they were retroactive and phased out those deductions. This is a serious issue of government ethics. Fortunately the vast majority of our investors were very honorable and did make their payments, despite the reduced tax benefits. The new private-placement investment sales portion of our business was devastated and had to be cut back by more than 90 percent because of the retroactive change of the rules by the 1986 tax law.

Ethics and morality are more clearly discernible in black and white when there are stable rules. When the rules change, then our normal idea of who should be the winners and the losers becomes meaningless. For instance, a borrower who puts a 5 percent down payment on a property should be at a greater risk than, say, a borrower who puts down 35 percent. In a normal economic slowdown, you would expect that the borrower with the small down payment would be more likely to lose his property than the one with the larger down payment. But in an all-out depression, such as Texas has been experiencing, both borrowers in this hypothetical situation would probably be wiped out. Ironically, the borrower with only 5 percent down in many cases had a better chance of working out his problems with the lender (i.e., getting a lower interest rate and in effect "rebuying" the property). Why? The more equity involved in the loan, the more leverage the lender has against the borrower. The lender figures he might as well work with the person with only a little equity and at least get something new out of him. But with the heavy-equity or conservative borrower, the lender will more than likely take the hard line. He has the advantage. The lender can foreclose and resell, maybe even at a profit, if the borrower has put a lot of equity in the property. In other words, the borrower with more invested during a depressed market is a much bigger loser than the more highly leveraged borrower.

Many times during the depression we ran into the "pay or die mentality" of lenders. The phrase "pay or die" had double meaning for many of the lenders in the Southwest. They needed every penny they could get as fast as they could get it because they, too, were in trouble. They were strapped with bad debts from oil and gas loans of the early eighties, and from the larger commercial banks from Mexico and some Third World countries. Banks were cutting back their staffs just like real estate and oil companies were making cutbacks. Every employee knew that his or her future was on the line. In the end, a good workout or a bad one depends on the people who sit down at the table together. Individual personalities do come into play, as do perceptions. Is the borrower still alive and kicking? Roy, from MBank, obviously thought Hall Financial was down for the count. But he found out otherwise.

A nonrecourse loan versus a personal liability loan is another good example of life not being fair in tough times—this time for the lender. In a nonrecourse loan, the borrower has no personal liability. In real estate partnerships in which the debt is nonrecourse, many limited-partnership sponsors unethically take as much of the rents as they can for themselves, spend nothing on the properties, then just give the properties back to the lender in horrible condition. On the other hand, you would expect borrowers with personal liability to care more about the properties. But in a time of dramatic depression, you'll find these borrowers pulling many of the same stunts as those with nonrecourse debt. When times get tough enough, borrowers with personal liability will often fall back on the old "you can't squeeze blood from a turnip" line of thinking. Many of them are truly broke, but others transfer assets, send money out of the country, and resort to illegal action to appear broke to the lenders.

In the eighties depression, many general partners took advantage of their limited partners by grabbing all they could get for themselves and walking off the job. One firm on the West Coast negotiated to become a substitute general partner on seven hundred properties in a workout with several lenders. But instead of working on restructuring the debt, this firm took all of the income it could take from the properties and left nothing for the limited partners. The properties were eventually foreclosed, but not before this substitute general partner had stripped the rents for a few months and deferred all maintenance. You might ask why the limited partners wouldn't sue in such a situation. Well, some of them do, but litigation takes time and money, and a positive result can never be guaranteed. Moreover, suing general partners who are truly fraudulent usually fails because they have already hidden their assets from creditors. Even if you win, collecting is another matter.

I also found that in a depression some lenders, borrowers, and/or investors alike fall into asking themselves what they can get away with. With a lot of borrowers, investors, and lenders thinking this way, the only winners are the lawyers who litigate the lawsuits between them.

There was once an unwritten law that "you don't file a lawsuit against a bank—even if you are right." You would be committing commercial suicide, taking the chance that no other bank would ever lend you money again. In 1985 in Texas, no one with any business sense would have considered suing a bank or using bankruptcy as a legitimate business practice. But in the depression, like in anarchy, the rules change completely or disappear altogether. In the last half of the 1980s in Texas, lender liability suits were rampant. Friends and business associates sue each other as a matter of course. Everybody seems to take to stiffing everybody else and hiding behind litigation shields. It has become almost impossible to discern the legitimate lawsuits opposed to the smoke screens.

Suing a bank was a sin in 1985, yet it became the norm in 1987. In the 1990s, when we look back at 1986, 1987, 1988, and 1989, even a Chapter 7 personal bankruptcy—straight liquidation—will not carry the same disgrace it once did. People will sit around talking and ask, "Hey, B.J., did you go bankrupt?" The man of 1992 will probably answer, "Oh, yeah, I went bankrupt during the Texas depression in 1988." Not such a big deal, so did a lot of others. In a strange way, the bankruptcy of many highly respected, old-wealth citizens has made bankruptcy nearly down-right fashionable in these parts. The important question is, did the individual knowingly take unfair advantage of other people along the way? Was he a thief or, even in the worst of times, did he maintain his integrity? Values are sometimes moving targets.

When we sued anyone for anything, it was serious, and only after other options were exhausted. Lawsuits should be a last resort. If normal negotiations fail, then litigation sometimes is the only choice. We always preferred our proven route to success: lots of homework and an aboveboard straightforward approach. More lenders than one have told me they didn't like my honesty in the papers. I announced we had a problem. We didn't hide from it. My advice would have to be that when you are really in trouble and you know it, you have to stop paying people, communicate immediately, and hold on to whatever capital you can in order to settle or work out an agreement with them.

When it came to litigation, generally the only time we filed a lawsuit was after someone else had filed first, and then we did it only if we had a legitimate claim. We didn't sue FSLIC. They sued us. But we countersued very, very hard. It was consistent with the way we would have done business in 1983 or 1984 or any time. Most of the debt we fought over was nonrecourse debt. We could have legally walked away from those problems. However, thinking long-term, we were trying to save our investors and the property. What we were doing also helped to save the lenders, although many didn't realize it at the time. But that was far from the norm in the late 1980s in Texas. Most people came down to the view that what they should do was concentrate on the personal liability debt to avoid personal bankruptcy; who cared about anything else? It had become the era of everyone fending for themselves. Initially everybody would be pals, the deal was great, and then, as soon as the developer couldn't make the loan payments, he would file a lawsuit saying he had been duped into the deal by the lender. Some of the incidents were ludicrous. I know of one case where an investor in a development filed a lawsuit against the developer saying he hadn't been apprised of the value of the development coming into the deal. This investor's occupation was, you guessed it, real estate appraiser.

Transfers of assets to hidden accounts or trusts have become a favorite pastime for many, though far from all, debtors, the point being to get as much wealth out of your estate as possible so you have more than just a little nest egg to start over.

In Texas, a family's or single adult's home or place of business in the city, up to one acre, is considered a homestead and is exempt from the claims of most creditors. Outside of the city limits, the homestead can include up to two hundred acres for a family and one hundred acres for a single adult. The only claims that may be made against the homestead are those for the purchase money mortgage, taxes on the property, and improvements to the property.

In addition, Texas is liberal in the protection of personal property. However, there is a limit of $30,000 for families and $15,000 for single adults on the personal property that can be protected by the exemption law. The list of personal property that is protected includes home furnishings; family heirlooms; tools, books, and equipment used in a trade or profession; clothing; two firearms; sporting equipment; pets; an automobile and one other mode of transportation such as a truck, bicycle, motorcycle, or wagon, or, if so desired, two animals, which may be horses, colts, mules, or donkeys, with saddle and bridle; the cash value of a life insurance policy if it's more than two years old; and a burial plot. In the late 1980s many real estate people were buying either a Rolls-Royce or Mercedes, paying cash for an expensive home on one acre, and generally preparing themselves for maximum use of the modern interpretation of the homestead laws.

During the depression in Texas from 1986 through 1989, the term "Loan Committee" was a euphemism for a workout or restructuring committee. This was a fact at Resource Savings, where I was interim president and CEO from May to mid-November 1987. But this situation was certainly not unique to Resource. Throughout Texas financial institutions in those days, loan committees were simply not making loans. The credit wasn't there and financial institutions weren't able to find ways to put money into productive loans that made sense for both the borrower and the lender. Problems with liquidity plagued the entire financial system of Texas.

Typical loan-committee meetings began for us at Resource each Friday morning at 7:30. We would go over loan after loan that was having problems. As time passed, the loan problems actually became worse and worse. Workouts were into second- and third-round changes, and the problems became more and more difficult to solve. This was an entirely different environment from what I had experienced in my previous fourteen years as a lender. Being experienced as both a lender and borrower, I had a particularly unique perspective.

I wish I could say there were redeeming qualities in what we were doing in those committee meetings. Often we thought we had things worked out, then a new set of problems would come along. Sure, we had a few honorable, good borrowers, but the fact is that even most of the good borrowers had become so cornered that their sense of ethics and morality had deteriorated. The rule of the day for many was: We are out for what we can get.

Morality and ethics seemed to continually reach all-time new lows in Texas in the late eighties. We even had some elected officials and high-level federal appointees who were borrowers at Resource and had signed personal guarantees, but when it came time to pay, they were quick to point out how powerful they were and that no one should push them too far. We pursued collection in an evenhanded manner no matter who it was. Resource Savings also had many very friendly borrowers who had been around for a long time and whom I knew in the business community. They would come in and say all of the right words like, "I know we owe you money and we are going to pay and cooperate." But when it came to action, we would get a slow stall and finally, "Gee, you don't expect me to do all of that for you. What about my other creditors?" The bottom line was that some of the good ol' boys were friendly in words, but not in actions.

There was a particular irony for me. The $145 million that I had voluntarily contributed went to pay nonrecourse debts. I wanted to help my investors and lenders; I thought it was the right thing to do. Then in the loan meetings at Resource Savings, I would listen to people tell me that they wouldn't pay their personal liability obligation to our federally insured financial institution because, gosh, if they did, they would have less money to spend on personal needs and to pay their other creditors. That logic didn't go over too well with me.

As an owner of banks and savings and loans in Texas, I realized that the whole industry was broke. The numbers showed that we were all really working for FSLIC or the FDIC. I accepted that with the spirit of challenge in wanting to do the best we could for them. Lenders had to become resigned to walk through the restructuring process, hopefully without any more legal cost than necessary and with the best economic benefit to FSLIC and the FDIC possible. The bottom line in the majority of cases was that contracts could never be fully and effectively enforced by the courts. Moreover, most of the savings and loan borrowers had no personal liability on their commercial real estate loans. Instead both borrower and lender depended solely on the real estate cash flow and value for repayment. In most cases, good faith between parties had just disappeared. In my morning loan-committee meetings, I often found myself thinking about the sadness I felt seeing the mainstream of humanity at its worst. It was financial anarchy. Our job as self-respecting, caring lenders was to maximize the ultimate financial recovery and do everything possible to minimize the costs that would be borne by the taxpayers. We knew that in time the government would take us over, but until then we'd work as hard as we could to collect the loans.

What is good, moral behavior for a debtor? What is good, moral behavior for a lender? Is it moral to stick to the letter of the contract and do nothing more or less than you have to? In "good times" it might seem easy to answer most of the above questions. Some standards do change with economic times, but basic honesty should never be compromised. You have to look carefully at your various fiduciary duties and responsibilities and moral obligations to different parties—lenders and investors—as well as look at legal obligations. But legal boundaries and what you can "get away with" ought not to become the morally acceptable standard. Step back and take an overall look at fairness to all parties. Keep relationships in mind—and a sense of human decency. It is always critical to keep full disclosure, openness, and honesty as paramount concerns.

Taking money from properties and giving it to investors is fine—if it is legal under the structure of the partnership, if it's properly disclosed to the lender, and if the parties involved agree that's a fair way to go. At the very least, you must be on sound legal and moral grounds. However, taking the money without proper disclosure or taking the money for your own account without disclosing it in an open manner is unfair and would certainly jeopardize future negotiations. It is important to try to do the best you can for yourself in terms of business results, but it is important to always be honest and open about it. It's one thing to win a legal battle and to fight hard, but quite another to do so by lying, cheating, or stealing.

The whole legal system becomes a bigger player during a depression. Lenders and borrowers alike spend huge sums on lawyers and litigation to protect their various interests and to attack each other's interests. Lawyers are like a massive invasion of ants fighting to get control of an anthill. Perhaps the difference is that at least the ants are doing something positive. Unfortunately for both lenders and borrowers, the cost of this legal procedural garbage produces no added net income to the property, pays no interest on a loan, and provides no productive benefit to anyone—except perhaps to the lawyers. Litigation has just become a necessary part of the game. The one profession that does well in this mess is the lawyers—that is, if they can collect from their clients. Although we never gave any indication that the several law firms with which we were doing business would have any problem collecting from us, one of them lost faith.

Our primary law firm in the restructuring began to look totally differently at us as a client during our roughest of times in 1986 and 1987. There was no question in my mind that they believed that we would end up in bankruptcy. I truly think that if you had asked the executive committee of the firm to rate on a scale of one to ten whether or not their big, long-time client Hall would end up in bankruptcy, with ten being the most likely, all of the members except Bill Sechrest, who worked most closely with us, would have voted a nine or a ten. Bill would have given us a one or a two. That's because Bill always believed we would figure a way out. He knew my commitment to it, and he was creative and committed to it, too. Plus, he is an optimist himself.

At the eleventh hour, when we were in the thick of negotiations with the government and many other commercial lenders, MBank, as a result of Roy's new ideas, told the law firm that their work with us was in conflict with work they did for the bank. He asked them to resign with the not-so-subtle threat that they would lose MBank's business if they did not. This was strictly a power play by Roy to hurt us in the negotiation, even though this law firm had always done work for us and for the bank. This law firm introduced me to the bank. The bank didn't find the business in conflict then. And Roy didn't just ask our law firm to resign on this particular case but on all of my commercial bank transactions. Unbelievably, the firm obliged. We were at the most sensitive time of the negotiations with all the commercial banks when our law firm quit on us. The law firm to which we had just paid millions of dollars apparently thought MBank was a bigger client with more promise. Ironically, MBank ended up broke a couple of years later and we didn't.

Adding to the problems in the 1986–1989 period was the fact that bankruptcy laws were for the most part rewritten in 1984, and all of the regulations were being tried and tested in the courts during this little economic hell we called a depression. From early on, the lawyers and court were testing out new ground.

There is no such thing as justice per se, only justice "under the law." Decisions come from people, not machines, and they are not the same every time. We found that out the hard way during our lawsuit with the U.S. government. After winning a decision in a Texas court, we took the same argument on the road to Colorado to face a different judge with a different way of thinking. It didn't help matters to be armed with a long-haired lawyer against a judge who looked right out of *GQ*. It drives home the point that you are just dealing with people, and they are each going to be different. Personalities are always going to come into play. Without question, though, even with all of its imperfections, we're lucky to have our justice system in this country. I believe it is a lot better than any other.

The following are my suggested ideas to use as a blueprint for business ethics in tough times. These are ideas that I believe are sound, good business philosophies. I try to live by them, Hall Financial Group tries to live by them, and they've helped us come through most difficult times.

1. **Fight hard, but remember thou shalt not lie, cheat, or steal.** These ancient principles from the Bible hold true today. I think the fact that our company followed this philosophy closely is the key to our successful workouts. It's important to fight hard for what is fair, just, and equitable—even if people may disagree. But so many people in a tight spot do lie, cheat, or steal their way out of it. It becomes commonplace, but it never becomes right. In the long run, people who want to come back again to borrow another day or do business in any respect will find that dishonesty works against them.

2. **Take a long view.** Don't look for the short-term benefit. Instead, look at relationships. Believe me, it is truly a small world. What we do today will come back either to help or to haunt us in the future. Look at the long-term business picture and take actions with the long view in mind rather than a short-term quick fix. Five and ten years from now where will you be? Is it important to take advantage of someone at this moment in time just to try to save a few dollars and risk a lifetime of reputation and opportunity? Obviously, the answer is no. My business has proven to me time and again that hardworking, honest actions are not in conflict with being aggressive and tough. It is not a sign of weakness to be fair and decent.

3. **Don't compromise values.** You are always better off to lose assets than to compromise personal values. Personal values and doing what is right versus wrong transcend the importance of any property. Anyone who compromises values begins to deteriorate and lose his or her sense of self-worth.

4. **Be honest with yourself, and others will always help you win.** Take a realistic look at yourself and be honest and open about your problems with others. Doing so is certainly a risk. It is no fun to strip your problems naked to the world, to admit you are not perfect and do have problems, but especially in volatile times, everyone has problems. Those who are willing to stand up and act in a fair, open, and honest manner will win.

5. **Never ignore something that's broken.** Fix things you see that are broken. Very simply, it seems that many people, in an effort to be what I call a Pollyanna optimist, just plain try to ignore

reality. No one should ever get so obsessed with trying to act positive in bad times that they ignore or walk over problems. We should find out what the problems are and fix them.

In short, being straightforward and a ''good guy'' doesn't mean you can't fight hard and be tough. Most of all, being honorable not only gives you a good feeling when you look in the mirror, but it is also, in the long run, good, solid business.

C H A P T E R 1 3
THERE IS NO FINISH LINE!

NO ONE RINGS THE BELL when a depression starts, and no one will ring a bell when it is over. The first lesson of surviving is to keep hanging on. It is critical to keep on keeping on and to keep the faith that things will and have to get better. Even when things do start to get better, there is not a simple cutoff between problems and good times. Depressions simply don't have fairy-tale endings.

While many real estate markets were still declining in 1989 as the overbuilding and tax-law changes continued to affect areas throughout the country, a very important exception was Texas. Texas was clearly beginning to move forward in a positive direction even though it wasn't widely known in the media. The year 1989 brought many signs that things were getting better, yet many loose ends remained from the troubling times that had passed. It will be well into the 1990s before things sort out in Texas, but it is clearly going in the right direction.

In 1989, operations in our apartments steadily improved. While all types of real estate did not improve to the same degree, we could see the turnaround had a firm footing in the real estate markets in general throughout Texas. But even as those markets were turning upward, the markets in Phoenix and other areas, where we had large concentrations of apartments, were still getting worse. The real turnaround and recovery in the market would begin in the various areas at different times. The key from our standpoint was to take advantage of all the opportunities we could and manage the process rather than having it manage us.

Relatively early in the Bush Administration, the President focused on the mounting problems of the savings and loan industry. Although I don't entirely agree with all of the plans in this area, I admire and commend the President and his Administration for their leadership and decisive actions. As the precursor to the final law, when the President made the plan public in February, the FDIC was ordered to take control of all insolvent savings and loans. That meant a virtual nationalizing of those savings and loans that had been successful enough to withstand the several earlier waves of insolvency. For me, this meant that Resource Savings would come under the control of the FDIC. That brought the overall savings and loan crisis home to me in a very personal manner. Although I would still own Resource, it would be controlled by the FDIC; eventually it would be put through receivership, and I would lose my ownership.

Resource Savings Association held $675 million in assets and had been very profitable during 1983 and 1984. In 1985, it made a modest profit, and by 1986, the losses began and increased substantially in 1987 and 1988. Like practically the entire savings and loan industry in Texas, Resource had finally failed. At one point the book value of my 100 percent ownership in Resource was $22 million; now I would lose it all. It failed because of bad loans that were backed by collateral that had declined in value anywhere from 30 to 70 percent. Resource, like so many other savings and loans with commercial loans, was overwhelmed by the deflation. While we were solvent longer than most, eventually we couldn't fight the pressure of loan problems either.

In February 1989, we knew after the President's speech that Resource would be taken into conservatorship. Beth Mooney, the president of Resource, and I were determined that our transition of control would be the best in the history of the FDIC. Like the officers in charge of the bridge over the River Kwai, we drove our employees hard during the weeks and months that preceded the conservatorship to prepare several large binders of information for the FDIC. We wanted the representatives assigned from the FDIC to find an orderly, organized institution that was willing to cooperate in every manner possible.

On April 6, coincidentally while I was out of town, the FDIC did, in fact, come into and take control of Resource. Unfortunately, it was a far more traumatic event than we had anticipated. In what apparently was an instruction-book methodology of showing force, the FDIC representative displaced key officers, abruptly having them move from their offices to smaller quarters with only a few hours' deadline. Unfortunately, within a short time of the arrival of FDIC personnel, the damage to morale was substantial.

The majority of individuals representing the FDIC in Resource were very logical, fine people to work with as individuals. One or two seemed to take advantage of the opportunity to be in a powerful position, especially at the beginning of the transition period. Initially there was a certain amount of unnecessary force and resulting frustration, especially given the good order and thorough preparation that Resource had exhibited. In time, the situation quieted down and smoothed over. I think the problem stemmed from the systemic reality of the scope of the problem, the sense of urgency to correct it, and the lack of time for firm management direction.

The Bush plan, entitled the Financial Institutions Reform, Recovery, and Enforcement Act of 1989 (FIRREA) was aimed at appropriating money and forming the Resolution Trust Company (RTC) to take over and resell or liquidate the failed savings and loans and their assets. Tax-paying citizens will have to pay 70 percent of the cost. It has been estimated this will be from $600 to $1,000 for every man, woman, and child in the United States. The size of the problem keeps escalating. Current estimates go as high as $900 billion, but most are in the range of $500 billion. It is staggering.

The RTC has retained the FDIC and its current staffing to manage the program of liquidating the assets under control of the RTC. To put the immensity of this task in perspective, it is interesting to consider that the FDIC in their fifty-six-year history has handled a total of $144 billion of assets. Just prior to the FDIC involvement in the savings and loan crisis, they were handling $9.9 billion of current asset problems. The FDIC was created as a result of the Great Depression in the 1930s. Today's problem is fifty times or even greater the size of what the FDIC was handling just prior to its involvement in this crisis and three times or greater the size of the $144 billion of assets it has handled in its fifty-six-year history. The problem is awesome. It is going to create some great transfers of wealth and some interesting opportunities. The positive side of this (and it is substantial) will be discussed more in Chapters 16 and 17.

Politically it has been appealing to suggest that heavy blame goes to criminals and frauds who ran many savings and loans. There is no doubt that fraud (including self-dealing in loans and other conflicts and abuses) has played a significant role in the savings and loan crisis. But think about it: If fraud were so rampant for such a long period of time, the question must be asked, "Where were the federal regulators?"

In 1986, Congress and President Reagan passed a tax law that essentially drove capital out of real estate and retroactively changed the law, causing defaults on many existing agreements. At the time this happened, I knew real estate, the financial system (savings and loans and banks), and ultimately the renters were in for a huge and unmerciful adjustment. The adjustment is far from over. In hindsight, I had no idea how bad bad could be. The fact is, on a nationwide basis, the impact of the lack of some type of tax benefits in real estate has been felt everywhere. Many people who pre-1986 used to state that they were only interested in economic, non–tax-oriented real estate really didn't realize that the long-standing tax aspects of real estate have been a vital part of value for years. In my twenty-one years of doing real estate transactions through numerous congressional tax changes, there were always some major tax components in the structure of real estate—that is, until the 1986 law which, through its complicated rules, essentially allows only so-called passive real estate losses to be used against passive income. After 1988, a major long-standing key component of real estate was virtually eliminated, and the resulting effects on declining values, defaults, foreclosures, and bankruptcies were a major part of the savings and loan crisis. The negative costs to the country in many economic and social ways and the disruption to people's lives caused by the tax-law change are massive and to date highly underestimated. The restoration of some tax benefits should be instituted by Congress to help resolve the current savings and loan overhang of assets and to stop the current deflationary free-fall in many U.S. markets. While Texas was the first and probably most severe, there is no need for other regions to suffer if constructive actions can help avoid the severity of the problems.

It is unrealistic to suggest that the tax-law change is the singular nature of the problem. We were in the midst of one of the biggest deflationary crashes and depressions in the history of the country—certainly since the 1930s and, maybe, even including the 1930s, in real estate values in Texas and the Southwest. Yet, strangely enough, that and a true understanding of the impact of the tax-law changes have been missing in all of the political finger-pointing rhetoric. The obvious fact that real estate values have declined from 50 percent to as much as 90 percent is a phenomenon that people should be but aren't talking about as the real reason for the collapse of the savings and loans. "What caused it? Why did it happen? How do we best handle it?" These are questions that should be discussed, but rarely are they even brought up. The true public policy issues regarding the savings and loan crisis have been all too often overshadowed by double-talk and rhetoric and placing blame.

All in all, there were a lot of problems and a lot of complexities that have caused the real estate depression and the savings and loan crisis. At this point, that's history. What we need now are solutions to this complex economic circumstance. We need business and government to work closely together to minimize the further damage. Business needs to be a constructive helping partner, or otherwise the final result is that taxpayers end up even more shortchanged than they already are going to be. The President's plan is the right starting point and we all should support it and help make it work. Just like with the problems Hall Financial and I have suffered, there won't be a bell that goes off and says the President's plan worked and the crisis is over. It's a process that will take time, but with hope it is going in the right direction.

Meanwhile, during this same time period, I, of course, had hoped that Paul Bilzerian would pay us the more than $40 million we were owed. What a difference that one transaction would have made. Not only was it very disheartening to not have the money we were promised, but to have been taken advantage of so badly at such a critical time was a real blow to my spirits. I had taken a risk and trusted the wrong person, but then so had Boone Pickens, Ed DeBartolo, Arthur G. Cohen, and Alex Spanos. In a funny kind of hard-to-explain way I still liked and felt sorry for Paul. He is a genius with a lot of problems, most of which he seems to have inadvertently brought on himself. Unfortunately for us, we had no choice but to carry on with litigation until we got a judgment or a reasonable settlement.

Litigation with Paul Bilzerian wasn't the only type of lawsuit in 1989. We also experienced a few investor lawsuits. The first one, with publicity attached, was filed by a family from Arizona. This was not only a surprise but also a personal disappointment, because the lawyer-accountant who made the investments and ran the family business had met with me in November 1988 seeking a payment plan for their delinquent note installments. While I offered to help and he pretended to be trying to "work together," he was secretly planning a major lawsuit in an attempt to push us to release his family from their debt payments.

The family lawsuit was filed in a sensational manner with lots of attendant publicity. An interesting thing about lawsuits is that they can be given to newspapers and used like a press release. The lawyer writing them and the client filing the lawsuit generally cannot be held accountable for libel or slander because they are protected by the fact that the statements in the lawsuit are allegations and generally protected under the law. People often use this to their advantage and engage in name-calling and strong sensational statements to get publicity.

Lawsuits, unfortunately, increased dramatically after the 1986 crash. Historically, our company never had many lawsuits, but after the 1986 real estate deflationary depression started, lawsuits increased geometrically. During the 1986 through 1989 period, Hall Financial Group and the partnerships had anywhere from three hundred to four hundred active lawsuits at any given time. The lawsuits varied considerably but were all characteristically a very unproductive activity and something that tended to drain management time, cost money, and rarely produced a good business-like solution for either side. In fact, during the unique period of the crash, we had more lawsuits than our entire previous eighteen years in business. Through hard work, careful management, and some luck, we were able to successfully resolve most of the lawsuits in a fairly short time and get things back to normal for the 1990s.

We attempted to settle lawsuits when appropriate, while being totally unyielding when a matter of principle was involved. Sometimes those settlements became difficult negotiations and were in some ways downright amusing. I had a conflict with a couple of co-general partners who, when times got rough, didn't put any money into the properties. In fact, during the six years that we have been general partners together, I had put in $3,800,000 to save the partnership and they had put in zero. We were in a lawsuit which I wanted to settle and they wanted to settle, but after extensive negotiations we were $50,000 apart. I had been willing to buy their interest out of the partnership for $1,200,000 and they wanted $1,250,000.

Since they were both Jewish and I am Jewish by background, I thought of a creative solution. I proposed to them two alternatives in the final negotiation. I suggested that they could take $1,225,000 and that would be a compromise for both of us. Alternatively, my creative suggestion was that I would pay the full $1,250,000 that they requested, but only $1,200,000 to them. The additional $50,000 would be paid to Jewish causes, and it would be on our mutual behalf. I suggested this could be a way that we could each do a *mitzvah* (a Hebrew word for "good deed") and, so to speak, give $50,000 to Godly causes. I was certain they would accept this second alternative, and while it cost me more, I felt it would be the best resolution for the dispute. After a lengthy negotiation by phone, I made this proposal to break the log jam, and there was a silence on the other end.

Finally the partner with whom I had been negotiating stammered and, in a very nervous, quick manner, said, "Well, Craig, that's very creative . . ." and then he asked if he could think about the alternatives and call me back in ten minutes. I assume that during those ten minutes he probably called his partner (the other individual in the lawsuit). I received the call back after almost exactly a ten-minute interval. Much to my surprise, the answer was that Godly acts would have to wait; they wanted the $1,225,000. So much for our $50,000 donation to Jewish causes.

Litigation in the depressed economy is one way that people can put off problems. By filing lawsuits and entangling business disputes with the courts' already overcrowded dockets, many people put off payments that they know are legitimately owed. The lawsuits are directly related to the economy and over time as the economy gets better, more lawsuits will be resolved and fewer new ones filed. While our society is, unfortunately, highly litigious, the depression times certainly multiply that business problem.

There is never a real "finish line" in the race of business or of getting through depression times. The hard struggles and the positive upswings keep the challenge in the game. One of the strange things about economically rocky times is that they get better almost without warning but not overnight and not all at once. Just when we were used to things not going well, we found, if we kept trying, things got better.

In addition to its various battles and setbacks, 1989 began a process of the true rebuilding of our company. We started acquiring real estate again and put together some of the most exceptional acquisitions in our entire history. While others in the market were basically stagnant, we started to quietly move forward. Unproductive complaining about the "unfairness" of the market certainly doesn't get the job done. Chaos and difficulties provide for great opportunities. There truly is a flip side to the tough times if you can persevere and survive.

In 1989, we acquired apartments based on prices that were one-third to one-half of their replacement cost (what it would cost to build the same property today). Currently these properties produce between an 8 and a 9 percent yield without any mortgage. We have been financing these with out-of-state life insurance companies and credit companies. There are no easy deals and there is virtually no local liquidity. But for those people who see the future and want to be resourceful about taking advantage of it, there are opportunities and ways to get capital to move forward. The way to get capital is to work hard at exposing lenders and investors to the benefits of Texas in general and individual opportunities in particular. If you work at it, success is very attainable.

We have had a whole series of successful acquisitions, including apartments, manufactured housing communities, and unique first-class parcels of land. One of our acquisitions in 1989 was a large industrial park that Xerox had developed. Not only did we acquire the entire industrial park, but we have been successfully and profitably selling parcels of it.

As a company, in 1989 we had our overhead at one of the lowest levels in years. At the same time, we started to carefully attract some of the strongest senior-level talent that we have ever known to be available in the marketplace. We have added several new key positions to the company and we're increasing our strength and ability to produce favorable results for our clients. With the addition of experts in certain areas such as land, we are increasing our ability to find and put together specialized investment opportunities of the highest caliber for investors. As real estate investment managers, it is important that we first build a base and then start to expand into new capital markets. Our base building included proving our ability to acquire outstanding real estate opportunities.

One of the most important elements that we have put into effect in 1989 is a renewal of our research and development efforts. We have research and statistics on every market area in great detail. Our attention to detail and demographics of each market is part of the strength of our new acquisition program. We began to expand our acquisition staff and, more important, while being entrepreneurial, we at the same time were being very prudent, cautious, and thorough in our approach.

Another important ingredient that has kept us in business is our property management. By 1989, we had initiated a program requiring all of the senior and middle managers of the corporate office to see at least two properties per week. I, personally, have been averaging more than six per week. What I have seen has amazed me. Our property management is absolutely terrific. We outperform every market area. Our specialty has been apartment management, and in that area I don't believe anyone is better.

We make mistakes and property management sometimes slips up, but now with the eyes and ears of fifty or so people from the corporate office walking around at least two properties per week throughout the country, an added sense of management's presence and interest is taking place. At the company meetings and throughout the field, we feel and see a company that is better in its performance and its management than it has ever been in its twenty-one preceding years. A positive feeling about our future comes from knowing that we can add value to our company and properties through superior management. Our intent is to keep our management at a very controlled level, managing primarily for larger clients with whom we have a long-term relationship.

As we look forward to the future, our capital needs are substantial. We see tremendous opportunities in the recycling of government-controlled real estate back into the private sector. We hope to be a major participant in helping the government as it sells foreclosed real estate and seeks private ownership sources. The future in real estate, we believe, is heavily oriented toward the large institutional investor, particularly pension funds. We will still work with a select number of sophisticated individual investors, but pension funds will be a major key to the future.

Looking back at the depression of the eighties from a personal standpoint, I feel that individually I have grown a great deal. From a company standpoint, we have also grown a great deal. There is no doubt that we suffered a huge, temporary financial setback, but that pales in comparison to the inner peace and perspective we gained. The experience that we have obtained and the self-confidence that we have gained are invaluable. The depression was truly a building period, and in many respects the last few years have been the most successful in the company's history and of my career. It takes far more skill and internal strength to save a company and not to give up than it does to ride the wave of a good, up market.

As I said earlier, there is no bell that rings to say that a depression is over. No one ends depressed times with a happy ending. With perseverance, even the seemingly impossible can be accomplished. A greater sense of appreciation and gratitude for what we have in this country comes about from the perspective of having lived through a depression. A lot of hard work and one-at-a-time successes are what a true turnaround is all about.

PART FIVE

REBUILDING THE FUTURE

CHAPTER 14
PERSONAL LESSONS

DURING MOST OF 1986, my life was a nightmare. In 1987, 1988, and 1989, times were still very tough, but they could never compare to the pain I endured in 1986. Many nights I would drop into bed at 1:00 A.M., exhausted from another full day with bankers only to wake up at 3:00 A.M. drenched in my own sweat, having relived the events of the day in my dreams and nightmares. Welcome to the Sleepless Nights Club. Certainly I'm not the only member, but in the worst of the late eighties, I felt like president, CEO, and chairman of the board of that club.

The number-one characteristic for membership into this dread club is depression. Usually when people think of depression, they think of being lethargic and sleeping too much. With me, and I now understand with many others, the opposite was true. It was like I couldn't shut off my mind even though I surely wanted to. I was always thinking about the problems and my responsibilities. I couldn't stop thinking about them— even during my little bits of sleep. We at Hall Financial were fighting for the company's survival, but most of all, we always knew that ten thousand investors were depending on us—they were the greatest weight of all. When I personally look someone in the eye and promise I'll do something, then with everything in my heart and soul, I aim to deliver. On the vast majority of our partnership debts I had no personal liability. It was as if I had personally looked each of those ten thousand investors in the eye and made them a promise we'd always do our best to protect their interests and we couldn't let them down. We had to do everything possible. Even though we couldn't be perfect and save every property, we had to save the whole of the situation.

I really believe that business is not a game of how much money you can make at other people's expense, but rather an art form of combining one person's business needs with another's business strengths for a common good—and, of course, an important result is profit. We wanted to see our deals make it to fruition, achieve that art form, not only Hall Financial Group, but more importantly, for our many investors who would reap the rewards. I couldn't bear the idea of seeing any of that destroyed.

Although we did everything we could to stay positive through the battle, that became an increasingly difficult task. I often made the situation worse than it had to be by being too hard on myself, which I still do. I would get angry with myself for not being able to handle the pressure better, kicking myself for being weak when I let things get to me. I really tried to be strong in front of people, but not being one to put on airs, the depression or anger usually showed through. Generally, my weaknesses, anger, and depression came through with the same degree of passion as did my strengths, happiness, and joy in better times. During this time, my associates and staff had enormous patience with me. For the patience and support my associates and staff have given me, I will be grateful always. I know I was not always a barrel of fun to be around. Looking back, I know I was dealing with real difficulties and real fears that I could not completely control. Perhaps sharing my emotional experience in this chapter and the lessons I learned will give someone else suffering similar depression the insight I needed so desperately.

My close friend and jogging partner, Marty Cohen, is also my medical doctor. In 1986, he became more and more concerned about my deteriorating health. He knew about my membership in the Sleepless Nights Club, and he became convinced that sleeping pills might bring me some relief. While I've never been too keen on medication—given my experience with phenobarbital as a child—I have to admit, the sleeping pills he prescribed were certainly the right thing for a period of time. I didn't take them every night, but would try to take them at least two or three nights a week so that I could at least regenerate my body. They worked like a charm for a while. I would sleep a full eight or more hours—only to wake up and find all of my problems still there. Needless to say, my body required the sleep. I learned that the pills were not the answer to my depression or my very real business problems, so after using the pills for a few months, I was able to replace their use with my jogging and learned to better compartmentalize and separate my problems.

During the worst of my depression, Marty suggested antidepressants. I tried them and, though they may work for some, they made me wacky. They were completely wrong for me. So next I tried a psychiatrist. After an hour or so in my first session, the doctor told me something that I now know to be very true. He said that it was okay to be depressed. I had real problems, not the kinds of problems that people normally take antidepressants for. My problems needed to have me, with all of my faculties, working hard to solve them. His simple words meant a lot to me. It is okay to be depressed, but I had to focus on solving my problems. He was very reassuring, and he suggested that if he were me, he wouldn't have time to see a shrink. He thought I should muster all the time I could to work out the problems. Most important right then, he said that I shouldn't waste time worrying about being depressed. That short time in his office helped me put things into perspective one more time. He agreed that the sleeping pills had been a good idea for the short term to help me ease out of the Sleepless Night Club and get back to work refreshed. It was a lot of advice for one visit and it served me well.

Later in 1988, my friend Rabbi Mendel Dubrawsky shared some more of his faith with me, and this same point would ring true again. He explained that his Chassidic Orthodox Jewish sect didn't tolerate depression. He said he accepted the reality of depression, but believed that it should be put in its place. In a sense, take a little bit of time to be depressed, then kick yourself in the tail, pick yourself up, and get back to working on the problems causing your depression. I realized, after all of my depression in 1986, 1987, and some in 1988, that depression needs to be controlled, that it is not a productive outlet. In order to deal with the real problems that tough times bring, you must first of all get yourself in a mental and physical condition to do so.

In addition to solving day-to-day problems during our hard times, I struggled more and more with the bigger questions in my life. In times of difficulty, people typically turn to their faith, searching, hoping for religion to bolster their inner strength. In my own case, I was born of a Jewish Orthodox father and a Catholic mother and, for a while, I was raised Episcopalian. As an adult, I ended up a very religious and spiritual person, taking the standards and values of my various backgrounds, but I've remained unassociated with any specific religion. I've always seemed to have a Protestant work ethic and have philosophically held a concern for the life-long struggles of the Jewish people.

I began to study the Talmud, the book of Jewish laws, during my most difficult times. I also pursued other religious readings, and one of my strongest interests was in the Book of Job. A friend of mine, a black Baptist minister, recommended I read about Job, who went through multitudes of tests. After these tests, Job's life would return to normal as his faith transcended the struggles between God and the Devil. I have a deep belief in the righteousness of God, in honesty and the value of life, and in my country. I believe in this economic system that helped me and so many others to prosper, and I have always had faith in myself. I guess it all comes down to believing in who you are and in what you are doing.

That faith may be sorely tested, but it must be preserved if you are to succeed.

I've always thought that if I didn't believe in honesty and in our democratic system, then there were a lot of easier ways to make money. But money is not my sole drive. I believe instead that doing business with quality, integrity, and according to the rules of the system—not doing what you can get away with—in the end pays untold dividends. When other real estate investors who owned savings and loans were being threatened with FBI prosecution, I never had anything to fear. I never had anything to hide. Honesty is an innate strength.

When a business battle escalates to crisis proportions, remember that you are no longer handling just another problem. You cannot expect to deal successfully with a major crisis by reacting to the problems in an everyday way. Tough economic times are like a war, and it is important to treat them as such. Define your enemy; know your true allies. Clearly establish your goals—both short and long range—and follow strategies that will inexorably move you toward those goals. Remember, war is not a normal condition, so be prepared for new rules and a different way of life, at least for a while.

This does not mean you have to sacrifice your own integrity or honesty. What you believe in must remain constant. What it does mean is pulling off the kid gloves and being prepared to fight harder than ever before. You may have considered yourself a hard worker, but in a real crisis, you'll find yourself giving up many pleasures you normally would have taken for granted. A fight for economic survival is not just another business deal that can neatly be separated from your personal or family life. This kind of war quickly engulfs every aspect of your life. Take it on with total commitment, or don't take it on at all.

The following are some of my personal lessons that applied to my struggles in our company's tough times. This is some of what I learned in my war:

LESSON I: STAY IN THE GAME—DON'T EVER QUIT

Stay in the fight and never quit. Never let your strength or determination dissipate to the point where you cannot rethink, regroup, and regenerate renewed power to fight again another day.

Don't quit. It is very easy to say, but much harder to do. Still, the most important principle for winning in business, or in your personal life, and the best piece of advice I can give from my experience is: Do not give up. Keep on working. Keep on keeping on. If you have to try a thousand different solutions, try them. Then try another one.

To win at anything, one must first and foremost survive. You have to be there to become a winner. In business, politics, and life in general there is a very fine line between winning and losing. In my own case, it would have been so easy many times just to quit and to rationalize that as the best thing to do. I could have become a loser easily. But I wasn't, and I think the main reason I wasn't is because I was just too stubborn ever to let events overcome me and then rationalize my failings. I couldn't make excuses to myself and I don't believe in quitting.

LESSON 2: NO MAN IS AN ISLAND—FAMILY IS WHAT COUNTS!

The stresses of the times were a great added burden on MaryAnna's and my marriage. Marriage in today's society, especially with people as intensely active as I am, is a complex institution with many ups and downs. Financially tough times are often hard on marriages. As this book is being published, MaryAnna and I are in the process of a divorce. It is sad, frustrating, and a heavy price to pay for the stresses of the tough years we went through. MaryAnna is a great lady and will hold a special place in my heart.

My children range widely in ages, and they took the problems on in different ways. The difficulties certainly affected our whole family. My youngest daughter, who was then six, would come to visit me at the office. The older girls used to call me from time to time during the day to see how I was doing. They were each concerned about the business but, more important, concerned about me. Each of our daughters has always worked while she was in school, but somehow my oldest daughter became convinced that she could no longer go to college because of all of our financial problems. It took a lot of talking to convince her not to quit school and work full time. All of the children took the newspaper coverage more personally than I did. Every untrue statement used to drive the whole family up the wall. Sometimes it made me feel frustrated to hear them complain about reporters, but it always made me grateful and proud to know that they were with me in spirit. Today I am closer to my children than ever before in my life and it feels great.

As I approached my thirty-sixth birthday, it was perhaps the lowest, most depressed time of my life. I felt like the weight of ten thousand investors and many other businesses that depended upon the continued operation of our company was squarely on my shoulders. While certainly I couldn't save things alone, I needed to be the one who was the leader and provided the sense of direction. I knew that we were blessed with many fine, talented people in our organization. The question was whether or not I could do my part and successfully lead them through the many difficulties that we were facing. Around this time, my secretary was receiving requests from people wanting to organize a surprise birthday party. MaryAnna suggested that I probably wouldn't want any gifts from people, and so she came up with the idea of having people just write me a letter expressing their feelings and support. I have always been a real people person and I like to get to know and to hear from people. Her idea began with employees and mushroomed into our investors and even people totally outside of the Hall family writing their support for what we at Hall Financial were trying to accomplish. It was an overwhelming outpouring of hundreds of letters that helped to keep my confidence and positive outlook going.

LESSON 3: IF YOU DON'T FEEL SORRY FOR YOURSELF, THEN YOU AREN'T HUMAN

Like most people who are high achievers, I am a mixture of extremes that can be both bad and good. I am a perfectionist and, without a doubt, my own biggest critic. It's fine to be critical and tough on yourself, but everything has its limits. On any given day during my crisis, I would blame myself for all of the problems, even though I knew rationally that the major problem, the market condition, was beyond my control. I was always particularly critical of how I was handling each problem—while focusing on one, I was worried about the other lacking my attention. I expected myself to be perfect. We all need to be realistic as to our limitations and abilities. At times, I certainly was not.

At the opposite extreme, I spent an awful lot of time simply feeling sorry for myself and not practicing that rule I'd so often preached to my daughters about life not being fair. As each unfair thing would happen to me, and another and then another, I felt as if I was participating in some giant experiment in human endurance. The pressures were immense and I confess to practicing a great deal of self-pity as a result. Over time, my attitude about feeling sorry for myself changed.

Everything changed when I came to realize that feeling sorry for myself was just a perfectly natural, normal human reaction. It suddenly hit me that I was really no different than anyone else. I wasn't the target of some personal cosmic disaster, I was simply hurting like a million other people who got bumped and bruised as they made their way through life, doing the best they could.

This new perspective didn't really solve any of my business problems, but it did allow me to live with and understand feeling sorry for myself. My ups and downs continued to be a kind of a self-healing process. Instead of wallowing in self-pity, which used to make me feel weaker and weaker, I developed an ability to think of all the people who had worked their way through even tougher situations, and somehow I experienced a regeneration that helped me stay in the fight. I felt lucky to be alive and to have the ability to face whatever anyone wanted to confront me with. We are all lucky to be alive and should never forget it.

LESSON 4: EXPECT THE UNEXPECTED IN TERMS OF WHOM YOU CAN AND CANNOT COUNT ON FOR SUPPORT

Perhaps one of the most difficult lessons that I learned was that all friends can't be counted on to stand with you. As I have said before, tough times do strange things to people; some of my friends began to distance themselves from me as my problems became public. Perhaps they were hoping the same fate would not befall them. It's almost funny looking back on it now. It was as if these friends thought I had some communicable disease, so they kept their distance. Banker friends especially deserted me like I had a plague.

The old Texas, where a man's word was better than a contract and a friendship was forever, will never be the same again. The economic disasters of the mid-eighties were too swift and too deep. Something had to give. Despite all of the people who deserted me, there were many business and personal friends who not only stood by me, but went out of their way to let me know they believed in me. These true friends are the most important treasure that comes in life. As I recall their expressions of support, the most remarkable thing of all was the backing I received from investors.

Throughout 1986, 1987, and 1988, investors were not filing group lawsuits against us, despite the fact that several law firms (known as "strike" firms) actively solicited our investors and broker-dealers to promote lawsuits. I was really bolstered by the fact that these strike lawyers were not able to drum up a single suit. (That changed with three suits of that nature in 1989, but still, in the context of ten thousand investors, it is a small percentage.)

Several hundred of our investors wrote letters of encouragement and support. We called these our "good news" letters, and they were really kind of a secret weapon in terms of maintaining faith and morale for me and the entire organization. After answering these letters, I put them on the credenza behind my desk. Just seeing the stack and watching it grow helped to keep me going when the world was falling apart around me. When I was in desperate need of a good thought, I would read a couple of those letters and they always helped me. I still keep them close at hand in three big binders.

LESSON 5: POSITIVE THINKING, FAITH, AND REALISTIC WORK ARE WHAT IS NEEDED

It is obviously unproductive to run around in a circle and to constantly generate negative thoughts. Achieving an inner peace of sorts is important in getting through tough times. Just as blatant pessimism is damaging, so is blind optimism. A Pollyanna, overly optimistic attitude alone will never carry you through. Certainly thinking positive is beneficial, but it must be combined with a realistic approach and lots of hard work. I don't believe there are any easy steps to achieving anything that is worthwhile. Important things are all earned.

My personal experience through all of the tough times convinces me that faith is essential if you are to succeed in any critical effort. I am not going to try to specify a particular kind of faith that works for everyone. Many of the people I admire most are active members of various formal religious denominations, and they gain tremendous strength from their beliefs. For me, the thing that helped was work and more work and continued faith that my honest effort would eventually prevail. I also have strongly maintained the belief that there is benefit in doing what is right rather than what is easy. I may not be able to define God the same way many others might, but I believe there are basic human moral values that should spill over into business and personal ethics. There are right ways to conduct your life—both personally and in business. Inevitably, I have come to the conclusion that the right faith for any individual is an extremely personal matter.

LESSON 6: SEPARATE YOUR PROBLEMS AND UNDERSTAND YOU CAN'T WIN THEM ALL

Each problem in a major business crisis must be addressed like an individual battle in a war. Each is important, but you must realize that the results of many battles are not noticeable. The true results are cumulative. Battles are the stepping stones that may ultimately add up to victory. You may lose many skirmishes, but as long as you stay in the war, you can still win. This is where strategy or game plan becomes all-important.

Face the fact that you can't win every battle. You don't need to. Instead, identify the prime targets that are best suited to your strengths and will most dramatically advance your cause. Fight these battles for all you are worth, because these will be the big wins. Winning these can help enormously in providing the momentum to win some of the other smaller battles.

LESSON 7: FOCUS ON PROBLEMS AND SOLUTIONS ON A PIECE-BY-PIECE BASIS

Planning is the beginning of any action. When you are in an economic crisis, you will probably react almost immediately. That's normal, but you will soon discover that you are not ready to move effectively until you have developed a plan that encompasses the entire situation. You need a true understanding of your needs, your priorities, your strengths, your weaknesses. You have to consider and adopt strategies and tactics. In short, you must decide what you are going to achieve and how you are going to do it.

Start by concentrating on the problems: Identify each of them, define them, and prioritize them. Your problems may seem overwhelming at times as mine often did. Sometimes one economic problem after another can lead to an avalanche—as it did for many in the Texas depression of the last part of the eighties. When this happens, there is a general loss of confidence as well as a loss of financial resources, each building upon one another very much like an avalanche. It helps to break down the problems into groups so that each task becomes surmountable.

No matter how complex or difficult things may seem, you can break them down into simple, basic problems that are not impossible to resolve. As your problems are more clearly defined, the matter of priorities tends to become fairly clear. It may prove obvious that nothing can be done about an entire group of problems until one keystone issue is handled. Then again, when a certain issue is resolved, sometimes a whole group of seemingly major problems will suddenly become only minor annoyances. Obviously, when you are faced with a mountain of problems, you can get a more manageable point of view by looking at each of the individual boulders and pebbles.

As problems become clearer and their priorities stronger, it is time to move on to solutions. Use all of your creative skills and decision-making experience. Remember, developing solutions is where you will benefit from a variety of experience, so call on all of your best advisors and make this a team effort.

LESSON 8: REALISTS ARE SURVIVORS—
TO THINE OWN SELF BE TRUE

The ability to look at the world in the harsh light of reality is a key to winning because the realist is the survivor. To win is to survive, and conversely, to survive is to win. It may sound very simple, but when you are under fire, you simply have to take each day one at a time and attack the problems that come with each. You have to switch from the aggressive builder of a business (the optimist playing offense) to the determined survivor (the realist playing defense). Eventually, survival will mean new opportunities and prosperity, but in the thick of the battle, you must remain focused on the problems and solutions. The first step toward being a realist is admitting your problems. It's not easy. But only after you know your problems are real can you begin to solve them.

For those of us who are trained to be constantly optimistic, to keep smiling no matter what just slapped us in the face, it is tough to reject old habits and get down to what can be a pretty negative reality. But you have to if you want to survive. You need to face the facts. One technique that may help when you sit down to think and plan is to imagine you are wearing a special set of mental eyeglasses. These glasses are powerful filters that let your mind see only real facts and pertinent questions. They eliminate all images of the way you wish your situation were. They screen out all doubtful conditions and wishful thinking. These glasses don't keep you from seeing realistic positive images, they focus on support and strengths as well as problems and weaknesses. They always present conditions and facts and people only as they are.

If your plans and strategies are created from the point of view of these special glasses, you can be sure they will be realistic and therefore powerful.

LESSON 9: KEEP YOUR SENSE OF HUMOR

During our tough times, we tried never to say the "F" word. That's right. Never say "foreclosure." A sense of humor is sometimes the best tool

for survival. Throughout a lot of our most difficult times, we would constantly come up with new—and ever more absurd—jokes to carry us
through. Most people may think of the "F" word as something worse
than foreclosure, but foreclosure from our standpoint was worse than any
four-letter word.

We managed to cheer ourselves up in many ways. We gave nick-
names to our lenders and key employees and even used costumes. Off to
our first court battle with Westwood on July 24, 1986, some of our associates dressed me in SWAT-team garb, complete with helmet. Another
time, they presented me with a cookbook, complete with recipes for FSLIC
Fries, Bankruptcy Beans, and Capital Call Cake. We planned occasional
parties away from the office and always managed to come up with joke
gifts or funny T-shirts that somehow revived our senses of humor.

The point is, if you ever completely lose your sense of humor about
your problems, you really have lost it all. Clearly, I had my good and bad
days through 1986 and the rest of the late 1980s, and perhaps for a long
period of time there were more bad days than good, but we hung on to
those personal human qualities needed to succeed, one of which certainly
is a sense of humor.

LESSON 10: YOU MUST BE AS TOUGH AND TENACIOUS AS YOU CAN BE

Your biggest enemy in tough times is usually yourself. Coming to terms
with yourself is a key requirement. You've got to face who you are and
put that perspective into the process. When you are involved in a critical
battle for survival, tenacity and selective focus are essential for success.
The capable individual will always attract more responsibility and more
work than one human can possibly handle. Don't let the avalanche weaken
your dedication. Quickly sort out those things you can capably and profitably handle, then work on the areas where you can make your most
important contribution.

Tenacity is another key to winning. Focus on your goal, whether
that is saving a property or saving your company, and don't allow dis-
tractions of name-calling, personal insults, and short-sighted trivia to get
in the way of your real progress. Remember, it is a mind game and these
insults are intended to wear you down. Don't let them. Sometimes you
have to put your ego in your pocket, let the other guy throwing the insults
make his point, and keep your mouth shut. Save your energy to focus on

making this particular deal work. Be tough and tenacious, but in a quiet and respectful way.

LESSON 11: PHYSICAL CONDITIONING IS A MUST

Marty Cohen helped me through the tough times in many ways, but perhaps none was as important as getting me into better physical condition. No matter what the activity, some sort of physical regimen is so important to surviving a crisis. It's therapeutic, it's stress releasing, and it helps make you stronger. No doubt everyone uses the excuse of not having time or not being in shape to begin with. Many days I wasn't in the mood to run, but that's where having a partner comes in. You boost each other along, the physical activity becomes part of your friendship, and if you miss a day, you are not only letting yourself down, you are letting your friend down.

If you are going to war, you must be fully trained, and that includes getting your weight down to a fighting level and putting your body along with your mind into its best possible shape.

As my business got better, I found that my waistline again began to expand. I still run, though less frequently, and when I do, I remember the lesson my crisis taught me that physical exercise (jogging, for me) really relieves stress and adds to productivity. I am not a very good runner; I'm slow and not in great shape. But even now, when things get tense in the office, I will often drive out to Bachman Lake in Dallas and make the 3.3-mile run around it. After the first half mile or so, it always seems like I am ready to quit, and that it will be impossible to finish. But I keep going, pick up my pace, and eventually I get a second wind. I eventually get past the picnic area at the halfway point—where it would be too embarrassing to stop because of the picnickers—and where the finish line (my car) is in sight. I start saying to myself, you can't give up. When I get to my car, I feel like I have finished an Olympic marathon. That short run means a great deal to me both mentally and physically. It is a great stress releaser, and I always find myself rejuvenated when I get to my office. It is funny to say it is a pleasure, because running that lake is also a big pain. When I'm pushing myself as hard as I can physically, my mind can let go completely of the problems of the day and focus on the physical goal that's within reach. Achieving that goal —getting around the lake to my car—is a little victory that can keep me going when I get back to the office.

LESSON 12: IT HELPS TO KEEP A JOURNAL

In January 1986, when our problems were just beginning to become public information, my wife and I had dinner with Don and Judy Williams. Don is head of the Trammell Crow Company and one of my personal heroes. He runs a huge organization superbly, but what's more important is that he's one of the most ethical people I have ever known. Don suggested at that dinner that I keep a journal to keep track of all of the problems and my thoughts. It was a suggestion that I am grateful I followed.

The journal took a lot of my time, but in retrospect, I know every minute was worth it. It was also a lot cheaper than psychotherapy. Ironically, with the completion of this book, I destroyed my journal. For me, the purpose of my journal notes, like the times they covered, is history. I'm now looking to the future. Throughout the book I've tried to combine my story and the story of the Texas depression with observations and lessons learned from this experience. Although it is hard to do justice to the magnitude of lessons learned both at a personal and business level, I hope this chapter will help bring home some value for you from the most important of those lessons. I have used my journal not only to record history but to analyze and learn from events. The profound personal effects of the tough years on my life are now a launching pad for new personal and professional growth and improvement in many new demensions. The journal provided a systematic way to organize the needed learning and growth process.

CHAPTER 15
BUSINESS LESSONS

IN APRIL 1988, Dallas's First RepublicBank Corporation jolted the financial world with news that it had lost $1.5 billion in the first quarter of 1988. Not long before that announcement and news that First Republic was seeking a record federal bail-out, I had a meeting with David Florence, who serves on the board of Hall Financial Group, Inc., and was on the board of First RepublicBank. David's father, Fred Florence, who had retired some thirty years before, had built Republic from a small bank to a regional powerhouse. All of this was before its merger with InterFirst, which formed First RepublicBank.

Our meeting took place on a Saturday. David was somewhat mysterious about why he wanted to get together, but as he began to explain his concerns, I saw a familiar pattern emerging. First Republic was having huge problems and this fact was well known at the time of our meeting. Their losses were staggering and publicity surrounding them in the *Wall Street Journal* and the Dallas papers was compounding the problems. As David told the story, it had a déjà vu effect on me. He wanted my advice about what the bank could do to deal with its problems. I agreed to meet with management as well as anyone else they would suggest and offered to provide any other help that I could. Given what I had gone through, and was still experiencing to some degree, I felt a great sense of sympathy and empathy toward the people in charge.

The publicity was causing a run on the bank. Hall Financial Group had all but experienced a similar "run" in the spring of 1986. We were fortunate that our investors weren't part of that run, though many others we dealt with bolted. So, as David and I talked, I remembered the hurt of having to deal with the community from a position of weakness. I remember the spring our employees couldn't get their paychecks cashed because, ironically, BancTEXAS, where I was the largest individual shareholder, believed we were so very near bankruptcy. In time it was one of the banks that went broke while we survived. Also ironically, we are again doing business with the new BancTEXAS. At the same time, large New York stock exchange firms began to call our employees and tell them our 401K plans would be lost if the company went bankrupt. Some employees got worried and started withdrawing money from the plans. Head-hunters phoned constantly trying to lure employees away from what they called "the sinking ship."

As David and I talked that day, he related many similar problems from First Republic's current experience. And First Republic had the added problem of its stock price, which was taking a severe beating on the NYSE.

Was First Republic alone in its problems? Certainly not. But like Hall Financial Group, Inc., in the real estate business, First Republic was very visible and represented the problems in Texas banking. They were the easiest for the press to focus on, and the harbinger of things to come.

Businesses often go through one or more crises like Hall Financial Group and First Republic have in the Texas depression. Many of the business lessons we learned apply not only to real estate companies, but to all businesses experiencing tough times. Here are just a few of the many lessons.

LESSON I: CASH FLOW IS KING

Virtually any business is cash intensive. Certainly major real estate investment, as we practice it, requires dependable cash flow either from earnings or borrowing or investment. Borrowings are a form of cash that without earnings and/or equity investment simply can't be depended on to be the source of cash. Cash is the fuel that keeps a business forging ahead. Cash allows you to attract and afford the best people to share the load as you grow. Particularly in real estate, cash gives you the competitive edge to buy the desirable properties.

Especially when your business is new, the importance of maintaining your cash flow cannot be emphasized enough. As a venture capitalist, I have worked with many new companies and have observed that they generally spend beyond their means—often they don't have proper spending constraints and controls in place to monitor cash flow. Cash-flow problems are the number-one killers of all new businesses. According to the Small Business Administration, nearly 85 percent of all new businesses fail. The businesses with the highest rate of failure are men's and women's specialty clothing stores in strip shopping centers—notorious for cash-flow problems associated with paying for merchandise up front and having to meet expenses from a weakened cash position while selling inventory. Retailers have to spend money to make money, and they have to spend money to grow, but often the spending goes unchecked for too long.

This same spending syndrome occurs in later stages of business when a profitable company falls on hard times. An optimistic leader, whether inexperienced or a veteran, will often fail to see the reality of his business problems. Caught up in the spirit of the business, focused on the future and on growth, many business leaders fail to see the realities until it's too late. Monitoring cash flow closely can help optimistic leaders be realistic winners. To live through a financial crisis, the optimist must realize it is not profit but cash flow that determines survival.

Again, survival is everything. Being close doesn't count. When we were in the thick of our fight with the government and lenders, negotiating interest payments on more than a $1.5 billion in loans, we had to be very mindful of cash flow. We had to make payroll every two weeks. Making payroll was often a very, very difficult event. Profit becomes irrelevant in a crisis. What really counts is having the cash to keep the business going. Below is what I learned about how to analyze cash flow.

Blueprint for Analyzing Cash Flow

Start with an analysis of the facts, and from that, you can develop a plan. This rather monumental job can be broken down into four steps.

1. **Get a "snapshot" of where you are today.** This is essentially a cash balance sheet, a personal and corporate realistic "self-inventory" of cash, short-term receivables, liquifiable assets, and a complete list of payables ranked by required payment date. This is your realistic picture of your cash or liquidity inventory.

2. **Put together a detailed five-year projection showing all foreseeable sources and uses of cash.** Project the first year on a month-to-month basis and the balance on an annual basis. What is most important about this step is being realistic about the numbers.

3. **Analyze the downside potential and everything that can be done to keep your cash flow out of a negative position.** This is where the "art" of cash-flow management comes into play. It needs to be an ongoing activity in order to keep ahead of economic changes that in a crisis seem to move faster than the speed of light.

4. **Put together a long-term debt restructuring plan if that is necessary to solve your cash-flow problems more permanently.**

Consider more fundamental issues such as interest rates, the size of your debt, and your probable earning power over time.

LESSON 2: DEBT RESTRUCTURING IS AN ART AND SOMETIMES IT IS NECESSARY

Most of us tend to develop knowledge and skills when we do not need them at the moment. We like to have broad-ranging abilities, and we want to be ready for whatever the future brings. Financial restructuring is a skill that Hall Financial Group and many other real estate companies have had to develop to survive.

It is difficult to know when to stop trying to solve financial problems by outrunning them—making new deals that allow old debt to be moved around, or simply by expanding debt in anticipation of inflation. If you try to outrun the storm too long, the results can be fatal. Well ahead of the moment of decision, you need to understand your options and have a good idea of what is required for successful restructuring of debts you can no longer handle.

First, a simple definition of "restructuring" is that it is an agreement between a borrower and one or more lenders to change the terms of existing loans, usually reducing the interest rate or lengthening the time for repayment or both. In extremely unusual cases, the lender takes a "haircut," or actually discounts the amount of debt. In any event, the purpose is to make it possible for the borrower to maintain debt payments. This usually occurs during a severe and widespread period of economic difficulty. The lender benefits by avoiding the high cost and disruption of foreclosure or bankruptcy. In addition, the loan conditions are, when feasible, usually changed to give the lender additional value to sweeten the deal. The value is received either at the time of restructuring or when the debt is ultimately repaid.

It is important to understand that, under normal circumstances, restructuring is rarely even considered by lenders. Lenders, after all, do what is in their best business interest—as well they should. But during widespread economic problems, such as during the mid- to late-1980s Southwest real estate depression, it is in the lender's best interest to restructure. On rare occasions, a lender may agree to work with a large borrower suffering a serious financial problem in normal or good times, but usually restructuring comes into play only during periods of widespread recession or depression.

The troubled borrower should expect to initiate the negotiation. And when you do sit down at the table, it may be only the beginning of a long and tortuous process. Lenders have serious responsibilities in regard to protecting their capital and are appropriately quite cautious about restructuring debts. Still, if a plan is presented that is realistic and creditable, there are ample reasons why the lender may accept it.

Restructuring is a complex art, and there are many important aspects to being successful. We believe the one absolute necessity is to show the lender that the new arrangement will be a "win-win" situation. Both parties must adjust to the new realities of the marketplace, and both must benefit. This requires considering what you can offer the lender as much as you consider what you can gain from a restructuring yourself.

Another important characteristic of successful restructuring is absolute fairness to all lenders with whom the borrower is involved. There must be a scrupulously honest disclosure to all so that no one lender feels another is getting a bigger piece of the pie. If they do, it's safe to say that they may consider pushing you into bankruptcy on the premise that they will be better off with a judge making sure everyone gets equal treatment.

We learned that the "value-added" approach of offering each lender additional value in the future for his concessions today was very effective. Most business people don't have any problem with the rationale for adding value in the negotiating package! They feel it makes good economic sense. But they do wonder, when the cupboard is bare, where extra elements of value can be found when a company is already in extremely serious financial trouble. That's a good question, and while the answer is not easy, value can be found in a kind of creative treasure hunt.

As we put together the restructuring package for more than $1.5 billion dollars of properties, we found ourselves using various approaches for the value-added elements. We referred to part of them as the "dime." Ken Leventhal made a big point of the fact that you should never come to the negotiating table empty-handed if you can help it. If you owe a dollar, but you haven't got a dollar, you can at least bring a dime. His concern was as much about the borrower's attitude as it was about actual value offered. It is important that the lender view the negotiation as a win-win effort. The concept was to give the lender all of the net income they would get if they foreclosed and owned the property *plus* something extra—the dime. The dime would typically be a monthly payment added to all the cash produced by the property, often with a minimum total monthly payment required.

Armed with that philosophy, we searched for value-added items we could afford even in those toughest of times, and we found them. While the examples that follow are, of course, from real estate, I'm sure a creative look at any business will find hidden treasures that can help balance the scales with lenders. Our major source of general partner profit from syndicated property investments traditionally comes in the form of a significant percentage of the profit on sale (after the limited partners have realized certain minimum returns and benefits). Of course, none of this profit was on hand from the properties we were struggling to save. But it was a good bet that if the properties could be retained until the markets came back, there would be profits. It might take a number of years and a tremendous amount of work, but that "back end" reward would almost certainly be of enormous value when it arrived.

So, in many of our restructuring plans, we offered to share with lenders the general partners' profit due on sale of the property. True, we were giving up a major percentage of our anticipated future profit, but without the assistance of the lender, we would lose the property long before that profit became a reality. The lender in turn would receive a direct share of the profit that its cooperation made possible. In addition, it would avoid the cost of foreclosure and management. This is a good example of a win-win restructuring plan.

As I explained earlier, when the Senate Finance Committee passed the tax bill in May 1986, I knew that the ability of the Hall Financial Group to generate cash-flow profits sufficient to create the dime we had negotiated with lenders was not going to be available. After a lot of thought and consideration, the final result was a need to do capital calls. Capital calls, depending upon the structure of the partnership, may be voluntary or pre-agreed and mandatory. In our case, they were voluntary.

We asked the existing investors to put more money in and offered those who put more money in a greater share of the future profits. For those who did not, profits were diluted—very similar to what a rights offering would be in a corporate format. The capital call was important to each partner and benefited them in that it saved the property and its future economics and also deferred a tax gain that would occur if the money wasn't put in and there was a foreclosure. In essence, there was a reason in terms of future value and a reason in terms of avoiding a current loss that motivated investors to be interested and cooperative. This process also helped lenders realize that everyone involved, general and limited partners as well as themselves, was working together to make the transaction work.

In one form or another, many workouts, whether for a retail store or a real estate transaction, need more equity. Whether it's a rights offering or a capital call, the concept is similar. The existing owners dilute their ownership position and new money comes in last but usually with greater preferences or priorities over the first money. Oftentimes in the capital-call situation, it is last money in, first money out.

The important point about total disclosure and a value-added approach is that while they may not seem overly important, they are symbols of fairness and appreciation, and they go a long way in cementing good business relationships that are at the base of all restructuring.

It is important to keep in mind the creditor's alternatives. A lender's basic alternative is a judicial bankruptcy. One of the things that needs to be thought through, while establishing the details of the plan itself, as well as during the implementation of the plan, is what each creditor would gain under a legal bankruptcy. A big part of organizing the plan is to look at creditors by classification and decide what their legal posture would be in a bankruptcy, then give them that same result at a minimum in the non-judicial form of a workout restructuring, plus something more as incentive. Treat all creditors fairly and in a consistent manner. In general, although there are exceptions, I believe both borrowers and lenders are better off if a formal bankruptcy can be avoided. The extra costs, additional required approvals, and loss of credibility for the company all harm both the borrower and lender in most bankruptcies. We learned there are various logical important steps to succeeding in a debt restructuring.

Blueprint for Steps Needed to Succeed in Your Workout

1. **Pick Your Team.** Your team needs to be put together for all of the stages that follow. You need the experts that can help establish the plan and provide information on alternatives—your specialized accountants and attorneys. You need your internal ombudsmen who can be the leaders and control a certain series of loans. An ombudsman is someone who assists in achieving fair settlements and, in this case, takes full responsibility for certain loans that need restructuring. The ombudsmen coordinate all of your team's efforts on the loans assigned to them. Then you need your entire company focused on the analytical process and the follow-up process to create the momentum that is required in a lengthy restructuring program.

2. **Collect and Analyze Data.** Putting together data of this type includes both a look at the current assets and liabilities as well as cash flow. Specialized outside help can be very useful in formatting and presenting complete and accurate cash-flow information. The best source, in my opinion, is the accounting firm of Kenneth Leventhal & Co. They are very experienced and they do an outstanding job in this area. It is as important for your

internal needs as well as for the informational needs of your creditors to understand exactly where you are and where you're headed. That will help you analyze what needs to be done in order to survive.

3. **Prepare the Plan for the Restructuring.** Once you have information on where you are and where you are going, with roughly a five-year projection of cash flow, you are now in a position to prepare your plan. The plan is basically a two-stage process. First, the pre-plan, which is prepared with the information you've analyzed on where you are and where you're going, and second, the post-plan, or what you need to do to bring things into balance. An important element of the post-plan is that you properly, and with the guidance of experts, treat all classes of creditors in the fairest manner possible in proposing modifications or restructurings in line with their legal rights in a bankruptcy. If you have done a good job of isolating classes of creditors and treating them fairly, the implementation of the plan will be much easier. If your plan itself is flawed, you will have to back up and revise the plan at the implementation stage to provide for proper equity or the plan will fail.

4. **Implement a Preliminary Agreement of the Plan—the "Letter of Intent."** Now that you are armed with a pre-plan (where you are and where you're going without change) and a post-plan (what you need in the way of help from your creditors and how you will improve the situation), you can proceed to implementing the plan. An important part of what creditors will look at now is what you are doing in the way of overhead cuts, how you are providing additional capital through a capital call or rights offering or similar vehicle, and what your overall business plan is in terms of its reasonableness and likelihood of success. Your objective at this stage should not be to get complete legal agreement from each creditor because that will simply take too long. Instead, you need to get momentum going in your favor. The best way to do that is to have creditors sign a simple letter of intent that binds everyone to the general terms of the plan and spells out the modifications they will make in their loans. Once signed, start to implement and pay them based on that letter of intent. The final documentation often will take a year or more to be completed, but the first agreement will bind everyone to the general terms. Except for Westwood, we never had a problem with a lender after signing the letter of intent.

5. Document the Plan. As I indicated above, while it may seem unusual, it often takes at least a year from start to finish to modify any given loan. The more complex things are, the more they can drag out. The documentation takes the longest time and can be a real headache. Even though everybody has agreed on some things, it takes the lawyers to finally get the documents prepared and signed and it just drags on and on. This is a time-consuming process with a lot of back and forth at an unfortunate, huge expense.

LESSON 3: IT'S NEVER TOO SOON TO CUT OVERHEAD

When serious trouble strikes, overhead becomes a cancer that grows and grows and feeds upon itself. You may think of dozens of reasons to delay immediate cutbacks, but the one reason to proceed, which supersedes all others, is that if you don't reduce overhead promptly and drastically, you will surely go out of business. Resist your optimistic reasons for why you should wait. I did this wrong, and most people do it wrong, so I can only urge you, if you're in this type of crisis, to do as I'm saying, not as I did.

Cutting overhead is like pruning a tree. In the long run it will make you stronger. You may feel like you are cutting the lifeblood from your organization, but it is a necessary and generally healthy part of your survival and subsequent rebuilding process.

But remember, the key is to do it sooner—not later. Face the hardest decisions first and get them over with. Know that if you don't make deep cuts, you aren't going to survive.

Blueprint Guideline for Cutting Overhead

1. **Start by eliminating the frills.** Cut out the owned or chartered airplanes, chefs for the executive lunchroom, first-class air travel, any extras. This was easy for us and should be an immediate step for anyone in trouble.
2. **Take a look at your company as a whole.** Are the profit centers really worthy of that name? Sell off or just disband entire areas that are not profitable. Examine your business piecemeal: what is making money, what is losing money, what is marginal? Make decisions for the short term, keeping in mind that in tough times you cannot afford investments for some future date. Cut everything that's not pulling its own weight today. Whole divisions are a lot easier and more effective to cut than just trimming back. Both are needed.

3. Make across-the-board reductions. Give department heads
absolute dollars-and-cents cutback objectives tied to overall
company needs and anticipated departmental workloads.
Executives should have reasonable latitude in how they cut back
in their own areas, but no latitude in terms of the total
achievement required.

LESSON 4: MANAGING MORALE IS A CONSTANT CHALLENGE

A lack of confidence among your customers or the public at large may
hurt you, but chances are you will have even more serious problems from
within your company. The reaction of employees, including many in management, can dampen morale, virtually stop momentum, and replace a
positive sense of direction with uncertainty.

All employees are vulnerable to the concerns created by fear of the
unknown. Their lives are suddenly dominated by cash-flow problems, a
lack of raises, the probability of future layoffs and overhead cuts, and
general confusion and insecurity. With the lack of positive focus, morale
hits new lows, and the spirit of the company languishes.

In our case, which probably wasn't unusual, our people went through
various phases. The first was one of shock and panic. There was enormous
concentration by everyone on our troubles, and constructive work suffered.
During the first year, some of the middle-management people left the
company along with a number of lower-level employees. Some were asked
to leave by necessity of overhead problems while others, whom we really
needed, left because of their fear that we would be out of business soon.
Morale was at a very low level.

In 1987, the second phase set in with some degree of renewed
positiveness. People were still concerned and apprehensive, but it seemed
like there was light at the end of the tunnel. Our workout with Westwood
and solution to the government problems in late 1986, combined with the
purchase of five different real estate general-partner companies during
1987, gave people new hope. Layoffs slowed down significantly, some
new hiring began, and there was overall positive improvement. Yet, toward
the end of 1987 and into 1988, people realized that other vital improvements
we needed still weren't there. We were again having layoffs, head-hunters
soliciting, and some of our most valuable people were quitting. The third
phase for us was a settling down to a more realistic view that the comeback
would be slow and steady, not an overnight boom. We took measures to
at least improve communication and, when possible, promote good morale.

We had dozens of superior employee associates with special skills that made it easy for them to jump to a more secure job. Some left, but the majority stayed through the worst of times and are still with the Hall Financial Group. Probably one of the major reasons they stayed was our constant effort to share all the facts with them openly and straightforwardly.

If you have offices all over the country as we do, write memos or newsletters frequently to get the facts out to the field. Associates in field offices don't deserve to be forgotten; they are just as important to your team, and you need to make an extra effort to keep them informed. Also, remember that whatever you write may turn up in the press or elsewhere at any time.

We also tried to make work fun. For example, our Houston office had a clever way to boost morale during property inspections. Harry, an adult-sized rabbit, made many of the property inspections of Houston properties. The property managers never knew when Harry would show up with his twelve-inch ears perked, ready to take a look at the property. Some property managers made fun of Harry at these inspections, but they later regretted it. At a year-end awards ceremony, the Houston employees put on a skit called the "Wizard of Hall," and I made a special unannounced appearance as Harry. Those property managers will never know if that was really me making all of those inspections. But Harry did make an otherwise unpleasant part of their job fun. He lightened up the atmosphere—though his white-paw test was certainly as tough as that of any other inspector.

LESSON 5: MAKE SURE YOU KNOW WHO IS ON YOUR SURVIVAL TEAM

It's important to know who's going to leave the company and who's going to stick with you during the tough times. Having complete loyalty within your team is crucial. But again, an honest approach is your best tool. If you have good communication with your middle and upper management, if you know each key employee well and keep him or her informed as to what's going on, you'll know whether you have his or her loyalty or not. Don't be afraid to talk about whether or not the employee wants to leave. It's better to know and let someone walk out the door than to have a half-committed associate who may leave when you need him or her most.

You are going to have some disappointments no matter what. Associates whom you figured you could count on may walk out the door if their bonus is late. Don't get emotional about it or dwell on it. Don't let disappointments distract you from the fight.

During all of 1986, head-hunters were raiding our company for talent. It's a fact that you'll have to deal with if you ever get into tough times. And when it happens, you may not be in the financial position to bargain in dollars. What you can offer is the leadership in trying to do what is right, and it's a big challenge. The key again is good two-way communication. It can be surprising to learn what your key people really place on top of their want-list. It isn't always money. You're more likely to score with increased challenge in the job, with more responsibility, and even with some well-deserved recognition. The best way to know for sure is to take the time to ask.

Retaining senior management should be your prime focus. They are critical to holding the company together for morale as well as functionally. Our senior management was extremely loyal. I owe a great deal to them. They stayed through every bit of the crisis and stood up to it all the way. Frankly, even some of the senior-level people who, because of overhead, ended up leaving have remained very supportive of us.

LESSON 6: LOSS CONTROL SHOULD BE THE PRIME OBJECTIVE IN TOUGH TIMES

In normal times, a healthy business manages for profit and positive results. Our orientation in our first eighteen years of corporate life was "How can we take advantage of opportunity?" Sure there were ups and downs, but overall, we took a lot for granted and our failures were comparatively few. What we thought were tough times were minor blips in a long upward trend. Managing in that environment is much different than managing in tough times. In normal times you can afford to be more generous with your associates, do more to help to protect investors, and generally be a super good guy with all creditors and associates involved with your business.

In a crisis, you learn that it's impossible to be perfect, you can't please everyone, and no person or company can possibly carry the weight of everyone else's problems. I agonized over the effects of many decisions. But in time I came to realize our primary objective had to be to minimize loss. We couldn't eliminate loss, but we could control it, and that became our overriding goal.

There was no doubt we would have casualties. Good people would lose their jobs. Investors who depended on our skills would be let down and disappointed, as we couldn't carry every property and many would be lost. This was a tough new realization for me and for the Hall Financial Group tradition. We couldn't save everything and everyone.

Controlling and minimizing losses is a different approach from the norm, but we learned to maximize the whole with survival as our primary goal. We continued to do our best to make good, educated decisions and to be consistent, as well as ethical, but no doubt, we made our share of mistakes. We did manage to survive intact as much as possible, and sometimes that meant accepting some very painful losses—losses of associates, property, outward esteem, self-confidence, investor capital, and sometimes relationships with people who misperceived our actions.

We tried to soften the blow for associates with severance paid as generously as we could afford. We also helped in every way we could in placing them in new jobs. For our investors, we've tried many things to try to cushion them against financial loss. We've bought new properties where possible and given them to existing partnerships that have lost properties. We've voluntarily assigned portions of general-partner interests in new deals to help investors recover losses. For a long time, I was confident we could voluntarily do things to make sure no one ever lost any money with us, but as the problems have grown, that's far less certain. Although we've always reminded people that investments have risks and there are no guarantees in life, we still care a lot and intend to go the extra mile. Our investors are, for the most part, very understanding of the causes for the market depression, and our extra efforts.

Loss control and survival of the whole can and should be carried out with an emphasis on caring for the people involved. Tough times do require a management style all their own, but it is important to remember that this state is not permanent. The key is to survive until the time when you can return to profitability and turn again to the offense.

LESSON 7: LAWYERS ARE A NECESSARY EVIL, BUT IT HELPS TO BE A PROFESSIONAL CLIENT

As a veteran of many legal battles and a connoisseur of legal concepts, I have come to know, respect, and admire a number of lawyers throughout the country. I find their work, particularly in litigation, an intellectual challenge and a fascinating arena in which to participate. Nevertheless, despite the true respect I have for some lawyers, I've long worried that our country is "over-lawyered." My recent experiences in dealing with lawyers and the legal system during crises leave me with grave concerns.

Examples abound of the waste and destruction caused by lawyers who squeeze every ounce of life out of many troubled businesses. There are, of course, exceptions where lawyers are a business's savior, but for the most part, in my opinion, the lawyers tend to harm rather than help in troubled times.

However, you simply cannot protect yourself against dozens of potential perils without employing lawyers. They are powerful because of the legal system itself. The system is a handsomely crafted closed shop. Either you work within the cost and time constraints lawyers have developed, or you take your chances.

Year after year, the volume of litigation and the number of lawyers in the United States have increased, to the point that it seems to have become a frequent point of discussion and concern, even in social conversation, that "we are a litigious society." We certainly are. This is due, in my opinion, to the general lack of morality in business, coupled with the widespread willingness of many lawyers to build business by taking on and even soliciting litigation no matter how shoddy or blatantly unreasonable the client's position. Winning is too often not defined as helping justice prevail. Ideals seem to be replaced by competition to see who can exert the greatest leverage and pressure on the other side.

During troubled times, litigation increases due to bankruptcies and the need for offensive and defensive uses of lawyers. Too many lawyers aren't particular about whose side they are on, or for the most part, how they achieve their clients' goals. Lawyers are advocates, and like the gladiators of olden days, most are like mercenaries for hire.

Lawyers inevitably are a part of any financial crisis. In the difficulties that Hall Financial Group experienced, frequently it seemed that the lawyers were the main players and sometimes they were part of the problem rather than part of a solution. But there are a number of outstanding lawyers who clearly were critical to the solution.

How to Be a Professional Client

"Professional client" is a term I came up with to describe a client who is a knowledgeable monitor and an active managerial participant in the process of any litigation on his or her behalf. Becoming a professional legal client takes a lot of time and energy, as well as a great deal of study, but it will pay off handsomely in any business where legal involvement is frequently required. This is particularly needed in the midst of financial crisis. The first step in becoming a professional client is to recognize that in your business you simply cannot afford to turn over legal matters to the practitioners and assume they will always keep your best interests in mind.

Of course you can do this, but be aware of the risks and do it with caution. For myself, I long ago decided to educate myself so I could play an active role in guiding and managing my own legal activities.

Because the legal arena is complex, becoming a professional client is not something you can accomplish in a week or two. Like any other important achievement, it requires a determined decision, followed by study, observation, analysis, discussion with selected mentors, experimentation, and practice.

Just in case you think the idea of "managing" professional services you purchase is unfeasible, consider the recent changes in the relationship between many patients and their medical doctors. Doctors used to be the absolute masters of the patient relationship. They put themselves on pedestals, made unilateral decisions, and gave patients only selective information. The patient was expected to follow orders blindly and implicitly.

Today, adult patients are openly invited to participate in their medical care. More doctors encourage questions. They offer patients choices and solicit opinions from the families. Time is more often set aside for discussion, and more doctors are trained in listening and communicating effectively. Doctors who don't do this are losing patients at a rapid rate.

The point is, even the most rigid of professions ultimately responds to the demands of its customers. In a crisis, it is vital that you get actively involved and do not leave the lawyering just to the lawyers. Good lawyers will actually appreciate your active interest.

Blueprint for Keeping Legal Costs in Line

I wish I could give you a long list of specific strategies that will keep legal fees reasonable. The reality is that when the desired result is so important, it's not the right time to be terribly cheap. Still, to be a good manager of the process, you can't ignore costs either. So, here are a few controls I can suggest:

1. **Hire the best.** You are better off paying more per hour for fewer, smarter, and more experienced people than you are trying to save money by hiring those who will work for a lower rate per hour.
2. **Keep the numbers of lawyers involved to a minimum.**
   Sometimes it's hard, and if you're under serious time pressure, you may have no choice. The key is realism. Balance your desire for strength in numbers with the knowledge that each extra body cuts the efficiency of the entire group. Ask specific questions: "Exactly what will the extra people do?"
3. **Remind your lawyers you are concerned about the budget.**

Lawyers tend to bill clients what they feel will be acceptable. Fortune 500 types of companies often get pushed unmercifully by law firms because nobody's watching the store. Make sure your law firm knows you care about costs. Tell them up front that you will spend heavily when you are convinced that results truly depend on it, but that you will resent costly activity that has little value. There are always ways to do things more efficiently. Let your law firm know that is your way.

LESSON 8: BE CONSISTENT AND OPEN WITH THE PRESS

I don't believe that having a high profile is a real benefit. Sometimes, though, it can be advantageous. I have had a high profile from the time I was written up at eighteen years of age as "Ann Arbor's Youngest Landlord." Perhaps even before that when I was "Mayor for a Day" in my early teens. In any event, the press has generally been fair with me, and I am grateful for that. Nevertheless, if someone asks me for advice on whether they should seek a high profile or not, I would clearly say, "If you've got a low profile, keep it."

Having a higher profile demands a lot of extra effort to keep it from getting out of hand. You cannot simply say "no comment" to reporters. You've got to react to questions or else you lose credibility and the ability to influence the outcome of their story. Without your input, you increase the chance of error and decrease the reporter's access to factual information.

One of the biggest mistakes I made in 1986 was to stop talking to the press for a period of time. You don't have to tell the press everything, and it's okay to say that you are not at liberty to discuss something or that it is your policy not to discuss a particular subject or dollar amount. However, to totally change your accessibility, to be communicative one day and the next day be silent, is a big mistake. It's a mistake I made for about ninety days. My best advice is to be open, consistent, and honest with the media, but use your head. In other words, be smart by recognizing that anything you say you may be reading or hearing out of context the next day. Reporters only have so much space or time so quotes or clips have to be at least somewhat out of context. A two-hour interview, for example, might have to fit into twenty inches of newspaper space.

Blueprint for Successfully Dealing with the Press in Tough Times

1. Communicate. Be honest, straightforward, candid, and careful. Don't say anything you don't want to see in print the next morning at breakfast. There is no such thing as "off the record" unless you know the reporter very well.

2. **Cultivate credibility.** It's okay and, in fact, it's *good* to say "I made a mistake" or "had we considered . . ." Don't try to do a commercial for the press. Present your story in a down-to-earth, factual manner.

3. **Don't be unavailable or say "no comment."** You can always say *something*.

4. **Don't be defensive.** If you're not trying to hide something, you don't have to be defensive. Remember, reporters have a job to do. Help them do it *with* you rather than *on* you.

5. **Don't ever tell a reporter that you spend thousands of dollars a year in advertising.** A reporter for a credible publication doesn't care and doesn't have to care. Ad sales and editorial in most (not all) publications are as far apart as opera and rock and they like it that way.

6. RELAX. You'll think better and make a much more credible impression.

7. **Branch out.** As often as possible, have others in your organization quoted in press releases and occasional interviews to broaden the scope of your organization. Be sure they are briefed first by your communications or media specialist so they will be comfortable, honest, straightforward, and can prepare necessary facts and figures. But I always believe the Chairman or CEO should remain the key spokesperson.

8. **Ask for a retraction or clarification only if the inaccuracies are extremely severe.** Otherwise, forget it. Most other people also will forget it unless you draw additional attention to it.

9. **Don't blame the next reporter for the last story.** Just communicate and help this reporter write a better one.

LESSON 9: COMMUNICATING WITH ELECTED OFFICIALS

When your adversary is a business, you simply try to go talk to them, and since they have a profit motive and you have a profit motive, you work together to figure out what's right. When your adversary is a government agency and it has been told by its attorneys both inside and outside that it cannot talk, you've got a big problem. Where do you appeal? I went to elected officials and senior Administration officials.

The fact is, I dealt with a number of Senators and Congressmen. I went to staff members of committees and staff members of Senators and Congressmen. I went to members of the Cabinet and Presidential Administration. The common element that shocked me and surprised me in all of these dealings with both Republicans and the Democrats was that they truly cared. Most people that I met clearly were in Washington because they cared and thought they could make a difference. A properly presented, thoughtfully prepared, and well-documented case on any major issue in this country can gain support and sponsorship. But how it is put together is critical, as is how the message is delivered.

The point is, our system does work. Our elected officials are elected to do exactly what they did in our case, which was to help solve major public-policy problem issues. We, the people, albeit through a roundabout and difficult-to-see manner, do in fact control this country.

The bottom line is we are very lucky to live in a system that works as well as our system does. Freedom is a wonderful thing. It doesn't just happen and it can't be taken for granted. Those elected officials who are representing the people or those staff members that they've chosen are amazingly interested and responsive to real issues, and we all have a lot to be grateful for in that regard.

I found sincerity to be as effective in Washington as I believe it is everyday in doing business. Being straightforward with people and telling them what you know, what you think, and why things are the way they are is all-important. That is what works. While it is time-consuming and takes patience, officials will try to do what is right if they are well informed.

LESSON 10: DON'T LOSE SIGHT OF YOUR OVERRIDING PURPOSE

When you go through tough times, you become so immersed in fighting your war, nothing else seems real. Problems take on a life of their own and it's easy to forget why you decided to fight, instead of giving up in the first place. It's a safe assumption that you decided to stand your ground in order to save your business. Your goals probably had something to do with clients or customers or investors and associates and pride and long-term achievement. So the only real value in beating back tough times is to earn the right to move ahead with rebuilding the business you have been fighting to preserve.

Certainly, you must concentrate on winning the war, but always keep a bit of your mind free to decide when it is time to declare victory and get back to the productive pursuits that are what business is really all about.

No one will ring a bell to tell you it is over. Rather, victory is a process. Nevertheless, as the crisis wanes and putting out fires begins to take up less of your time, you have to make a conscious decision to change your emphasis from defense to rebuilding. You need to take time to focus on the business of your company, to make sure quality hasn't been sacrificed during the hard times, to reinstate old standards or create new ones, to make your company more productive. It is equally important to spread this change in attitude throughout your organization.

Once you start your comeback effort, you may quickly get the feeling of being a split personality. One minute you are running a positive organization; the next minute you are running an almost overwhelmingly negative organization. It seems like the world is one problem after another.

You really have to walk a tightrope within your own organization. It is understandably difficult for employees to rationalize the turnaround developments. You communicate. You give raises where you can and you create new ventures and more work as fast as possible. You display great caution in expanding the work force, so while work may be brighter, it is certainly not easier.

Adversity truly does bring opportunity. American business history is full of companies that have survived tough times and then have gone on to bigger and better accomplishments. You need look no further back than Chrysler or Apple Computers for shining examples of comeback strength.

In our own case, Hall Financial Group, Inc., is coming back strong and we plan to be a solid contributor to solving the real estate problems of the Southwest and the savings and loan crisis on a national basis. In looking at the problems that caused the crisis at Hall, it became evident these were primarily market driven. We, of course, made some mistakes of our own and we've learned from them.

In looking forward you must also look inward. How long has it been since you asked, "What business are we in?"

In business schools there is a lot of talk about knowing what business you are in. As far as I know, most undergrads still read the classic myopic marketing case dealing with the demise of railroad companies because they failed to realize they were in the transportation business rather than the business of running trains. The problem with this is that people who are managing a small- to mid-size company that is doing well are far too busy chasing business to spend serious time analyzing.

But when you are starting to turn the corner after really tough times, you'd better find the time to take a good look at "Who Am I?" "What Am I?" and "Where Am I Going?"—all from the organization's point of view. To resume successful operation, the company must lead from strength. Yet, the strengths an organization had before a crisis may have been lost or diminished, or market conditions may have made them less valuable. The time to find out is before you try to move into high gear.

Redefining your business involves more than just knowing your strengths and weaknesses. You need also to accurately gauge the current needs of your marketplace and your own position in the market. If you have been through tough times, the companies you do business with may have sympathy for you and increased admiration for your capabilities. Or they may think your performance has been poor and your future is in doubt. The facts are important, but the perception in the marketplace is what will really count. It's all in how you handle it.

Looking at our organizational strengths, we see strong abilities in analyzing, packaging, and marketing real estate and in raising large sums of investment dollars to supply major capital formation needs. In terms of market needs, real estate limited partnerships with a tax orientation are gone due to changes in the tax law, as well as market problems. But there still is a property-management business and a continuing opportunity to develop a delivery system to meet the needs of special-interest investors in a worldwide marketplace for real estate–related assets.

Examining the depression and the financial devastation that has occurred in the market, we also see a new need for organizations that can act as financial intermediaries in helping to move assets from the temporary hands of lenders and government regulators back into more permanent ownership. This ability is needed to stabilize the banking system and the real estate community as a whole. It is also needed for the long-term benefit of consumers who want and need real estate at affordable prices.

We are participating in meeting this major challenge. As this book is being completed, we are buying lots of Southwest properties and working on new ideas for capital formation. We are again raising capital and providing superior asset management and property-management services.

For a long time, people threw me cliches like ''You'll come back stronger than ever.'' Frankly, I didn't believe them. How could we possibly raise more money than the $320 million of equity in 1985? How could we possibly come back and buy more than $725 million of property as we did in 1985? Today, I believe we will, in time, reach these levels and higher. We have vision, the ability to create and form capital and solve problems, along with our orientation toward quality operation of properties. We are not out to be the biggest or to surpass past records. We are simply going to try to be the best and grow as large as we can while maintaining strong financial control.

LESSON 11: RESTRUCTURING YOUR CAPITAL BASE IS NECESSARY TO GROW

Once the survival problems are put to bed and the company has restructured its debts, you are left in a generally weakened financial condition. You are working for your lenders and limping along for the most part. The limping along phase is not one that really is in anyone's interest, but once the lenders have grabbed all they can, there isn't much left for a positive turnaround. This could bring a slow, unpleasant death.

In that state, it's hard to take on new activity, and without that the company will simply be a lackluster performer for a number of years.

To help this situation, step back and take another look at the structure toward the end of the loan-restructuring process. Now you're looking at it based on your business plans and the positive things you can do: what do you need in the way of capital to regain market position and credibility and momentum? Once your needs are established, the question is: how do you obtain that position? Each situation will be different and there are no generalities that completely apply to all situations.

Most often some kind of dilution of the current ownership of the company will be necessary to recapitalize and give the company the vitality to go forward. In our case, the May Petroleum merger provided the vehicle for going forward and the new capital, as well as momentum to move us into the future. Because I owned so much of both companies, the dilution was fairly minimal. After the merger, my children's trust would own 9 percent and the outside public would own approximately 17 percent. This small dilution worked to build new capital, to provide tax benefits to the structure, and to create a new public vehicle that would help us gain credibility and tap into additional capital for future growth.

For other companies it may mean bringing in a partner, doing a joint venture, doing a public offering, or any number of other financial structures. The real point is, once the company's debt has been restructured, getting new capital even at a high cost of dilution is probably a good thing to do if you've got the game plan for turning back to positive business activities.

LESSON 12: WATCH OUT FOR BUSINESSES THAT ARE TOO EASY TO ENTER

Put simply, builders always build whenever lenders make money available. Lenders make money available when they have excess supply of deposits and need to find a place to make loans. Unfortunately the real estate markets are determined more by supply and demand of money than the needs of consumers. This inevitably leads to oversupply and cycles—although not normally as bad as the one we've recently experienced—that are generally harmful to the market.

The best real estate tends to be in areas that either have environmentalists who put the brakes on new construction, such as California, or on an island, such as Manhattan. Where there are limitations on new supply or limitations on the business, there are better opportunities. Industries where you have a franchise or a name brand that has some sense of exclusivity or almost a monopoly on the market are better businesses than those that offer easy entry. In restructuring your company, try to get into product lines where you have a niche and do something different or better than everyone else within a local geographic market.

LESSON 13: MAKE QUALITY THE NEW BATTLE CRY

Before our tough times set in, my most important function was setting the philosophical and conceptual mission of the company. Now that we are back on a positive course, I am once again trying to concentrate on that longer-range point of view. I am excited to say that since our recovery we are forging new ground. We are trying to better understand our customers' needs and desires and meet them. We are going back to the basics of our business—good management of properties and superior asset management for our investor clients. Our creed is to concentrate on service and quality in meeting the needs of our markets.

It is my strong commitment to see our company achieve the highest standard of quality because we believe that profit and growth are both by-products of quality and service. If we understand our market needs and then meet them, we will succeed. Otherwise, we deserve to fail.

How do you know what quality is and if you've achieved it? For starters, executives need to get out from behind their desks and personally visit the consumers of the product. Surveys and reports simply cannot communicate the way real people do. When I began to have the time, I started going around the country and looking at our properties, meeting with our staffs, talking to residents. You have to get out where business is really done to know your business.

It's tough to do this. You can schedule one of these "field trips" for yourself every month, but it is too easy for urgent business at hand to get in your way. So you have to make a commitment, make it as important as the rest of the agenda at hand. It might even help to assign a "sponsor" to this task, just as other middle managers are "sponsors" for their areas of priority and vie for your time.

The big value of executives going into the field is that the facts they discover, and the actions they take to follow up, will help field managers truly understand the company philosophy and objectives. Areas like quality mean different things to different people. It may be difficult to quantify what you want to achieve, but that is exactly why it can put you way ahead of others in your business. Work with your customers and your entire operation until you pin it down. Quality is worth continuous attention and effort, and it must start at the top.

CHAPTER 16
TEXAS WILL RISE AGAIN

MOST OF THE GREATNESS that made Texas remains today, even after the crash. Yet ironically the crash itself, which temporarily devastated my business and many others, has laid the groundwork for what I believe will be a sustained and super-strong new Texas built solidly on the bedrock of the crash. The opportunities in the 1990s in Texas are even more exciting than those of the magnetic Texas which brought me there almost a decade ago.

THE TEXAS SPIRIT

In the late 1970s, I first began to visit Texas. We bought some property in 1977, and then more in 1979, at first all in Houston. As I began to spend time visiting various areas of the country looking at real estate or talking to lenders and others in the business communities, I naturally would compare one market to another. For me, Texas always stood out as a unique area.

Texans are different. There is a spirit in the air that I felt early on, before moving to Texas. And, after having lived in Texas for only a short time, that spirit became more and more evident.

It has been said that it takes seven years to become a true Texan. In my case, on the one hand, I was accepted very quickly into the Texas community and, on the other hand, there are still those who believe that unless you are a native, you'll never be a Texan. The Texas community is an amalgamation of many former Yankees (the northerners who, like me, moved to Texas) and the hard core of native Texans. The blend can sometimes produce even more rabid, pro-Texas types or, as I like to refer to myself, naturalized citizens. Not only have I been a Texan for well over seven years now, but I've also paid my dues during the great Texas depression. Notwithstanding the dues, I really enjoy being part of the Texas community.

In Texas, especially Dallas, the question isn't so much "Who are you?" or "Where did you come from?" as it is "What can you do to be part of our community?" The point is, standing on ceremony of your bloodline or the accomplishments of your family is stifling for a progressive community. When I moved to Dallas, it didn't take long before I was active in community fund-raisers and serving on several charity boards. That is very different from the opportunity in some areas in which community leaders tend to be a bit more stuffy or elitist about inviting a newcomer to serve on a board or committee. It's true that I brought with me a track record of civic and charitable commitment in Michigan, but it was more important that I was enthusiastic about making an active commitment to Dallas.

Texas is open to new people and new ideas. It is an area that exists because of the people. Dallas, for example, is flat, has no navigable water surrounding it, and simply has no geographic purpose for its existence. Yet it grows, thrives, and prospers. The reason is that historically, the people of Dallas had the spirit to make it a great city, and the people today continue that spirit.

It's the Texas can-do spirit. People in so many areas of the country stifle themselves by concentrating on what can't be done, but not in Texas. A positive, we'll-get-it-done attitude prevails. Texans are pro-business and pro-growth. Instead of offering negatives or complaining about why something can't happen, Texans think big and ask, "Why not?"

This unique, positive spirit perhaps at times gets out of hand. Part of that Texas spirit may have led to some of the excesses in the real estate and savings and loan boom that have now turned to a bust. But no matter what the negatives may have been in the past, that positive spirit is the ingredient that will help Texas recover in strong and intangible ways that statistics simply can't measure. Texans will not go crying to Washington or anywhere else for handouts. They will simply fix the problem.

An example of this is Houston. Houston was heavily dependent upon the oil business in the early 1980s. In the fall of 1982, when oil prices started down, Houston was in trouble. Today, Houston leads the country in new incorporations and has had an entrepreneurial free enterprise expansion that surpasses every other city in the United States. It is a pro-business, pro-entrepreneurial city. Houston is coming back strong and not because it got help from Washington or anywhere else.

It is coming back because the Houstonians have the Texas spirit and Texans help themselves.

In Texas, nothing is impossible. The will of the Texas spirit is one of the strongest intangible, yet very powerful assets that will not only help Texas to get through this depression, but also help Texas to grow to far-greater heights in the future.

When MCC (Microelectronics and Computer Technology Corporation), a think-tank research group, was looking for a location for its high-tech research facility, cities across the United States were competing for its attention. Everyone wanted the prestige of a high-tech research group that would be funded by many large corporations across the United States. MCC was presumed to be a company that would create many jobs for the winning city that was lucky enough to attract them.

When it came down to the final selection process, it looked like San Diego would be the winner. San Diego's government officials had offered MCC some excellent packages and wooed them as best they could. When the decision was made, it was Austin, Texas, that was picked. The reason Austin won in that particular competition is another example of how Texans help themselves.

In this case, Bum Bright and a few other prominent business people formed a group that raised several million dollars by allocating a portion of the necessary amount to each of numerous major Texas businesses and requesting it via a personal telephone and letter campaign. I was contacted and told that my share was allocated at $10,000, and I readily wrote my check. It is part of the price of being a Texan to help out, and it's a price we all gladly pay. We responded to create the incentive of a financial package to attract MCC to come to Texas without government funding. This is just one of many stories that shows the extraordinary steps to which Texans go to help support Texas. Texans take care of their own and Texans are progressive about marketing for new business.

Unlike many other regions of the United States—or the rest of the world for that matter—Texans don't complain. They jump in with both feet and try to fix their problems. It is this can-do spirit that built Dallas in the middle of nowhere and will make it survive and prosper in the future. It is that can-do spirit that will make Houston and Austin and San Antonio and all other Texas cities throughout the state strong again and continue to make them stronger and stronger.

IF TEXAS WERE A COUNTRY

Maybe one of the reasons that Texans are different is rooted in the fact that Texas once was its own country in the 1800s. If Texas were a country today, it would be the twelfth-largest economy in the world and rank tenth in terms of gross national product—just behind Canada and China. With 267,000 square miles, Texas has more than 23 million acres of forest land, 91 mountains a mile or more high, 624 miles of beaches, and more lakes and streams than any other state except Minnesota. As a country, Texas would be the thirty-seventh largest in the world. There are 17 million people in Texas (not all of whom, surely, are considered Texans yet) and proportionately more working age baby boomers, now aged twenty-seven to forty-two, than the rest of the United States. That's a lot of buying power!

And, through the year 2000, with an increase of 3 million people, the U.S. Census Bureau expects Texas to be one of three states that accounts for more than half of all population growth in the nation. By 1995, Texas is projected to surpass New York to become the second most populated state, second only to California. Consider this: in 1981, 14.8 million people lived in Texas; more than 17 million lived here by 1989; and by the year 2000, we are expected to have 20.2 million. Apparently, the word has gotten out.

It's not unusual to think of Texas as a country on its own because most native Texans regard themselves as Texans first, foremost, and always. On a worldwide basis, city/communities are strongly competing for business on their own. Cities like New York, Los Angeles, Paris, Berlin, and Tokyo compete individually, as do Houston, Dallas–Fort Worth, and San Antonio, but Texans are state proud before they are city proud. When it comes to competing for business, Texans really know how to sell Texas. In fact, Texas and Texans mean business. There is a lot to sell here, and a big part of what we have to offer is the people themselves.

Texans have an international reputation for being proud, but they have a lot to be proud of. With a pioneer heritage, they have a strong work ethic, and their ancestors built a lot with very little. I think that has a great deal to do with the Texas spirit.

However, as with most things, there is also a not-so-positive side to Texas pride. Yet I am enough of an optimist to believe that with the events of the last few years, the arrogant side of that pride and the narrow side of the good ol' boy network are gone. They are replaced with the positive, self-help side of Texas pride and the best of "the good ol' and new people network," based on a foundation of solid, honor-bound Texas relationships. I believe Texas's open, honest, can-do pioneer spirit today is at its best.

IS TEXAS DEPENDENT UPON OIL?

Historically, Texas has enjoyed great strength from natural resources. The oil boom and, before it, the agricultural and cotton industries have contributed to the natural-resource prosperity of Texas. However, with the bust of the oil and gas industry in the 1980s, Texas has had to retrench. A new balance of diversification began to take place in the late 1980s. Today, Texas has a growing manufacturing sector, significant advances in scientific research centers, new high-tech industries, and expanding service industries. The Texas economy in the past few years has become more diverse and resilient. It was the Texas spirit, work ethic, and risk-taking that made those natural resources succeed as economic engines for Texas, and now those same elements are focused on diversification. Today 78.4 percent of Texas's work force is employed in transportation, insurance, finance, trade, retailing, education, real estate, public utilities, and other service-related fields. When the real estate depression made development impossible, many developers turned brokers or went into leasing and management, often having to learn the ropes in one or another new area of real estate services. Above all, Texans are survivors.

Oil will continue to be important, but it will not dominate like it has in the past. In 1981, oil and gas accounted for 27 percent of the gross state product, whereas in 1988, it dropped dramatically to only 15 percent. Agriculture, too, will have its place, but it is not the financial force that it once was. Texas will emerge building its business climate on an internationally competitive basis. It is the diverse business interests that will build a stronger and better Texas than ever. In Texas, business and the free-enterprise system are alive and well. Texas spirit is still the key.

Texas has long been established as a pro-business community. Since the beginning of the decade, even while reducing the dependence on the energy industry, the economy has gained 950,000 new service jobs in the process. The depression of the eighties was not one of unemployment, but a depression of declining values. The decline in values actually will help the future growth of Texas. Among the Fortune 500 companies, 482 have investments in Texas.

WHY COMPANIES MOVE TO TEXAS

Many companies have chosen Texas as their new headquarters. The reasons, of course, vary, but interestingly, the relocations of companies such as American Airlines, Associates Corporation of North America, J. C. Penney Co., GTE Corporation, and Fujitsu America, Inc., all occurred at a time when the relative cost structure of Texas was much higher than it is today. In fact, in the mid to late 1970s, the cost of living in Texas was, compared to many markets, considerably on the high side. The reasons companies moved to Texas then are just as valid today, only there are additional economic benefits. Some of the reasons companies relocate to Texas are as follows.

1. **Pro-business attitude.** Texas is a pro-business state. The laws state-wide and regulations in local communities, for the most part, promote and enhance business rather than hinder or restrict it. Austin and Dallas nationally rank first and second for the highest frequency for business start-ups.
2. **Location.** Texas is midway between the East and West coasts of the United States. It has direct flights to Europe, Asia, and all major parts of the free world. For a company that is national in scope, Texas provides the most central location.
3. **International air and sea ports.** Houston, of course, is a major port city, being on the Gulf of Mexico. It is a major source for imports and exports and shipping throughout the world. Dallas–Fort Worth, too, has its ocean but it is the ocean of the air. Centrally located in the United States, the Dallas–Fort Worth International Airport is the largest airport in the United States in land area and the second busiest. It is second in the world to Montreal as the largest airport in land area. It has tremendous room for expansion and provides the ultimate in the new type of port. The Dallas–Fort Worth area is less than three hours from either coast. The new Alliance Airport, which is the nation's first airport designed specifically for industrial use, is being constructed in Fort Worth and will be able to accommodate the largest jets projected to be operational for the foreseeable future. In fact, with a total of three new area airports, the aircraft operations in the Dallas–Fort Worth area are expected to double by the year 2005.
4. **Cost of living.** Texas has the third-lowest cost of living and the lowest average fuel and electric energy costs in the nation. Low

housing costs are also a major inducement for relocations. For example, the median housing cost in Dallas–Fort Worth in late 1988 was $84,700 versus $92,600 in New York and $190,900 in Los Angeles.

5. **Tax structure.** Texas has no state corporate or personal income tax, and the state attracts many businesses and individuals for its favorable tax treatment.

6. **Labor environment.** Texas is a right-to-work state. While the major unions are here, they have fewer members than any other industrial state proportionate to the population. There is a ready supply of capable and motivated nonunion labor.

7. **Not a "welfare state."** Texas believes in people taking care of themselves and working. The welfare in Texas stresses taking care of those who cannot take care of themselves rather than those who simply take advantage of the system. For that reason, those who do not want to work and want only welfare tend to move to other states.

8. **Availability of excellent opportunities for higher education.** There are major nationally acclaimed colleges and universities, including the University of Texas, Texas Christian University, Southern Methodist University, Texas A&M, and Baylor University, to name a few.

9. **Real estate bargains.** All the reasons above caused companies like American Airlines and Associates Corporation of North America to move to Texas in the 1970s. Now there is an added incentive to relocate to Texas in the 1990s—the real estate bargains. The J. C. Penney Co., for example, spent $140 million in moving costs from New York to Dallas but they will recover that cost in two years of savings on their rent and other office costs. Moreover, the employees can find good, inexpensive housing, and the overall cost of living is favorable. For companies and their employees, the real estate bargains are a major added incentive for relocations in the nineties.

WHO HAS MOVED TO TEXAS AND WHAT IS THE EFFECT?

Recently Texas was selected to be the site of the superconducting super-collider. This will eventually be a multimillion dollar project. It is antic-ipated to create thousands of jobs. Also, there will be a lot of favorable spillover of jobs and opportunities as well as an economic infusion for the Dallas–Fort Worth market with the resulting relocations of scientific experts and support staff.

Exxon Corporation, the third-largest U.S. corporation and the world's largest oil company, is moving its headquarters from New York City to the Las Colinas business community in the Dallas area. GTE recently decided to move its headquarters to Texas and the company has estimated that it will save $700 million in the first five years as a result of its move from Stamford, Connecticut, to Dallas's Las Colinas. Many other national companies are moving their headquarters or regional offices to the Dallas–Fort Worth area, including Kimberly Clark Corporation; Greyhound Lines, Inc.; Holt Rinehart & Winston; Uniden Electronics; Albertson's; and even the U.S. Bureau of Printing and Engraving. Dallas has the fifth-largest concentration of Dun & Bradstreet "Million Dollar" corporate headquarters in the United States. Relocated companies will find that Texas has a good work force and a very favorable tax system. They will also find that Texas has a good quality of life. The weather is good, the location is central for travel to anywhere in the country, and the opportunities abound for combining business and pleasure in a new, growing, dynamic community.

Texas will be on the move again in the 1990s. Ironically, the crash of real estate will, in and of itself, be one of the major benefits to the next step of Texas growth. As a company from the Northeast, Midwest, West Coast, or even another country looks around the world for a place to locate, the state's real estate market will be like a magnet drawing them to Texas. In the early 1980s, companies were relocating in Texas, but the expense was high. Real estate was expensive for the families that moved to Texas, and office space was expensive for the company. Today, of course, it is just the opposite. Compare the office rent in New York City at an average of $40 a square foot to $12 a square foot for prime downtown space in Houston and $14 to $15 a square foot for prime downtown space in Dallas. Boston is at a cost of $28 a foot, and other U.S. markets are in the range of $25 to $30 a square foot. In Dallas, Houston, and throughout Texas, companies can find ample supplies of prime class-A space at bargain rates.

Dallas–Fort Worth has its airport, Houston has its port, Austin its education system, and San Antonio its leisure and military industry. Each of the four main hubs of Texas has its own special draw. Yet, the major draw, believe it or not, is the can-do spirit of Texas in general. All of these factors help Texas prosper by providing unusual business and social opportunities for relocation.

Companies moving into Texas should be prepared for a change of culture. Many of them have no idea how different Texas is from the rest of the world. Some people move here and, within six months to a year, they don't adjust, so they go back to wherever they came from. Those are the exceptions. The first year or so is an adjustment and a cultural shock. Then something happens. It is hard to explain, but after somebody has lived in Texas for a year or so, it just gets into their blood. It is contagious. Whether you are a factory worker, a business executive, or an entrepreneur with a large or small enterprise, Texas gets into your blood.

You better be prepared to be a contributor when you move to Texas. Texans don't like people who sit on the sidelines. In Texas, when there is a problem, we all chip in, whether it is time, effort, or money, to do something about the problem. Texans don't stand on ceremony or get hung up on society or politics when it comes to solving problems. Texans get together and fix things.

In the recent depression, I know of numerous people who had been transferred here just a few years earlier who have lost their jobs. Unfortunately, in my own company we had to cut back many associates who came with us from Michigan. Our situation was not unique. These people didn't leave and go back home. Once people are in Texas for a couple of years or longer, then generally they want to stay here. Texas becomes home. Texas is a unique culture that brings people alive and makes each person feel like a valuable contributor to building his or her future.

Having grown up in the Midwest and always feeling somewhat out of step there as an entrepreneur with creative, progressive ideas, for me, Texas is home. Texans don't know the meaning of "it won't work" or "it can't be done." Texans are positive, enterprising, and despite whatever the world can throw our way, survivors and winners. Texas is a great place to live and work. Right now Texas is an outstanding place in which to invest. The opportunities are great and the prices are extraordinarily low. Most importantly, the upside in the future is extremely positive. Texas will rise again!

THE NEW BANKING SYSTEM

As the new buyers of banks have come into Texas, they have proceeded with a sense of great caution. In time there will be a need by these new bankers to take some risk and start lending money again. In 1988 and 1989, the banks were sorting out new ownership, with First Interstate taking over Allied Bank, Chemical Bank taking over Texas Commerce Bank, First City being taken over by Robert Abboud, NCNB taking over

First Republic, Bank One taking over MBank, and many more. Initially some of these takeovers have been government assisted in a manner in which there is no incentive for the bank to take risks and begin to aggressively make new loans, at least for the first year or two. But, in time, each of these new banks and new bankers will have a need to develop loans and new business to make their investments profitable.

By 1991 and 1992, the banking system in Texas should be greatly reliquified. That means that there will be more dollars available from the banks for loans (something that has been missing in Texas since 1986). As the banks increase their liquidity or cash positions, they will have a desire to make loans. As the new banks get their feet on the ground and know the market, slowly but surely things will get back to a more normal banking system.

Although Texas has survived the lack of lending and the lack of liquidity, both deficiencies have caused a further deflation than might otherwise have existed. Once the washout of the economic difficulties has occurred (which generally has taken place) the base for the comeback is in place. The base that currently exists in Texas is strong. Those who have made it through the last few years, while they are weakened in some ways, do have the ability to regain market share and be worthy of new credit that will become available as the banking system becomes more liquid and more competitive.

THE MANY FACES OF TEXAS—REGIONAL OVERVIEWS

I'm not the only one predicting that Texas, based on unique diversified strengths, will rise again. A report by Merrill Lynch Global Securities indicates that investors should again strongly consider the Texas markets as good places to invest their money. It states that Texas is on the mend and the recovery will leave the state's economy stronger than before, with the Texas economy predicted to outperform the nation's economy for the next ten years. And *Newsweek* magazine's January 23, 1989, issue stated, "In Washington a bumper crop of Texans—starting with George Bush—are in a position to help nudge the state's resurgence along." City by city, Texas has a wealth of varied assets simultaneously complementing and competing with one another, which only serves to enhance the comeback strength of each market area.

Dallas and Fort Worth are perfect examples of fiercely competing cities which, together, greatly enhance the strength of the market area from a national or international viewpoint. Dallas, in its quest to merit international recognition as a world-class city, has become a leader with respect to diversified amenities. Dallas boasts a new internationally acclaimed symphony hall, a new museum, extensive theater, nationally recognized restaurants and hotels, as well as the Dallas Mavericks basketball team and the Dallas Cowboy football team. The Dallas Apparel Marts and the World Trade Center are second in attendance only to New York's fashion district and Dallas is one of the top four convention cities in the nation. Dallas also has a burgeoning film industry and was made internationally famous with the long-running, award-winning television show "Dallas."

Although Fort Worth natives have a reputation for trying to keep the high quality of life in their city a secret so that it won't be disturbed, Fort Worth was named by *Newsweek* magazine in 1989 as one of America's best places to live and work. Fort Worth has internationally acclaimed museums and unique convention and visitor attractions, from the restored historic stockyards area with Western entertainment to a $3 million water garden in the heart of downtown. Unusually rich in character and cultural amenities, including opera, symphony, and theater as well as four museums, the city called "Cowtown" is the home of the Van Cliburn International Piano Competition.

According to a March 1989 story in the *Dallas Morning News*, "Houston—which for the past few years suffered more than any Texas metropolis after collapsed oil prices dragged the state economy into a deep hole—this year should lead what will be the state's strongest economic growth in half a decade. . . ." Houston is coming back strong primarily because of an increasingly diversified economy, the foresight of civic leaders with that Texas spirit, and the oil industry's partial recovery. Although oil is said to account for approximately 60 percent of the city's economic activity, medical services, petrochemicals, engineering, high-tech industry, aerospace, and the Port of Houston are all major performers, according to James P. Gaines of The Rice Center, an urban research institution affiliated with Houston's acclaimed Rice University. Houston's civic leaders have saved and spent wisely, having recently built a $105 million convention center with revenue bonds to be retired with hotel/motel taxes, a $76 million theater complex entirely privately financed with donations, and a $20 million art museum, also privately funded. Houston is the home of NASA, the Johnson Space Center, and the Astrodome. Houston is, in fact, leading the Texas comeback.

Houston's nonfarm employment and manufacturing job growth are steadily increasing and most other major cities in the Gulf Coast region are posting job gains. Petrochemical plant expansions have even created a building boom in a number of Gulf Coast cities, including Beaumont and Corpus Christi, contributing to the employment increase.

The East Texas region is recovering with its forest products industry upturn, resulting from an increase in timber prices and decrease in Canadian timber imports. Thankfully, oil prices are holding steady and employment in the energy industry has become stable. The Texarkana economy has rebounded and the Tyler and Longview-Marshall areas are experiencing increases in education and health services.

Texas A&M University in fast-growing Bryan–College Station recently added about 400 new faculty and staff to meet the needs of record-breaking enrollment.

Tourism is a major growth industry in the state's capital, Austin, and in San Antonio with its famous Riverwalk in the center of downtown. Austin is a beautiful and growing city anchored by state government and the University of Texas at Austin, which has a population of approximately fifty thousand students. San Antonio draws thousands of visitors to the Alamo, the new downtown shopping mall on the Riverwalk, and Sea World, which is the world's largest marine park. The soon-to-be-built Opryland, USA, country music theme park, which will occupy one hundred acres, is expected to attract more than two million visitors annually.

A new economy is also emerging on the Texas-Mexico border. Maquiladoras are manufacturing and assembly plants located in close proximity to the border, primarily on the Mexican side, which produce for the United States market. They can efficiently manufacture or assemble parts made in the United States or other countries and they provide steady employment for many Mexican people, most of whom previously had been seasonal, migrant workers. The maquiladora program, initiated in the late 1960s by the Mexican government to promote economic development, is a success for both sides of the fence. As a result, Mexico has liberalized restrictions on foreign investment.

The border area is enjoying a strong and steady growth trend spurred by the maquiladoras, according to reports by the Texas Comptroller's office. The job base is increasing and expanding, especially in the McAllen, Laredo, El Paso, and Brownsville areas.

The economy in the Plains region, which includes Abilene, Amarillo, Lubbock, Midland, Odessa, San Angelo, and Wichita Falls, is experiencing job growth in health and educational services as well as in local and state government. Hard hit by oil and gas industries problems, the Plains region is beginning to recover, finding strength in other diversified industries.

The connecting thread in all of these areas is the spirit, the optimism, and the "won't quit" attitude of Texans. "In a state that was built on attitude," says *Newsweek* in that January 23 article, "renewed optimism is the first essential step toward recovery."

THE LOSS OF CAPITAL AND THE OPPORTUNITIES FOR NEW CAPITAL

When the New York Stock Exchange declines, stock values decrease and investors lose money. When the real estate market declines in any given area, the same basic result occurs: Investors lose money. What happens to the decrease in value?

The answer is that capital is diminished as value declines. Value and capital are rather esoteric concepts—how do you determine what something is truly worth? It really amounts to the fact that the value of an asset is determined by the amount a buyer is willing to pay and the seller is willing to accept. It's obviously easier to ascertain value in the New York Stock Exchange than it is in real estate markets, but in either case, capital can be lost in huge amounts as values decline.

In a typical recession, such as many that we've had since the 1930s depression, some capital is lost. Usually market values decline by 10 to 30 percent and people lose net worth and assets that may set them back five, ten, or fifteen years. That setback is a cleansing process that takes the excesses out, in any financial market, and sets the stage for the recovery to a greater and stronger growth.

The crash in Texas was different. The capital lost in Texas was not comparable to a level of five, ten, or fifteen years earlier, but was much more severe. For instance, a friend of mine lost a $4 billion savings and loan. That $4 billion savings and loan had been in his family for three generations. In fact, his grandfather also had founded a mortgage company in 1908 which was owned by the S&L. Today it's owned by the U.S. government.

Another way to look at this was described to me by a banker at a recent lunch meeting. He was discussing the severe capital loss in Texas and its ripple effect. He described how many rural banks in Texas had been built up by multigeneration family ownerships. In the 1970s and early 1980s, frequently the current generation bank president of a rural Texas bank, who might be in his fifties, would sell the bank to a holding company located in Dallas or Houston. As part of the sale he received stock in the holding company, which was often an institution like InterFirst, FirstCity, Republic, or Mercantile Bank. He made a big profit and suddenly had $5 million in stock in the holding company. He finally was able to do all of the things that he always wanted to do, like invest in a local real estate office building, buy part of a friend's operating business, maybe work a little less, and buy a larger home.

Then suddenly, with the crash in the economy, the stock of every holding company bank was wiped out. All of the assets that the bank president had acquired were in jeopardy because he had used his holding company bank stock as collateral and borrowed on it. If, for instance, he borrowed $2 or $3 million on $5 or $6 million worth of stock, he would now find himself unable to make payments on those debts and he would lose his office building, his friend's business, and probably be at risk on the mortgage of his home. The domino effect of the loss of capital is not just a loss of the so-called value of the $5 million of stock that he might have originally held; it's also the loss of the assets for which he borrowed and increased his leverage in order to buy. This is truly an example of the Texas problem and the Texas situation.

This hypothetical bank president is really representative of so many Texans. He has lost generations of family capital and far more money than he ever had assets to back up. The capital loss sets Texas back not five, ten, or fifteen years like a normal recession, but back perhaps, in some areas, like the most severe depressions that we've seen in history. No one has yet been able to estimate the huge devastation and amount of capital loss throughout Texas. The ripple effect that the capital loss had on Texas has been huge.

The opposite of capital loss is capital opportunity. Despite all of the loss of capital which may reach back generations, there is going to be growth in Texas for all of the reasons discussed in this chapter. The key, however, is that capital is needed for that growth. This provides two types of opportunities. First, an opportunity for capital infusion to make an extra high return for a temporary period of time by being one of the first sources of funding being put back into the market to help in solving the problems. The opportunities for money are great.

The second type of opportunity is for those companies that can provide the service of matching up the capital needs with the capital that exists. Investment capital today, more so than at any time in history, is a worldwide marketplace. What is needed is the efficiency and technology to bring capital and investment opportunities together. That is the type of thing that I intend to have my company focus on and specialize in: How to take advantage of the opportunities in Texas. If I were an investor anywhere in the world, I would look at the accelerated and exaggerated loss of capital in Texas, due particularly to the complexity of Federal involvement, as one of the greatest opportunities for a transfer of wealth. Those people who get in and find the right places to connect their capital to assets will find great rewards over the next few years.

DUMPING VS. NOT DUMPING: THAT IS THE QUESTION

One of the most important issues for Texas from 1986 through 1989 was whether or not the government should liquidate in a short period of time or "dump" the real estate on which it was foreclosing. The alternative was to hold it for a longer period of time. Many people in Texas were concerned that dumping huge volumes of real estate would depress the market further, escalating the downward deflationary cycle. In 1986 and 1987, I was among those who believed that dumping would be hazardous to the already unstable market.

The dumping versus not dumping debate caught fire during the legislative hearings in Washington with the so-called Savings and Loan Bailout Bill. The Resolution Trust Corporation (RTC) in fact ended up with all kinds of restrictive language, slowing down the liquidation of real estate. Hot debate over the issue of dumping billions of dollars worth of real estate in the Texas market and its negative impact became very popular in 1988 and 1989, in the media as well as in the halls of Congress.

As Congress was debating language which provided for antidumping provisions in the new law, I personally became convinced that liquidating a lot of real estate fast probably was the best thing to do. Why had I changed my mind? It was not really inconsistent, although it may seem so on the surface. The fact is that had we dumped real estate in 1986 or 1987, the deflationary spiral would have been severely extended and the marketplace would have been devastated. The changes in 1988 and 1989 were substantial and warranted a change in the dumping vs. not dumping debate. Operationally, occupancies and rental rates started to recover in late 1987 and had been steadily and strongly improving throughout 1988 and 1989. Moreover, on a worldwide basis, a growing amount of smart capital was ready, willing, and able to move into Texas at reasonable prices. These were people who wanted a good deal but were not going to wait on the sidelines. Reasonable prices can liquidate huge volumes of real estate in today's market.

As an overall premise, I share the views of Bill Siedman, head of the FDIC, and Secretary of Treasury Brady, who in different ways have both espoused the view that selling real estate, as long as they can sell at current, fair market values, is the best thing the government could do for the market. I agree. The sooner we can recycle real estate at reasonable market-value prices to get the private industry back in the ownership and management business, the more efficient the whole marketplace will be for consumers, taxpayers, and industry alike. The longer government holds the real estate, the more likely it is to be burdened by huge administrative costs, lots of controversy on how to sell, and incur greater operating losses from an inability to effectively maximize current value as an operator. When the government goes home at night it doesn't stay up and worry about making payroll on any given property. The FDIC recently stated it needs at least 5,000 people just to hire property management companies and real estate brokers to sell real estate. Those 5,000 people may be good, well-intentioned people, but they simply aren't going to have the same motivation that I—or any number of others who put their capital on the line, as well as their reputation and ego, to make something work—would have. Private industry needs to get back into the ownership and operation of real estate in Texas at the soonest possible time. This is critical to the overall best long-term interest of Texas. The irony is that the legislation also includes language which is actually counter to dumping and could tie the hands of the RTC, which is truly unfortunate for everyone involved.

THE GREAT TRANSFER OF WEALTH

Although to some extent holding property past the depths of the crash in 1986 and 1987 will benefit the government, inevitably there will be a transfer of wealth from the taxpayers of this country, who subsidize the federal financial insurance funds, to the buyers of banks, savings and loans, and real estate assets throughout Texas. To a lesser extent, in other markets that have not plummeted as far, nor have as much of an upside, the transfer of wealth in the 1990s will be substantial. This great transfer of wealth provides unique opportunities for small and large investors alike. The opportunity to buy grade ''A,'' well-located real estate assets that normally would not be on the market and the opportunity to buy bargains at a fraction of their replacement cost for the handyman, fix-it-up investor are available for those who know where and how to find them. The 1990s belong to those with the courage and foresight to sift through the approximately 70 billion dollars of real estate assets to be sold in Texas alone or the many banks and S&Ls to be transferred. The opportunities are unprecedented in our lifetime and offer a rebirth of the days of the California gold rush.

A double benefit is going to occur. First, great bargains compared to previous prices. We are buying real estate today at half or less of the amounts of mortgages. Real estate value has decreased from 40 to 60 percent throughout Texas. The key is the second part of the equation, which makes it all work, and that is that Texas, as an overall economy, will be very strong in the 1990s. Demand for real estate is already on the move upward and will continue. The point is, nothing is a bargain if it simply is a low price and the operating results don't justify a higher value. It's only a bargain if the trend is moving in the right direction and that's what is occurring in Texas. For these reasons, I have great optimism that the 1990s will be a period of one of the greatest transfers of wealth in history; from the taxpayers absorbing the loss, to the buyers of the bargains in Texas. The 1990s will be a period of great opportunities for worldwide capital to invest in the future of the Texas economy.

CHAPTER 17
WHY REAL ESTATE WILL BE A GREAT INVESTMENT IN THE 1990S

FOLLOWING A SPEECH THAT I gave recently for the International Association of Financial Planners, two of the questions were: "Why aren't real estate limited partnerships passé as a concept?" and "Isn't real estate dead and gone as an investment vehicle?" Those questions probably represented the overall mood of that audience and many other investors in 1989. Why, indeed, would anyone want to buy real estate in the 1990s?

Limited partnerships have become synonymous with tax shelters that cause many people to think of high front-end fees and, in short, a "rip-off." Many investors have lost a lot of money in limited partnerships in the late 1980s. While that is true in fact, the partnership vehicle isn't to blame, nor is real estate itself to blame, at least not in a "forever" sense. As discussed throughout this book, the inflation of the late 1970s and early 1980s caused excess capital to create overbuilding. The result was a severe temporary deflation in real estate values. Add to that the 1986 tax-law change, which alone caused values to decline by 15 to 30 percent. In the case of Texas, add the oil price crash. But depressions do not last forever, and the down times can be the opportunity to create the basis for immense wealth. The downward side of a cycle is often exaggerated to an extreme because values decrease below their lowest intrinsic value to an unbelievable bargain zone.

Even though many of us throughout the country who invested in real estate have suffered losses, I feel fortunate to be in an investment industry that, in my view, has an outstanding positive upside future in the 1990s. With a careful and knowledgeable approach, real estate will be a safe and sound way to make a great deal of money in the next decade. I think we are in a period of time that will experience one of the greatest transfers of wealth ever to occur in the history of the United States as a result of the 1980s depression in real estate and the entire financial system.

TWO TYPES OF REAL ESTATE: PRE-CRASH AND POST-CRASH

Real estate investments before 1986 are pre-crash investments and they differ greatly from those made after 1986 or in the post-crash period.

While the physical real estate characteristics are the same, the investment picture is quite different. Before the crash, real estate had a very inflationary bias. Investors regularly would pay higher and higher prices with the view that the future would always bail them out. The inflationary bias was one that was not without logic. Certainly, in retrospect, it's easy to look back and say, "Boy, did that person overpay" or "Gee, that was a stupid purchase." But the fact is that the inflationary bias that was with us throughout the late 1960s, 1970s, and into the early 1980s, for the most part, worked for the active investor. Many times investors who did not buy a property because they were worried about its price would end up a few years later kicking themselves for missing the opportunity. Hotel values in Hawaii soared, prices for office buildings in New York soared, prices for apartments in Texas soared, and real estate everywhere was up, up, and continually up throughout the late 1970s and early 1980s.

The other half of the equation was the tax laws. The tax laws have been a major investment incentive for real estate during the last couple of decades as an important component of the benefits that investors sought. Even if an investor was not looking for tax benefits, the competitive investor would price a real estate investment with tax benefits in mind. Therefore, tax implications acutely affected the pricing and the nature of leverage and financial structuring of real estate. The entire financial engineering of real estate has been heavily influenced by the tax laws, not just since the 1981 tax law, but for decades. It has been an important inbred part of the system.

During a period of several tax-law changes from the mid-1970s through and including the Economic Recovery Tax Act of 1981, the tax laws for real estate were not only favorable, but actually became increasingly more favorable over time. In 1981, one could conclude that Congress believed real estate was a business that needed capital formation, and the legislation encouraged a greater emphasis of tax benefits for investors in real estate. All of that, of course, not only came to an abrupt halt, but also included a retroactive adjustment in 1986—part of the cause of the crash.

Therefore, real estate pre-crash had a totally different set of objectives for investors. Many investors weighed heavily the continuation of inflation and tax benefits as major motivations to invest. Even those who wanted real estate to have other attributes had to compete with the inflation and tax orientation. In my opinion, it did get way out of hand. It was hard to compete and prices were moving faster than cash flows, perhaps not unlike expanded price-earnings ratios in a stock market when things are getting to a lofty level just prior to a major crash. In hindsight, you could see this pattern for more than a decade from the mid-1970s, but how could anyone ever know where the bottom would really turn out to be?

The real estate crash and adjustment has been and, especially in Texas, will continue to be severe and painful. The human tragedy and complex sorting out of our financial system will leave their mark on this country for years to come. Not only will every taxpayer pay a portion of the cost in the S&L bail-out, but many investors who depended upon the consistency of Congress have paid a high price caused by the retroactive tax changes.

In many cycles, there is overreaction on the upside and an equal overreaction on the downside. The new post-crash real estate is a very different type of situation from that of its pre-crash brethren.

The post-crash real estate, for starters, is at a much lower price. It generally has lower leverage. Post-crash real estate investments are designed for cash flow and capital appreciation with little, if any, tax-benefit orientation.

Bought in a manner and at a price to be a highly safe investment, post-crash real estate is strongly oriented to the economics provided in any investment that is purchased at a real bargain, substantially below its intrinsic value. In short, post-crash real estate can be absolutely outstanding if bought carefully.

Pre-crash and post-crash real estate are very, very different and ought to be looked at with this in mind.

THE SAVINGS AND LOAN BAIL-OUT WILL BE THE GREATEST TRANSFER OF WEALTH SINCE THE 1930S

With the collapse of the financial system in Texas, and in the savings and loan industry across the country, has come the government bail-out. The government controls billions and billions of dollars of real estate, with more coming under its control every day. As mentioned previously, it is currently estimated that the Resolution Trust Corporation was initially charged with $300 to $500 billion in assets (and eventually maybe as much as $900 billion), including more than $100 billion of foreclosed real estate. In the entire fifty-six-year history of the FDIC it has handled $144 billion in liquidations. The entire FDIC liquidation staff just prior to the RTC law was working on $9.9 billion in total bank failures.

As foreclosures mount, the government will be under increasing pressure to recycle the real estate back into private hands. Whether anyone wants to fight about the semantics of the term "dumping" versus selling at the market rate, versus holding property, properties will have to be sold at bargain-basement prices as the government needs to raise cash by selling huge volumes of assets. The simple fact of the enormous oversupply will dictate the necessity of bargain opportunities (i.e., a giant garage sale) to clear the inventory.

The savings and loan crisis has caused dramatic change in the financial circumstances of many people and institutions. The legislation that resulted from the crisis will cause a great transfer of wealth. There will be many winners and many losers.

THE LOSERS IN THE SAVINGS AND LOAN CRISIS WILL INCLUDE THE FOLLOWING:

1. Pre-crash owners of savings and loans and banks in the worst geographic areas could be wiped out. In other market areas they will be hurt, partly by the depression itself and partly by the overreaction of Congress in putting new restrictions on financial institutions. Even the well-managed savings and loans and even their counterparts, commercial banks, will feel the adverse effects of the crash.

2. Consumers who benefited from the excess competition of too many savings and loans and too many banks will, in the long run, be losers because the consolidation will give the financial-service industry the upper hand. Where there might have been four different banks on four different corners in any busy area of Texas, in the future there may be only one left on one of those corners. That one bank will increase its service fees and lower its interest rates on deposits, replacing the highly competitive marketplace that had existed on that corner during the last couple of decades.

3. For the most part, pre-crash owners of real estate will be big losers. Obviously, if your debt on a property is twice as much as you would pay to buy it today, you are in a bad position. That's the way most of the pre-crash real estate stacks up in

markets like Texas today. The exceptions, however, are those pre-crash properties that have been restructured. When owners of real estate have faced the problems and worked closely with their lenders to restructure the assets, they can be turned from losers into winners.

4. Perhaps saddest of all is the fact that major losers will be the taxpayers of this country. It has been estimated that every man, woman, and child will have to pay an additional $600 to $1,000 in taxes as a result of the bail-out legislation. The bail-out of the financial industry is just a partial cost of the real estate crash and depression of the last half of the 1980s.

THE WINNERS IN THE SAVINGS AND LOAN CRISIS WILL INCLUDE THE FOLLOWING:

1. The savings and loans and banks that are bought from the government at bargain prices will provide outstanding investments. The ability to make this type of transaction work takes knowledge and experience in the financial-services field, or, at least, the ability to invest with someone experienced in the industry who leads a group of investors.

2. Large consumer-oriented banks, whether they are national or regional, can be great winners in this time of dramatic change. Particularly, a national consumer bank such as CitiCorp will find opportunities to gain market shares and add retail branch networks at a fraction of the cost they would normally pay. Regional banks such as Bank One based in Columbus, Ohio, or NCNB of Charlotte, North Carolina, are both examples of smart, well-organized, growth-oriented banks that are taking full advantage of the opportunities. Bank One bought the second-largest retail banking operation in Texas, MBank. NCNB bought the largest, First Republic. Both MBank and First Republic were commercial banks that had failed and been put through receivership by the FDIC. In the case of savings and loans which have led the crisis, there are numerous examples of buyers who will make a great deal of money. Part of the benefit for new buyers and existing financial institutions that are expanding is that after they are finished dividing up the best branch locations and banking networks throughout the markets that are in trouble, the balance of the failed competitors will

simply be closed and liquidated by the U.S. government. The result
will be near monopolies in many markets.

3. The well-structured, worked-out pre-crash properties can be
winners. Ironically, some of the restructurings and workouts will
make transactions more economical than they would have been
otherwise. Literally, luck will play a key role as well as the skill
and efforts by those involved in the restructuring. Restructuring is
a process that does not have an obvious logical pattern to it, and
while some transactions will do fairly well, others will turn out to
be extraordinary favorable.

4. Perhaps the biggest opportunities of all are for the new asset
buyers. This is true whether you are an individual buying a
personal home or a second home as an investment or a big
company trying to buy a large portfolio of real estate. With
knowledge and proper experience about what to buy and how to
finance it, the opportunities for the next few years in this
recycling of more than $500 billion of assets are extraordinary
indeed. There will be many other winners, including pension
funds, foreign investors, institutional players, and those
sophisticated individuals who invest either on their own or with
experienced sponsors. The new asset buyers will be big winners.

If in the next year or so we have a dramatic economic slowdown or
a national recession, it will drive down the consumer demand for real estate
and increase the deflationary pressures. Texas will feel it a lot less than
areas that have not experienced a wrenching depression. The time to buy
is when the oversupply and the recessionary decrease of demand for real
estate have totally squeezed all sense of optimism out of the system. The
more the government controls the process and the greater the financial
collapse of the overall system, the more the bargains come into being. But
the timing of the cycle by geographic location is critical. To sell huge
volumes of real estate, the government simply has to offer bargains. Favorable real estate investments don't mean overnight windfall profits, but
they do mean a massive transfer of wealth over time.

EVEN NORMAL REAL ESTATE CYCLES
PROVIDE OPPORTUNITIES

The famous investor Baron Rothschild once said, "Buy when there is
blood in the streets." Certainly in the late eighties and early nineties in

Texas there has been and will continue to be blood in the streets. What happened in Texas in terms of value declines is currently happening to a lesser extent in Arizona, the Northeast, Atlanta, the Southeast, and may even happen in California. The deflation won't be the same in severity or intensity in every area of the country, but in many areas we will experience a real estate decline in the early 1990s. For us, this spells opportunity. The blood is running in the streets and for those with foresight it is not only a time of great opportunity but, ironically, a time of great safety from a buyer's perspective. It is a much safer investment to buy a building at half of the replacement cost that is currently earning 8½ percent cash return without a mortgage than it is to buy a property for twice as much even if it is earning 9 or 10 percent. The reason is simple. Markets change, they are constantly in motion. What is hot today is probably cool tomorrow and vice versa. This is true cycle after cycle although the current one has been more of an extreme down cycle.

The time to buy is when the markets have gone through the most gut-wrenching pain and everyone is pessimistic. Recently, I was on a panel at an Urban Land Institute meeting held in Dallas to address how government agencies can sell the real estate assets back into private hands. Congressman Bartlett, the head of the FDIC in this area, a number of prominent bankers, lawyer Bill Sechrest, and another real estate entrepreneur were on this panel. The interesting result of the meeting was the realization that even the spirit of Texans, the most optimistic people in the world, had been broken by this depression. People were not predicting great things for the future; they were cautious and reserved at best. Yet our operating results in Texas have been moving upward in a dramatic fashion. That means more opportunity for us. When everyone is truly optimistic, that is a time to sell. When the world is on hold, he who ventures thoughtfully ahead of the pack can be a big winner.

While I haven't always practiced in the best sense what I'm preaching, I think the markets in these tough times have given me a new sense of appreciation for contrarian investing. In real estate, knowing when to buy and when to sell is critical. Recently, I have traveled to Arizona and California to talk with lenders and entrepreneurs. Interestingly, even though the market and economy are very bad in Arizona, the general attitude is still that "we're not another Texas." People talk about the so-called California influence and how great Arizona is in that it is immune from real estate downturns. All of that tells me it is still too early to buy in Arizona and it makes me worry about what we already own there. California may even be worse, in that the optimism with which people pay high prices for real estate in California seems totally frightening. Yet, California is a unique economy and a unique market, so one must be careful not to judge California too quickly.

In the mid-1970s there was a severe recession that affected the overall economy, including real estate. Perhaps the most severe impact was on the East Coast and, in particular, the City of New York. New York was essentially bankrupt, and the news accounts of its demise as a city could be read in newspapers throughout the world. The investment banker Felix Rohatyn helped to restructure New York in a manner similar to a major complex corporate bankruptcy.

During this very uncertain and difficult time in New York City, rents were tumbling in the office market. Many developers and owners of properties were washed out of the business. Olympia and York, an aggressive and successful real estate company from Canada, saw this as opportunity. They purchased several office buildings from a large New York developer for $320 million with a $50 million down payment. Many people in the real estate business thought they were crazy.

In less than five years, the Olympia and York purchase had appreciated in value to more than $2 billion. Buildings that had been purchased for $75 or less per square foot in some cases were renting for more than that per year. A refinancing package of more than $2 billion and a number of sales catapulted the Olympia and York company into its current position as the preeminent worldwide real estate firm. By having the courage and foresight to buy at the seemingly worst time in the toughest market, Olympia and York increased their significant holdings to a vast fortune with that one acquisition.

Just like the New York downturn of the mid-1970s, the flip side of the Texas depression is the Texas opportunity. In fact, because the downturn was artificially pushed down further by the illiquidity of the financial system collapse and government actions, the upturn will be even greater than that of the New York market. In some ways the only comparison is the 1930s, and yet the recovery in the 1930s was far different because it was a national crisis and the money supply was contracting. Texas and the Southwest should come back stronger and in a shorter time than the country did in the 1930s. Of course, the 1930s provided a huge depression in the financial system and business in general as well as in real estate. Yet even that crisis provided the basis for some of the greatest real estate fortunes in history.

THE AVERAGING DOWN METHOD OF GETTING EVEN

Most people don't want to buy after they have just lost money in the same type of investment. People rarely take a fresh look at an investment area and say, "Maybe the reason I lost money has now become the reason to expect a great opportunity." The same situation that caused the deflation will eventually lead to a massive upside cycle of a shortage. For example, now that the tax laws have changed, capital going into real estate will be limited to economically driven investments. The result will be that less equity capital will come into real estate development unless the economics improve. This means that first vacancies fill up, then shortages occur, then rents go up—a lot. Existing properties, particularly if they are well built and in prime locations, will go up in value a great deal as markets improve. At Hall Financial Group, Inc., we intend to be aggressive buyers in Texas and, eventually, other areas of the country as they start to come out of the deflation that is still in process.

It's unfortunate that many of us lost a great deal of money as a result of the real estate crash. Who would have thought that Congress would retroactively change the laws? Who would have thought that inflation would turn to deflation seemingly overnight? Who would have thought that Houston, the strongest market in the country in 1980 and 1981, would be the weakest by 1986? We can all sit around and feel sorry for ourselves or we can get up and do something about it. The other side of the coin is that the elements that generated loss are now providing opportunities to recoup the money that we lost as well as make a lot more. If one were to invest the same amount of money initially invested that caused the losses, I have every belief that the averaging down of buying post-crash real estate would provide for a break-even in short order. The same amount of money invested, in all likelihood, in three to five years, would not only recover the past losses but would also be making a substantial profit. If an investor invested only enough to buy the same amount of asset in total volume, which would probably equal half as much in cash as the original investment, the investor would more than likely at least break even within five years, even with the worst of pre-crash investments.

In my mind, the right thing to do as an investor is to re-evaluate the difference between pre-crash and post-crash real estate and to average down the prices. This is an age-old method of stock investing that has been effective for many people. It can work in real estate as well. Take some of the emotion out of it and look at the practical facts, and it is obvious that this is a time of exceptional opportunities.

THE REPLACEMENT COST THEORY OF
REAL ESTATE INVESTING

Comparing a purchase price to what it would cost to build new competitive real estate in the same general location is one good yardstick for establishing real estate values. During the pre-crash time period, people paid between 90 and 120 percent of replacement costs. Generally, it is understandable that a developer and builder who take all of the front-end risks of building a property should expect to make a profit (i.e., an amount over 100 percent). Today, however, due to the severe temporary depression in values, properties can be bought for a lot less than it would cost to replace them. This provides both a downside projection that very little new real estate will be built in any given market until the rents increase substantially, and the upside of knowing you have bought a bargain. Before new rents are high enough to justify an economic decision by a builder/developer to build new buildings, those investors who have bought into the post-crash opportunities of today will first have seen their rents and investment returns increase dramatically. This, of course, depends on the existence of user demand for the real estate.

User demand will increase with time for well-located, Class A real estate. The key is to buy the real estate in great locations at competitive prices that are a lot less than it would cost to reproduce. We are buying apartment buildings at a third to one-half of their reproduction cost today and office buildings at a quarter to one-half of their reproduction cost. We are buying land at a tenth to a third of its price of three to five years ago. In short, there is a bargain-basement sale going on in the early 1990s as the government clears inventory, just like an overstocked supermarket. For those investors who know how to pick the best merchandise carefully and prudently and structure it in a conservative manner, the future for real estate investments is extremely positive.

Prices that we are paying for apartments today are one third of the prices paid in the early 1980s. Recently, we have purchased several apartment complexes at prices ranging from $16 to $32 a square foot. We are buying only the best quality and well-located properties. We believe their upside will be stronger and the safety factor generally better. Office buildings are even more depressed, but we are very cautious in buying office buildings. Each office building is highly unique and requires detailed analysis. We recently bought an approximately 100,000-square-foot office building at $24 per square foot, which is approximately 25 percent of replacement cost.

If we are right that the Texas market and the economy during the next five to ten years is going to come back strong, then the opportunities today are great. The comparison of today's prices to replacement costs offers an interesting perspective. Replacement costs are more likely to go up than down. Even though existing real estate has deflated in value, the cost of raw materials and labor to replace real estate in the future will be a moving target on the upside. While it is not economical to build today, the rent gap between today's rents and those needed to justify construction will be an increasing gap as replacement costs increase. This will help to make existing real estate more competitive. In other words, while we might buy a property now for $16 a square foot that would cost $50 a square foot to replace today, in five years with inflation, the replacement cost easily could be $75 a square foot. Of course, by then we will own the property at approximately 20 percent of the replacement cost. It is this kind of opportunity that makes the market exciting now.

WHAT TYPES OF REAL ESTATE WILL PROVIDE THE BEST OPPORTUNITIES?

Although each given market area will differ, generally, the crash has been led by a decline of apartments, condominiums, and residential homes first, followed by the office buildings, the industrial, then the retail market, and finally and worst of all, land. In most markets land becomes the most overly discounted asset due to its illiquid nature and the belief that at the bottom of the crash no one will ever need the land again. Many types of real estate will offer opportunities, but all of them require knowledgeable, careful, and thoughtful analysis. There is no one type of real estate that is an obvious winner over others. There are opportunities in each area, but it's worthwhile mentioning some of the differences and some brief conclusions on the types of opportunities available.

1. **Single-family homes and condominiums.** For many individuals, buying a single-family home is the largest investment they will ever make. It seems frightening to buy a home in a market like Texas when everything has recently been declining in value. One might wonder if he or she isn't making a big mistake by thinking about buying a home at a time like this. The opposite is absolutely true. This would be a wise decision. Buying single-family homes or condominiums to live in when the market has

started to turn up, but before the area becomes too successful again, makes great sense.

Likewise, buying your neighbor's home, so to speak, as an investment can be an excellent opportunity for many individuals. Buying extra homes or condominiums and renting them and holding them for appreciation can be a great way to participate in the transfer of wealth from the taxpayers, who pay for the bailout, to you as an investor, who benefits. The savings and loans and banks through the government will be selling many single-family homes and condominiums at bargain prices. Buying at auctions and spending some time to learn the local markets will provide great future opportunities. One way to be successful is to be an active investor. However, if you're not going to have the time to manage the property yourself and to understand the local markets, then you are better off investing as a limited partner with an experienced sponsor. Both types of investing offer excellent opportunities.

2. **Apartments.** The first area to turn down in most markets when real estate begins a cyclical decline is apartments. Apartments also are leading the way back in Texas and in most market areas. They are predictable and have a strong upside. Many apartment properties bought today can produce a 7 to 10 percent cash flow and more than double the initial principal investment in three to five years. In short, this is a time of great opportunity for typical apartment investing.

In addition to typical apartment investing, there are apartments that have unique attributes of needing a turnaround. As described further below, buying opportunities for turnarounds and added value can be an excellent way to enhance one's investment return.

3. **Manufactured housing communities.** Another excellent opportunity during the down times is to acquire manufactured housing communities. These communities are an outstanding stable source of cash flow. Once they are full, people rarely move. During the worst of the downturn in Texas, people did move because their mobile homes were foreclosed by the credit companies. This provides a unique opportunity to buy well-located mobile home parks at terribly depressed prices. We've developed our own specialized strategy for this type of investing, which is described below.

4. Office buildings. One of the last areas to go downhill is office buildings. Many tenants are locked into long-term leases, which give office buildings an artificially high return from an investment standpoint and make them very risky to a new investor. One must analyze an office building based on current market rents. In the case of many Texas properties, for example, there are leases at approximately $20 and $25 per square foot that will decrease when they reach the conclusion of the lease to a new rate of approximately $15 per square foot. Office buildings are complex and hard to analyze and have taken a severe beating in the marketplace.

Long term, they offer a great store of value and tremendous opportunities. They are investments that should be for the sophisticated, institutional marketplace, and even then they must be very carefully and thoroughly analyzed. Perhaps more than other types of real estate, location is key. Many suburban office buildings that are poorly located will turn out to be terrible investments even at a fraction of their replacement costs. There are traps in buying real estate just on numbers or replacements, and one must add the ingredients of market knowledge and careful analysis.

5. Retail. The retail market, like office buildings, varies considerably. In retail it depends on whether we are talking about strip shopping centers or large shopping malls, and of course, as with office buildings, the locations are critical. Overall, the retail market held up longer than apartments or even office buildings, but its decline has been significant as the economy itself began to result in lower spending by consumers. A combination of overbuilt retail markets and consumers spending less on their shopping has caused numerous retail developers to find their tenants moving out in the middle of the night or groups of tenants threatening to leave as they demand rent decreases.

The retail market, carefully analyzed and with the right locations, does offer great opportunities on the upside. Particularly in areas where the economy is going through a temporary cycle such as Texas has been, there will be some unique property opportunities. It is important for the most part, however, to avoid two-story strip shopping centers and similar types of marginal properties that were only partially successful in the heyday of inflationary real estate values but will, at best, be the last type of real estate to come back.

6. Pre-development land. In the heyday of inflationary times and high real estate values, the greatest amounts of money were made in pre-development land. Fortunately, the Hall Financial Group, Inc., stayed out of the spiraling land game. While we may have left millions of dollars on the table, we also avoided the risks and liability that have since crushed many aggressive land speculators. Today we feel completely different about the land opportunities and we are aggressively investing in land.

The area that is perhaps hardest hit in a down time is land. The opportunities with perhaps the highest upside when the market cycle turns back will be land. The key is not to speculate or buy just any land that is at a bargain price, but to buy land that has a specific need and development potential in a three- to seven-year horizon. This predevelopment method of investing in land works well because we can determine what land values will be on a conservative basis when development is ripe for that particular area and type of property. In other words, we know what office and apartment land are worth. While obviously there will be a lack of new construction for three to five years in most of the markets in which we are buying, we are now focusing, from the land standpoint, on those locations that will be the first to build new assets. In other words, we focus only on the best of prime land that has development potential, not long-term speculative properties.

An example of this type of transaction is an industrial park called Waters' Ridge in Lewisville, Texas, a northern suburb of Dallas. This is an industrial and retail complex of extremely high quality. Land in that area was selling upward of $8 per square foot to users for building class A industrial showroom or warehouse types of buildings. We purchased the entire 400-acre site for $.72 per square foot. Within three months after our purchase, we sold 38 acres for $1.77 per square foot, yielding us over $1.7 million in profit on that one transaction alone.

Land can be very profitable during this down period of recycling. It is the largest single concentration of real estate assets held by the government that needs to be sold. It also has, perhaps, the greatest number of pitfalls and risks. Primarily those risks are analyzing all of the conditions of the land and picking the right locations, which are the kind of risks we like, because they are controllable by effort, knowledge, and general market experience.

THE VALUE-ADDED AND TURNAROUND APPROACHES
TO REAL ESTATE INVESTING

In a contrarian down market, perhaps more than at any other time, the profitability of finding turnaround opportunities, or opportunities to add value, is at its best. Properties that can be enhanced in value by improving them physically or operationally, with a marketing program, and/or by revising their financial structure, are in several of these areas turnaround opportunities. My first book, *The Real Estate Turnaround*, describes in great detail this theory of investing.

At Hall Financial Group, Inc., we try to find assets to which we can do something to make them better than the status quo. It is called "value added." If we don't bring something new to the party other than investment capital, it's nothing more or less than investing in a commodity such as sugar, soy beans, or pork bellies. Instead, we want to bring superior management and the ability to see something that perhaps others in the market do not see. For instance, if there is an old apartment building that is performing poorly and, because of the economy, has been allowed to run down, most people would look at its economic cash flow and value based on those numbers and the cost of fixing it up. That's logical, but it's only part of what we would look at. We've seen any number of old apartment buildings in what we consider in-fill land locations. By in-fill, I mean that they are already in developed areas. Some need to be torn down and redeveloped, perhaps from an old dilapidated apartment to a new strip shopping center and small office complex. The point is creativity, new concepts, and ideas to add value to the physical real estate are the ingredients that can enhance returns and make the most money.

During the contrarian down time there are great opportunities of this nature. Another example, and one which we are actively pursuing, is the opportunity of buying old, dilapidated mobile home parks. Mobile home parks are very hard to get zoned. Old trailer parks are often community eyesores that give a bad reputation to an area. When we go in and buy an old trailer park, we often spend more money on improvements than we do on purchasing the park itself. By the time we are finished, we have a clean, modern, five-star manufactured housing community complete with lakes, a new clubhouse, a new road, and everything brand new from landscaping to signage, for less than half of what it would cost to build it from scratch. Also, if we were to build it from scratch, we would have trouble finding the land in locations as good as some of the older trailer parks because communities simply don't like to zone land to allow mobile home parks. This is just one of our niche strategies to make money during the current times of opportunities.

WITHOUT TAX BENEFITS, WHO WILL BE THE BUYERS OF REAL ESTATE?

One might ask, "Who will be the real estate investors of the future?" Particularly with the tax-law change and the overbuilding—what investors will participate in this seemingly complex mine field? We believe the future lies in the hands of primarily institutional investors and pension funds. With tax advantages gone, pension funds are able to invest with a more level playing field. Their capital pool of $2.5 trillion dollars today will be more than $5 trillion by 1995. Many pension funds are targeting allocations for real estate of 10 to 15 percent. If 10 percent were to be allocated to real estate, the effects would be awesome. Approximately one half of the wealth in the United Sates consists of real estate. Pension funds currently have only about 5 percent of their holdings in real estate. No one predicts a 50 percent allocation to real estate or even the 25 to 35 percent level frequently seen in European pension funds. But a move from 5 to 10 percent while the portfolio doubles represents a potential *300* percent increase in demand from the pension-fund sector. The long-term nature of pension funds and the inflationary hedge of real estate are an obvious match. The opportunity exists for individual investors because they can decide and act faster than committees.

Real estate is truly becoming an international market, and the foreign investors will be a major part of the future of all U.S. real estate. The United States in the 1990s will be a worldwide place to shop for bargains in real estate. Our sense of urgency is to get in early and buy property at low, favorable prices in order to hold and own that property long enough to see major increases in value. Then we will sell. We believe we will be taking profits in a three- to seven-year time frame. The demand by pension funds, other institutional investors, foreign investors, and sophisticated individuals will be growing dramatically for real estate in the 1990s. Our role as a real estate advisor and manager will be to add value for our clients. We will provide a combination of superior in-house market research and acquisition capabilities, outstanding value-added property management, and the integrity that we have shown even in the toughest of times. As investment managers in real estate, we believe our recent experiences with tough times have seasoned us well to help investors profit in a solid and careful manner in this most unusual time.

We are very excited about today's opportunities. The upside of the depression that we have been experiencing is the greatest opportunity for a transfer of wealth we'll probably ever see in our lifetime. We hope to help others be winners in this time of opportunity.

WHERE WILL THE BEST INVESTMENT OPPORTUNITIES BE IN THE 1990S?

In the post-crash era of real estate, the best opportunities will be in the markets that suffered the most severe impact from the deflationary crash. While I have described my optimism for Texas, it certainly will not be the only market with great opportunities in the 1990s. Texas may have the best and the first opportunities to reap rewards, as the new post-crash real estate markets begin their long and solid comeback, but many other markets will be exciting as well.

Probably the next market to offer great opportunities with an exciting upside will be Arizona. Arizona in many ways could be considered "Texas II." Arizona started its decline a year or so after the Texas decline was under way and has yet to bottom out, but it is probably close. The market bottom in Arizona will not be as severe as it was in Texas, but nevertheless, from the standpoint of that economy, it will be a devastating decline in real estate values. At the same time, the long-term economic factors in Arizona, specifically Phoenix and Tucson, are extremely favorable. Arizona has been a great growth area for the last two decades and promises to have favorable growth through the turn of the century. Like Texas, the real estate decline was not caused by a lack of growth or demand, but a combination of overbuilding and a drastic tax-law change. With this in mind, Arizona is an excellent place for investors to look in the early 1990s.

Throughout the Southeast there are markets that in the early 1990s are still in the midst of their own deflationary downturn. Unlike Texas or Arizona, those markets may not have quite as severe a decline, but as they bottom out in the early to mid-1990s, they too, will have great upside opportunities. Atlanta, Georgia, is a market that is overbuilt in office and apartments as well as other types of real estate. In the long run, however, Atlanta will be one of the fastest growing and strongest economies, and certainly an area in which investors should take a good, hard look.

Other markets are harder to predict at this time, but the deflationary wave that began in Texas is spreading even to the northeastern New England states and all the way to the West Coast. California may even experience its own form of decline and this could, at some point in the future, lead to opportunities to buy quality real estate that has otherwise been priced at levels that are simply unrealistic for the wise investor. The New England states are still early in the decline, so it is more difficult to evaluate how prices will go and how favorable values will be in the future. Even New York, which seems to have been so strong for the last fifteen years, may experience a considerable decline in the 1990s as a combination of new construction, the tax-law change, and the possibility of increasing Wall Street layoffs all come together. We will be watching those markets closely but not rushing in too early.

In short, there will be many geographic areas throughout the country that will offer opportunities to buy at cyclical lows in the early 1990s. This severe cycle, which is certainly at its worst in Texas and followed somewhat closely by Arizona, will also have a strong impact throughout other areas of the country. As those areas bottom out, there will be opportunities and the smart money will be looking for the signs of the operations improving while the psychology is still at a low ebb. Those are the keys to where to invest in the 1990s.

CHAPTER 18
WHAT'S IT ALL ABOUT?

IN CRISIS, WE ARE ALL pushed to our limits. These times bring about change in each of us and in the world around us. We will never have absolute control of our world, but we can and do make choices. One of the first choices we all can make along our path of life is whether to live life or to merely exist. Many people choose just to exist, to skate through life with limited risk, with limited use of their senses, and usually with limited rewards. Others, with the courage to grab life and live it to the fullest, have a shot at something deeper, something bigger, something more. But wanting more requires risking more, and many times retreat can look appealing when the pressures get harsh—such as much of the late eighties was for me.

Years ago, in my days as a budding poet—and a budding landlord —I wrote a poem called "The Hard Road," which is reprinted at the beginning of this book. Its meaning is applicable to the experiences that I've recently come through. The poem talks about the choices in life that often challenge us at the important crossroads between doing what is easy versus what is right. Deep down inside, we often know the difference, but as humans, we take the easy road more often than not. For me, the whole struggle of my life, right or wrong, has been that struggle to take the hard road, to do what I believe is right. Oftentimes, as in 1986, this was an unpopular and a lonely journey. But there is something within me that continues to scream: Keep on going and do not give up!

In 1986, I thought it was my moral duty to stand up for my investors. I could do that only through risking my personal fortune. I also risked my reputation by taking the front-and-center approach instead of quietly giving back properties to lenders, as so many others in my profession did. I risked my self-confidence as I was battered daily by friends and foes alike. But I believed in this country's financial system, and despite my problems with the government and with certain regulators, I continued to believe that the problems between regulators and financial institutions and between financial institutions and their borrowers could be worked out in a rational, logical process.

In addition to the concerns for my investors, my company, and myself, I became increasingly concerned for the whole financial system. Again, I took the hard road and spoke out, not just for my investors but for the needs of the overall system. I spoke privately to many leaders in the government, with senior members of the established bureaucracy that controls our financial system, and I testified before members of Congress. My concerns were for the needs of the system, the lenders, the government insurance fund, and the overall economic fiber of our region.

Part of my message was one of encouragement and to face the realities of the unique, severe, deflationary real estate crash. Few people wanted to admit the problem early on. Another part of my message was one of forbearance and moderation between regulators and lenders and lenders and borrowers. First, I thought we should try to contain the problem. Then, for the honest, responsible, well-managed lenders and borrowers, encourage further business by adding capital and value to give everyone some breathing room until the market improved. Together, our investors, with capital calls of more than $40 million, and I put more than $185 million back into the properties—all on mortgages without personal liability. Certainly, saving these properties helped us, but clearly it also helped the lenders and the banking system.

As time went on, we at Hall Financial Group, Inc., were fortunate and our financial condition improved. The vast majority of the Hall partnerships were worked out, and for the most part, investors and lenders alike will come out quite well in time. We have not and will not end up with a perfect scorecard, but we've done everything humanly possible to help our investors. I found great support in Washington and with many congressional staff members and agency employees who are very dedicated to this country and our system. We were also blessed with the extraordinary efforts and assistance of attorneys, accountants, and other professionals guiding us through the complex restructuring. The need for a realistic approach to the severe economic problems in Texas was heard loud and clear around the nation. The solutions to complex problems are rarely simple. While the world is full of critics and, at times, I've been one, I can now say the regulators, in particular the FDIC in its new role, are doing the best they can in a crisis.

The real estate crash in Texas was the precursor of a national real estate deflation. The excesses of the heated real estate market in the 1970s and early 1980s stretched the market to the limit. As I finish this book, there seems to me to be many similarities on Wall Street in the leverage buy-out (LBO) markets. A deflationary collapse of the aggressive LBOs of the last decade could well be the next wave in a rotating industrial and geographic deflationary depression that has already hit farming, oil and gas, real estate, savings and loans, and banking. If I'm correct, then many of the lessons Hall Financial Group learned should be of interest and hopefully use to the LBO industry and investment bankers in the early 1990s.

The Hall Financial Group, Inc., has renewed its strength and, most important, continues its fine-tuned dedication to property management and service to the residents and owners of the properties. In 1989, the new program we started in which all executives of the Hall Financial Group, Inc., visit at least two properties a week has been great. I've been averaging about six a week and I can say with great pride that we've got a highly professional and enthusiastic management team in the field. We have also worked closely with both lenders and regulators in an effort to rebuild the industry. We hope to be a positive force in reshaping the future of the real estate industry. Looking ahead, I'm excited about the future of the Hall Financial Group, Inc. I'm confident that we will continue to be at the forefront of exciting opportunities in the Texas market. In time, there will be opportunities in Phoenix, Atlanta, and other currently depressed markets. Occasionally, I dwell on the severity of my personal financial setback and the reality that we have not had a perfect scorecard in our attempt to bring all investors to an absolute safe harbor. But then I thank God for all the blessings that we currently have. And I feel at peace knowing we have done our best.

Success isn't measured strictly in dollars and cents. Doing what's right rather than what's easy is what counts. Caring about your fellow human being and doing something about it is what life and living are all about. The best measure of our worth is the test we each have when we look at ourselves in the mirror. If you are true to a code of ethics and morality that has a righteous sense of respect for the dignity of mankind, and if you dare to walk the hard road even in the worst of adversity, then hold on to your hope and faith because you will always be a winner. That's what real success is all about.

The next decade in real estate will be great fun. The profits, I am absolutely convinced, will be enormous. Those with some courage and willingness to take risks will be very well rewarded. Money and profits come to those who work at it and don't accept failure, just like success in the deeper values of life. Certainly, surviving a depression doesn't end with someone ringing a bell. Rather, it is a process of gradual improvement with new positive things and old problems all mixed together. If everything in the real estate markets were "back to normal" overnight, then the opportunities would be short lived. The recovery process is a healthy one and we're in the early stages with the best opportunities available now and in the next few years.

I feel that with the conclusion of this book, I have shared a part of myself, a part of the process that was so important to the survival and turnaround of the Hall Financial Group and me. The challenges were not only the survival and stability of the limited partnerships and the Hall Financial Group itself, but a personal challenge and struggle to understand what life is all about, and to survive with my personal ethics, morality, and faith still intact. As I look back, I like what I see and I believe that what we did was right. We took the hard road and we fought for our investors, for our lenders (even though many of them might not have thought so), for the marketplace, and for ourselves as the Hall Financial Group family.

For me, taking the hard road and hanging on in the toughest of times is the only answer. As I close this book and this chapter of my life, I am thankful for being able to tell this story of a slice of unique history and of my personal story of surviving. I am thankful the news of my death was exaggerated and not an accurate reporting. I hope this story will inspire others to live, not just to exist, to walk the hard road when you have to, and most of all—to never give up.

EPILOGUE

The Chinese proverb "May you live in interesting times" reminds me that I have, and that I've been blessed with success. Sometimes the times can be a bit more challenging and interesting than any of us would like, and "boring" or "normal" would sound better. Yet for all of the ups and downs and challenges everyday, I thank God for being alive and I feel lucky.

As books take a long time to go through the publishing process, here is an update on events that have occurred subsequent to the main story.

1. **Personal side**. In late 1989 MaryAnna and I filed for divorce and separated. Unfortunately, the events of the last four years took their toll, and it seemed that our marriage had become a casualty of the tremendous stresses that we both went through. I hope and trust, however, that we will remain lifelong friends. Our children are all doing well, and we hope that the difficulties and challenges of the divorce and the stresses and strains of the last four years will be growth experiences for each of us individually and collectively for our family.

   The events described in this book and other personal family matters have caused me to pause and reevaluate my life. As a result, I have determined that while business is important, my priorities need changing. I am working on taking better care of myself, being the best dad I can be, being the best friend I can be, being a supportive member of my community, and being more balanced as a person. Business is exciting and fun, but the richness of the world is much broader based. We all need to take time to smell the roses.

2. **Business**. Business has improved greatly, in particular with the Texas economy improving. Yet with the completion of this book,

we at Hall still have our share of partnership workouts to complete and even some corporate and personal creditor situations to finish up. We are hanging in there and things are getting better, but there is no panacea.

Unfortunately, for many businesses in Texas, both borrowers and lenders, things have continued to deteriorate in 1990. Even though the markets are getting better, it is in some ways too little too late. What is often needed is a sense of cooperation and some breathing room from lenders to borrowers, but that doesn't seem to be occurring on a wholesale basis. The times continue to be difficult for many people, and the end of the washout will probably and unfortunately result in more personal and corporate bankruptcies.

3. **Opportunities**. The 1990s are already starting out to be very exciting. Truly the flip side of the problems is the greatest bargain basement sale of real estate if you know what to buy. We're fortunate to have the knowledge and contacts to put together great opportunities with our new institutional, Japanese, and sophisticated U.S. investors. In the first quarter of 1990, with our new partners, we acquired over $90 million of real estate assets. We're very excited about the opportunities in the 1990s.

As I conclude this book, in many ways Texas is concluding a chapter in its history. So, too, am I concluding a personal chapter in my life. "The Hard Road," as my poem describes, continues to be both my road and, I believe, the path of Texas. The crash, depression, and challenges build perspective and more foundation for a stronger and hopefully wiser future, with a richness in human spirit that comes from facing life head on and never giving up.

ACKNOWLEDGMENTS

No man is an island. Few, however, have been as lucky and as blessed as I have been with a wonderful family and so many talented and loyal friends, associates, and colleagues. I would like to try to express my gratitude in this acknowledgment section, so, with the apology to those who deserve my gratitude but inadvertently are not mentioned, let me begin by thanking the following:

My family
Love and thanks go for so much to my daughters, Marcia Anna, Melissa Elizabeth, Brijetta Lynn, and Kristina Emilia Independence, and to my parents, Herbert and Ellie Hall. Special thanks also to MaryAnna, and to her parents, Dorothy and Martin Panchula.

Those who helped write this book
This book took three years and could not have been written without the help of many people. First, there was Don Williams with the original suggestion of keeping a journal, then Eric Kirst, who helped me formulate and start writing. In 1987 the very talented writer Sally Giddens wrote an article about me that was published in May of that year. After that article, I asked Sally to help with the book and she worked on it from mid-1987 into early 1989, including several drafts and, particularly, the first half of the book. Her outstanding writing style helped greatly to influence me in a positive way in this book. Then there is Dedie Leahy, who has been a media relations consultant with the Hall Financial Group and a friend of mine since late 1980. Dedie helped review the project and edited it more times than she or I will ever care to remember. Annemarie Marek helped provide editorial guidance, research, and excellent constructive suggestions on a great deal of the material. Her efforts from beginning to end have been critical. My father, who had previously helped me edit the last two

books that I have written, also lent a helping hand, particularly to the chapters on lessons. Then there was the help MaryAnna provided in editing and rereading section after section. My two assistants, Tricia Richards and Cheryl Cromer, not only typed and retyped this book twenty or thirty drafts worth on each and every word, but they helped in the editing, researching, and sorting out of the numerous drafts. They have also lived as part of every word of it. Great thanks goes to Jim Fitzgerald for an outstanding editing job from St. Martin's Press. Jim's efforts helped make the book more meaningful to readers. Jan Miller, my agent, helped make the whole thing possible by being a matchmaker supreme. She correctly identified the right editor and the right publisher and has been a great help in the project. In addition to the people who worked directly in one way or another on the book, many friends read drafts at various stages over the last three years and took the time to offer excellent suggestions. Just a few of the people who spent a particularly extensive amount of time in this area helping are Melinda Jayson, Roland Freeman, Jim Simpson, Greg Dukes, and Jeanie Baggett, each of whom contributed many excellent suggestions.

Outside directors

The guidance, support, and integrity of the outside directors of the Hall Financial Group, Inc., and Resource Savings Association have both been critical to my last few years. Stephanie May, David Florence, Rex Sebastian, and Ron Krause, of Hall Financial; and Billy Gutow, Larry Levey, Dr. Martin Cohen, and Mike Kilbourn, of Resource, each deserve my gratitude.

Investors

Our ten thousand investors deserve to be mentioned by name but space cannot reasonably permit it. Several hundred of these investors have written me support letters, and for that I shall be eternally grateful. Each and every one means a great deal to me. The investors as a group have been of critical support and without their help we could not have gotten through this very difficult time.

Broker/dealers and registered representatives

Many of the broker/dealers and registered representatives provided excellent support in continuing to help us help the properties during this difficult time. Again, there are far too many to mention by name (more than 250 broker/dealers and 5,000 registered representatives). Just a handful of the supportive registered representatives include the following: Joe Allen, Kar-

ren S. Allen, Frank S. Archre, J. Richard Arellano, Maurice Betman, Jo
Anne Brown, Thomas J. Brown, Peter Butler, Bill E. Carter, Thomas P.
Casey, Mike Connelly, Thomas A. Corbett, Jr., D. Francis Dasher, Jon
C. Davis, David G. Elsworth, Robert Flynn, Mark Fuller, John E. Gorely,
Dennis Joppe, Bill Keen, E. Michael Kilbourn, Nico Letschert, R. Griffith
McDonald, Hal Mayfield, Alan L. Nero, Gerald Neve, Peter Nunez, Ra-
mesh M. Patel, Steve Pfancuff, Donald J. Postma, William H. Powers,
Jr., Lawrence Riegner, Charles J. Root, Jr., Michael J. Sahadi, Marc
Schliefer, James Shank, Luther Shoemaker, Elliot S. Simon, Bob Skeldon,
Billy Spain, Blaine Swint, Michael Tiberg, Guy F. White, David E. Witt,
Timothy E. Zimcosky. I have included only a small portion of the broker/
dealers: Arkoma Management, George Hays; Berachah Securities, Shelton
Thorne; B. C. Christopher/Morison Securities, Inc., Jim Lockman and
Lynn Whitcher; Chubb Securities, Thomas M. Hardiman; First Columbus
Equities, Inc., Jerry Maxwell and Paul Breen; Huntingdon Securities,
George Hastings and Hugh Black; Kavanaugh Securities, Inc., Gene L.
Parker; KRK, Limited, James Kouzes; Mariner Financial Services, J. Will
Paull, Bob Boone, and Clark Colton; A. C. Masingill & Associates, Jeff
Sharp and Gaines Walker; Planned Investments, Marvin Pheffer and Kath-
ryn McDonald; Sentra Securities Corporation, Gary Hill and Larry Papike;
Southwest Securities, Ray Wooldridge; Stephens Financial Group, Inc.,
Stephen C. Browere; VSR Financial Services, Inc., Donald J. Beary and
Mike Stanfield; WFG Securities Corp., John Lockrey.

Lenders
Many lenders worked with us in helping get through what was an unpleasant
and tough experience for the both of us. Again, I feel frustrated by not
being able to mention every name, but particular thanks and respect go to
Michigan National Bank and its team led by Farris Kalil; Meritor, led by
Bob Bifolco; First Bank Systems, led by Dick Frandeen; National Bank,
of Detroit, led by Pete Ward; and so many more.

Regulators and government officials
Without the help of many elected officials, as well as many regulators,
we would not have made it. Since I have been careful throughout the book
not to mention Senators or Congressmen other than those who have already
been noted in the media, I will not do so here. Those who did help,
however, I want to know that I am grateful and do appreciate it. Jim
Wright, of course, has been written about in the book and in the media
and from my perspective he is a man who has given a great deal for this
country and deserves not only my gratitude but that of the United States

for many, many important contributions. I thank Speaker Wright and the Congressmen, Senators, and their staffs, and members of the Administration who were so supportive and worked so hard to try to make the system work. Members of the Federal Home Loan Bank Board or the Federal Home Loan Bank System, including Shannon Fairbanks, David Martens, Roslyn Payne, Angelo Vigna, David Gustafson, George Barclay, Roy Green, and John Price. So many more deserve a lot of credit for doing a fine job for this country and my gratitude for being helpful to us.

Attorneys and accountants

Without the wisdom, guidance, and strength of counsel, no one could make it through the kind of difficulties we went through. Great thanks go to Alan Feld, Smitty Davis, Marydale DeBor, Bill Sechrest, Jim Simpson, Jack Stilwell, Ivan Irvin, Mac Strother, Dan Berry, Mike Logan, Al Conant, Melinda Jayson, and, on the accounting side, Kenneth Leventhal, Ken Townsend, Al Hague, Richard Ellis, and many more.

My many friends

Close personal friends who, through their decency and caring, provided me a great sense of counsel, support, and a reason to keep on keeping on: Ron Krause, Jack Butler, Rabbi Mendel Dubrawsky, Beth Mooney, Marydale DeBor, David Florence, Herb Wietzman, Colleen Hall, Marty Rom, Ted Strauss, Jim Klingbeil, Jim McCormick, and Dr. Martin Cohen, who are among those many close support people who were always there for me.

My second family

The following friends and associates were part of the Hall Financial family that lived through the period of time covered in this book. There are another couple of thousand names of current associates for whom space won't allow their being singled out, but rest assured, my gratitude to all of them is strong. Those members of the team who particularly lived through the tough times were: Mark Depker, Ronald Berlin, Robert Flynn, Karen Sucher, Mary Lee Miller, Daniel Wand, Christine Erdody, Marti Kohnke, Paul Zak, Pamela Sullens, Jeanie Baggett, Scott Kenney, Richard Proffer, Thomas Jahncke, Patricia Foley, Cheryll O'Bryan, Stanley Ferenc, Mary Bozyk, Nancy Baldwin, David Haraf, Michael Robbins, Willis Baker, Sandra Boscarino, Gary Thayer, Donald Braun, Vicki Thompson, Gerald Manko, Mike Bawulski, Norma Arabia, Alma Cahill, Margaret Verhelle, Nannette Engle, William Davis, Linda Dhar, Maureen Giammara, Danny Eversole, Norman Lang, Patrick White, Susan Ebbing, Mary Miller, Terri

Leirstein, George Norrick, Judith Ellenburg, Eleanor Parker, Masten Harris, Joyce Chatrand, Deborah Johnson, Michael Parsley, Laurie Millott, Janet Carlton, Scott Zahn, Jeffrey Kelly, Roland Workman, Sherry Cochran, Jonathan Graham, David Graber, Patrick Pomorski, John Buster, Arthur Johnson, Marcia Hammonds, Muriel Reynolds, Patrice Binkley, Valerie Reber, Patricia Richards, William Serna, Geraldine Kennedy, Judith Burton, Mary Eaglin, Rick Martin, Gerhard Schubert, John Tarvin, Rick Anderson, Carlos Barrios, Lawrence Elliott, Shannon Ferguson, Arthur Jones, John Reid, Kathleen Quinn, Nelda Jones, Lydia Silva, Craig Thornsbury, Cynthia Kincaid, Lawrence Brown, David Kerns, Kimberly Griswold, Tron Van Le, Kerry Ridgley, Donald Fitzgerald, Louise Lee, Kathleen Welsh, Delores Tucker, Pamela Crowder, Keith Taylor, Tammy McGuire, Harriet Swartz, Deloris Bordner, Susan Bradley, Patricia Brennan, Myrtle Brown, William Burmeister, Sandra Conley, Edward Davis, Betty Duerr, Bruce East, Donald Ellison, Margarita Fabian, George Fiedorczyk, Gayle Frano, Eileen Fulmer, Dorothy Goodman, Robert Goodman, Joann Herr, Leon Herr, Rick Houselog, Joseph Lalla, Elizabeth McCrea, Ronald Mindham, Eldon Moore, Debbie Nolan, Betty Nydell, Mary Papenhausen, Ernesto Renteria, Diane Russell, Christi Shanks, Thomas Shuler, Marvin Swartz, Donald Vanatta, Connie Weaver, John Weber, Deloris White, John Zipf, Vera Zipf, John McKeone, Timothy Brown, Ann Davis, Joy Chandler, Cheryl Cromer, Kyle Drake, Elizabeth Gonzalez, Marla Shelhorse, Robert Hutto, Mary Ann Hammel-Clark, Emma Miller, Jeffery Lighton, Janet Rusnak, Louie Armstrong, Patrick Patterson, Minnie Ramirez, Ellen Richmond, Jesus Solts, William Jansen, Michael Wabin, Judy Goddard, Raul Guerrero, Roger Sharp, Shellie Cross, Patricia Long, Roger Tennehill, Mary Wallace-Hebert, Sharon Tucker, Judy Young, Todd Fitzerman, Karen McClendon, Janelle MacDonald, Carol Schmidt, Peter Nunez, Teresa Stubblefield, Neal Katz, Clark Chavez, Alfred Brooks, Linda Doros, Cynthia DeLeon, Linda Moore, Barbara Trumpp, Carol Kosnik, Nancy Loetzer, Dolores Beck, Ilse Moster, Gary Rothballer, Mary Jacobsen, Pamela Smith, Shanda Gunn, Steven Schultz, Diana Wilson, Jose Rosa, Loyda Rosa, Charles Hastings, Harley Palmbos, Margaret Roberson, Lillian Blazek, Federico Albavera, Betty Bryant, Leticia Gomez, Barbara Mares, Dawn Fleischer, Betty Beatty, Ida Benford, Patricia Perez-Podesta, Ronald White, Stuart Harvey, James Smith, Anthony Colosimo, Nelly Escobar, Ralph Klatt, George Grandsard, Ronald Hampson, Gary Leclair, Tomo Matanic, Clatron Perkins, Sharon Perkins, Joseph Quentere, Gary Tegtmeter, Timothy Cislo, Norman Robertson, Dolly Stapleton, Steven Wherley, Deborah Young, Catherine Wilson, Nancy Ackles, David Benson, Michael Turner, Scot Standefer, Joseph

Toulouse, Robert Smith, James Faulkenberry, Roberto Mijango, Benita Soriano, Juan Soriano, Doris Wiest, Cherilyn Duncan, Shirley Bate, Renee Burrus, Cesario Padron, Gene Sigler, Sarah Sparks, Carolyn Outson, Georgette McAlister, Linda Davlin, Winfield Turk, Lorraine Dugray, Kimberly Bender, Felix Smith, Victor Abensur, Lorraine Dirks, Mary Stolarik, Samuel Chacon, Helen Turk, Mark Blocher, Janet Roznowski, Carolyn Timms, Mary Cummings, James Owens, Doris Straight, Kenneth Keels, Ozie Seawell, Karon Goodrum, Michael Schuster, Robert Niedecken, Adam Simpson, Thomas Herbelin, Amy Jorgensen, Ramiro Gomez, Mary Marshall, Lynn Brown, Cesar Martinez, Judy Horne, Linda Bowlin, Marian Nolan, Denise Bousantt, Ilse Schmitt, Ted Palles.

Richness in life does not come from material possessions. A rich man is one who can count numerous deep and dedicated relationships of a human and spiritual nature. The good fortune that the many people mentioned and many others have brought to me through their friendship, guidance, support, advice, and counsel has enriched me in countless ways. Part of what this book is all about is the key to the door of human relationships. I am very grateful to so many people for so much.